Partings Welded Together

Partings Welded Together

POLITICS AND DESIRE IN THE NINETEENTH-CENTURY ENGLISH NOVEL

David E. Musselwhite

METHUEN · LONDON AND NEW YORK

First published in 1987 by
Methuen & Co. Ltd
11 New Fetter Lane,
London EC4P 4EE

Published in the USA by
Methuen & Co.
in association with Methuen, Inc.
29 West 35th Street,
New York, NY 10001

Photoset by
Rowland Phototypesetting Ltd
Bury St Edmunds, Suffolk
Printed in Great Britain at
the University Press, Cambridge

British Library Cataloguing in
Publication Data
Musselwhite, David E.
    Partings welded together: politics
    and desire in the nineteenth-
    century English novel.
    1. English fiction – 19th century –
    History and criticism
    I. Title
    823'.7'09   PR861

ISBN 0 416 06162 1
        0 416 06172 9 Pbk

Library of Congress
Cataloging-in-Publication Data
Musselwhite, David E., 1940–
    Partings welded together.
    Bibliography: p.
    Includes index.
    1. English fiction – 19th century –
    History and criticism. 2. Politics in
    literature. I. Title.
    PR868.P6M87   1987   823'.8'09358
    87-11238

ISBN 0 416 06162 1
        0 416 06172 9 (pbk.)

For my parents
All of them

Contents

Acknowledgements

It will be clear from what follows that I am less than enthusiastic about the way in which literary studies are pursued in this country, both on the right and on the 'left'. It gives me all the more pleasure, therefore, to acknowledge warmly my thanks to Leon Burnett and Elaine Jordan, of Essex University, for having read and commented on earlier drafts of several pieces in this book. Most warmly felt thanks too to Maurice Hindle, at the Tower Hamlets Institute of Higher Education, and William Rowe, of London University, for the great support and enthusiasm they have shown while I have been preparing the final text. Both combine a love of literature and a sense of what matters most that is rare indeed. I would also like to register here, again most warmly, my thanks for the help given me while working on the Brontë material by the former curator at Haworth, Ms Sally Stonehouse and the current curator and librarian, Dr Juliette Barker and Ms Sally Johnson. Thanks, too, to Jean Poynter and Sylvia Sparrow, here at Essex, for having typed out earlier drafts of some of the material here but, on this practical front, my greatest debt has been to Colin Ferryman who has, on more than one occasion, rescued whole pages of text from the memory of my ageing Osborne I.

David E. Musselwhite
University of Essex
1986

'Pip, dear old chap, life is made up of
ever so many partings welded together.'
Joe Gargery, *Great Expectations*

'I can't stand objections.'
Gilles Deleuze (attributed)

1

Introduction

The title of this book – *Partings Welded Together* – is meant to convey a number of things. The two most important are the following:

The first – though not necessarily the most important – is that the following essays and their being 'welded' together into a single volume are essentially provisional groupings of what I regard as being more properly lines of flight. There are coherences here and even the beginnings of a rudimentary thesis – for example that as we move through the nineteenth century we can see the gradual construction of a model of the unconscious and its workings that will become, in the work of Freud, the 'Oedipus complex' – but I know better than anybody that many of the joints in my argument are shaky and question-begging. Most of the chapters have, at one time or another, been anathematized by friends and colleagues. To an extent I have courted this anathematization for it seems to me that that is the price one has to pay to work any kind of place within a discipline that is numbingly conformist and disinclined to take risks. This is not to beat my breast too much – for what real risks am I taking as I write this 'Introduction', for example, complying with all the protocols of the trade? – but I hope that the essays included here will create some disturbances, some reassessments, some annoyances and irritations, hopefully some smiles and pleasures.

The second point that the title I have chosen is intended to draw attention to is that the works studied here must also be regarded as the 'welding together of many partings', as the hard and sometimes brittle forging of coherences and cohesions out of materials set on flight and dispersal. The notion of the 'decentred text', or the 'absent centre', no longer disturbs anyone – though I remember it creating apoplexy in staff–student seminars not so long ago – and, indeed, its invocation now too often seems little more than a tease (as in those fluttering allusions to the 'real' or to 'history' as the 'absent cause' of some specific work or other). Nevertheless many of the readings that follow have tried to trace the dispersal of the texts that they address and to find their determinations in, at times, quite remote and unexpected places – in France, in Belgium, in Egypt, in Switzerland. One effect of this, I hope, is to disabuse us once and for all – some hope! – of the 'essential Englishness' of the 'English' novel. But there are other dispersals, too, that I have tried to trace and celebrate: the dispersal of identity, the fracturing of time, the conjugation of genders.

There is a third sense in which the following essays may be regarded as a number of 'partings': that is in the frequent use I have made of the work of a number of recent theorists, particularly of Derrida, Foucault, Lacan and, above all (I shall return to this in a moment) of Deleuze and Guattari. There are also important debts to the work of Pierre Macherey, Renée Balibar and Ernesto Laclau. My readings, therefore, can be seen as a series of experimental 'applications' or 'testings' of the theories offered by these people. But I have tried to do a little more than just 'apply' these theories – the effect of such applications on uninitiated readers often being no more enlightening than a three-card trick. What I have tried to do is use my readings of the various texts as practical, 'hands on', introductions to the theories themselves. Chapter 3, on *Frankenstein*, for example, is meant to be an easily accessible introduction to Derrida's early work on 'écriture' and the 'supplementary body' as it is to be found in his essay on Rousseau in his *Of Grammatology*.[1] Perhaps immodestly, I think this is as good an introduction to Derrida and to 'deconstructionism' as you are likely to get. At the end of the same chapter I have drawn extensively on

Foucault's account of the 'invention of man' to be found in *The Order of Things*:[2] in neither case — Derrida or Foucault — have I given an 'account' of their work — there are too many such accounts in my opinion — but I have tried to give an example of the kinds of reading their theories can generate. In many ways, indeed, the *Frankenstein* chapter is close to being a pastiche of Derrida and this should be borne in mind when one discovers the 'mistakes' and 'excesses' of this chapter: I am not trying to provide a 'correct' reading but to set a methodological ball rolling, a 'parting' in other words. I had better add now that, as far as I know, there are no mistakes or excesses in that chapter — not even the mistakes are mistakes or the excesses excesses. If the *Frankenstein* chapter is a pastiche of Derrida then Chapter 4, on *Wuthering Heights* is, in many ways, a pastiche of the work of Renée Balibar's *Les Français fictifs*[3] where she considers, in her chapter on Camus, the specific effects of a writer's education on his or her later work. As I say in that chapter, Balibar's work is outrageous: it brings back with a vengeance that old empirical category of 'influences' and, in many ways, my study of Emily Brontë and the account I give of the origins of Heathcliff is the crudest possible example of the exploring of 'influences'. If that is so I remain unrepentant for I think the research involved in this chapter — the 'archival retrieval' I understand the current buzz-word to be — was not only incredibly exciting in itself but also made possible and, I hope, convincing what I regard as the most sophisticated *theoretical* passages in this book as a whole. To parody Barthes, for a moment, one might say that 'a little empiricism may take us away from theory, but a lot of empiricism takes us back to it.' Chapter 5, on *Vanity Fair*, is possibly the oldest piece included here and the only one to have been published elsewhere. It is difficult in places in its discussion of the breakdown of representation and the relation between desire and the body. Even so it seems to me that, even to the reader new to Deleuze and Guattari's[4] notions of the flows of desire and the 'body without organs', the discussion of the 'schizophrenic' split in Thackeray figured in the relation between Becky and Jos Sedley is not only fairly easy to understand in itself but is also a fairly accessible introduction to such notions. Chapter 6, on Dickens, again returns almost to the mode of pastiche: ideally I would like the reader to think he or she is reading Deleuze and Guattari for I have tried, I hope with some success, to slip my reading of Dickens in and out of the pages of their *Anti-Oedipus* and *Mille Plateaux*: I would like to think it is a strategy that would meet with their approval. Finally, though it comes early in the book, in Chapter 2, on *Mansfield Park*, I have tried to illustrate the strategies, delineated by Ernesto Laclau, by means of which a would-be hegemonic class appropriates to itself the popular-democratic mobilizations of the masses.[5]

That last sentence – indeed the reason for it being last – is a terrible mouthful, I know, and this takes me onto the next point.

I like to think of myself as a fairly good teacher and this means that I would like to be understood. All of the chapters in this book have been given as lectures to undergraduates and one or two of them to secondary school audiences without causing, so far as I know, any great distress. Nevertheless it has been put to me that much of what I have written is 'difficult' and that I 'make too many demands upon [my] readers'. It is, of course, professionally flattering to have one's work described as 'difficult' but I am genuinely sorry that this should be the case. I often feel terribly apologetic about writing yet another book on the English Nineteenth-century Novel – it's so *boring*! Well, no it's not and I really think that a lot of what I have to say in the following pages is quite exciting and happy-making as well as being very relevant (I'm not sure that that is a word one is allowed to use at the moment) to what I consider to be the quite appalling predicament we find ourselves in in Britain in the mid-1980s. This being the case I would like as many people as possible to read what I have to say and understand it. I don't want this book to be accessible only to 'post-graduate' readers: what a horrendous thought that is! This being so I am going to write not one, not two, but what in effect will be *three* introductions.

The first will be a simple introduction to the essays that follow. I realize that in doing this I run the risk of spoiling all the fun and maybe even exposing how little I really have to say but I think it is important to break with the almost intolerable claustrophobia of so much academic criticism, especially of much that passes for 'radical' or 'marxist' or 'theoretical' work. Much of it is belletrist to the extent of being totally at home within an aestheticist and decadent establishment totally incapable of countering the Thatcher 'wind of change' either intellectually or practically. What is not belletrist is often terrorizing and dogmatic and pre-emptive.

The second 'introduction', which I will furnish as Appendix I (see pp. 227 ff.), will consist of a very simplified and schematic introduction to the work of Deleuze and Guattari. I offer this with some diffidence for I have not read all their work and much of what I have read I do not always understand. Nevertheless their work seems to me to be of such importance and such originality and excitement that I would at least like to try to share it. Those who would like a fuller introduction to their work might look at Jean-Jacques Lecercle's *Philosophy through the Looking-Glass*[6] and a delightful taste of it can be gained from the two essays that appear in *On the Line* published by Semiotexte.[7]

The third 'introduction', Appendix II (see pp. 240 ff.) will take the form of a critique of Fredric Jameson's *The Political Unconscious.*[8] Jameson's title suggests that he shares many of my own concerns but, that having been said, I find that we differ on practically all else. I deliberately did not read Jameson's book until mine was finished and certainly I did not set out to challenge his work. Nevertheless as my work is so indebted to Deleuze and Guattari and as Jameson's work has been seen as a challenge to their work, I now feel that I cannot avoid making some comment on the sheer travesty of Jameson's account of Deleuze and Guattari and what I regard as the disturbingly reactionary implications of what is offered as the latest thinking by America's 'leading marxist critic'.[9]

It is always an enormous pleasure, as well as being a relief, to come to the end of a piece of work which has been tentative and explorative and then to find that someone else has all the time been working along very similar lines, fired by the same angers, impatient with the same things and concerned with the same objectives. In my case this pleasure and relief has come from being introduced to the recent work by Philip Corrigan and Derek Sayer, *The Great Arch*,[10] the subtitle of which is 'English state formation as cultural revolution'. Summarizing drastically, what Corrigan and Sayer's particular object of investigation is is the way in which 'the state' organizes and legitimizes itself not simply by overt force nor by promulgating integrative ideologies but by the massive and disseminated operation of myriad forms of regulation and machining that classify, designate, identify, gender, homogenize and normalize so that those material differences and practices and behaviours that resist these operations are relegated to the status of the unthinkable, the aberrant, the unimaginable. The 'state' is not some monolithic despot sitting on high and ruling by main force but – and the pun is theirs – a collection of 'state-ments' that make it possible only for some things to be said while all that threatens the coherence of such a collection – what Foucault would call an 'archive' – is consigned to silence, is rendered literally 'unspeakable'.

Corrigan and Sayer's book is a massive piece of historiographical scholarship and my claiming fellowship with them opens me to the charge of seeking to bask in reflected glory, for my own work consists of no more than a number of readings of what are very much a group of set texts of the normal 'English Literature' curriculum. But two things: what struck me about *The Great Arch* was the anger that had clearly been inspired in the authors by the 1984 miners' strike (an anger fuelled even by that phrase – the 'miners'' strike: why not 'Mac-Gregor's' strike? or 'Thatcher's' strike?[11] – but it is precisely this manipulation of language that Corrigan and Sayer's book is about, as is, indeed, this one). My own work has also been written against the background of the 1984 strike and it would distress me if that were not apparent. The second thing that struck me about Corrigan and Sayer's book was its 'moral' outrage, its indignation. Now, like them, I am writing in what I think is a marxist or radical tradition and my readings are 'political' – as, indeed, all readings must be. But I have not tried to follow a 'line' – and I am all too familiar with the charges of being 'anarchistic', or 'eclectic' – and I would like to think that, in the end, the major thrust of my book is in fact ethical – very much in the sense that Foucault describes Deleuze and Guattari's *Anti-Oedipus* as a 'book of ethics'. We are frightened and unhappy and confused and terrorized by the 'state-ments' that are the 'state' and one of the principal concerns of the following pages has been to 'comb back', as it were, some of those major 'state-ments' that are some of our best-loved, as the phrase goes, novels, to show as best I can, all that their 'systems of narration'[12] have tried to hide, to render unsaid, to silence.

Which takes me to the next point of congruence I find between my work and that of Corrigan and Sayer – our impatience with the notion of 'ideology' – that 'execrable concept' as Deleuze and Guattari describe it. The 'unsaids' and 'silences' I have tried to locate in – sometimes in spite of – the texts studied here are not just those discursive 'blindspots' of ideology that Macherey and Althusser tell us 'literature allows us to read' but, rather, practices, conducts, behaviours, possibilities that are, in many ways, exorbitant to the very thought, the categories, the grammar, the 'state-ments' we have at our disposal. The 'state' does work by 'ideas', 'ideals' and by 'ideology' – they are, indeed, what it proffers us. But more importantly – and Corrigan and Sayer urge this again and again – the 'state' operates most effectively by engineering, by marking, by machining, by, even, 'hammering'. Ideological inter- pellation is too kind and gentle a term for this painful tooling of our sexuality, our 'individuality', our 'places' – in every sense of that term. And language is machinic, too, and this is possibly one of the strongest themes of the essays in this book. 'Feminine', 'masculine', 'housewife', 'worker', 'unemployed', 'father' – these are not designations only, but *effects*: they bear upon deportment, upon musculature, upon conduct. Language constitutes 'sentences' in the strongest sense of that term: we are 'sentenced' to being 'male' or 'female', 'father' or 'child' – even 'alive' or 'dead'. It is this material effect of language that makes it part of the infrastructure of a society rather than a mere superstructural echo or shadow. As Deleuze and Guattari say:

> How poorly the problem of literature is put, starting from the ideology that it bears . . . it [ideology] is the most confused notion because it keeps us from seizing the relationship of the literary machine with a field of production.[13]

or, as Corrigan and Sayer put it:

> we are talking not just of 'ideologies', but of the regulated formation of identities and subjectivities (male as much as female).[14]

Corrigan and Sayer describe their work as the study of 'the im- mensely long, complicated, laborious micro-construction and recon- struction of appropriate forms of power'[15] but though they term this process, quite correctly, as a 'cultural revolution' they, in fact, look very little at what we would normally regard as straightforward 'cultural' works – such as, for example, literary texts, which are the object of my concern here. In this sense, then, I regard the readings that follow as in some ways complementary to that searching analysis of forms of order and regulative practices – laws, institutions, sociological concepts, historiographical categories – which makes up *The Great Arch*. But, not to be too modest, I think what I have also done is address even more directly than they have done what they several times suggest is the most important problem of all, that is 'the presence of "the idea of the state" within us, in the multiple ways it totalises and individualises us'.[16] Elsewhere they state:

A central dimension – we are tempted to say, the secret – of state power is the way it works within us.[17]

The problem is put most clearly in the following:

The enormous power of 'the State' is not only external and objective; it is in equal part internal and subjective, it works through us. It works above all through the myriad ways it collectively and individually (mis)represents us and variously 'encourages', cajoles, and in the final analysis forces us to (mis)represent ourselves.[18]

I would want to argue that a most important agency for that process of internalization, or subjectivization, of the 'idea of the state' was the nineteenth-century novel. In the first place novel-reading itself *works* what Corrigan and Sayer suggest is one of the fundamental contradictions of the bourgeois order – that which yields what they call its 'social schizophrenia'[19] – that paradoxical determination to both 'homogenize' and 'individualize' the occupants of the social space – especially the masses. Reading a 'best-seller' is both a highly private act and an act of social solidarity. (I think it is only fair to myself to point out that it is precisely this 'schizophrenic' project of 'homogenizing' and 'indiwiddle-izing' that I draw attention to in my essay on Dickens.)

But the novel operates in other ways too, many of which I am concerned with in the following pages. The novel does, of course, present arguments and ideas and values – the domain of ideology. But it probably works most effectively where it is most 'transparent', in its concern, for example, with 'narrative' itself, centred as it so often is on the trajectory of a 'character's' 'life': all three are specific constructs, underwriting, making possible, certain patterns of motivation and behaviour and proscribing others. Among the questions raised in what follows are how can behaviours be ordered otherwise than as a sequential narrative? What can it be like not to be a 'character' or an 'individual'? How limiting is the notion of a 'life'? What *other* sexualities are possible apart from those termed 'male' and 'female' or 'masculine' and 'feminine'? So many forms of (mis)representation and so many forms of the internalization of 'the idea of the state' which requires, constitutes, in fact *is*, the registering of identities, the division of sexes, the structuring of 'lives'. And nowhere is the process of internalization more virulent than in the notion of the 'family' – with daddy/male/despot, mummy/female/slave, and the child to be gendered, individualized, regulated. The family as a nucleus of rivalries, threats, deferred promises and severely coded places centred on a despotic signifier and a lack: the phallus to be castrated and envied. The family and its taboos which at the end of the century are formulated in the Oedipus complex is the principal means by which the 'idea of the state' comes to be internalized and subjectivized.

> Father, mother, and child thus become the simulacrum of the images of capital ('Mister Capital', 'Madame Earth', and their child the Worker), with the result that these images are no longer recognised at all in the desire that is determined to invest only their simulacrum. The familial determinations become the application of a social axiomatic. . . . In short, Oedipus arrives: . . . . It is our intimate colonial formation that corresponds to the form of social sovereignty. We are little colonies and it is Oedipus that colonizes us.[20]

One of the principal themes of the essays that follow is the account of how from Jane Austen to Dickens – the process continues in George Eliot and Hardy – the exuberance and the threat of the forces let loose by the development of industrialism and the French Revolution – I have in mind the creation of a new urban populace on the one hand and the affording of new human possibilities on the other – are steadily but ineluctably worked within a new axiomatic, a new set of rules and constraints, of prescribed places and possibilities that made them both manageable and self-monitoring. At the political and social level it is achieved by deploying such notions as 'class' (see Chapter 2, *Mansfield Park* and Chapter 3, *Frankenstein*), the nature of 'knowledge' (see Chapter 3, *Frankenstein*), the 'role' of 'women' (see Chapter 4, *Wuthering Heights*), 'representative democracy' (see Chapter 5, *Vanity Fair*), the distinctions between 'public' and 'private' (see Chapter 6, Dickens). At the personal and psychological level – and I have tried to show various stages of this happening in the essays that follow – the potential of desire, which should be social and productive, can be seen to be slowly asphyxiated by the elaboration, first bit by bit (see my remarks on *The Old Curiosity Shop* pp. 193–4) and then more sustainedly (see Chapter 5 on *Vanity Fair* and the discussion of Dickens's 'Autobiographical Fragment', pp. 153–68) of an 'Oedipus complex'. Desire, which belongs to the domain of production – it *is* production – becomes trammeled up in the tawdry and preposterous paraphernalia of a classical theatre.

A word in edgeways here concerning 'my methodology'. Recall 'Partings . . .': I am not trying to tie everything up in some absolutely convincing overall theme. I am trying to set some hares running. I am not sure that Deleuze and Guattari are 'right' and maybe the 'Oedipus complex' is universal – though I find that a ludicrous idea – and therefore the 'anticipations' I see in some of the texts I have studied derives from that universality. But I haven't just picked up my *Anti-Oedipus* – difficult as it is, itself, by now, a sorry collection of 'partings' – and just swatted everything that hove into view with it. In the case of each of the texts I have looked at here – with the exception of Dickens's 'Autobiographical Fragment' – my readings began as just that: 'readings': I didn't go looking for bodies without organs and 'corps morcelés' and I don't think I have 'forced' my readings into a preconceived pattern. There is much of the Leavis in me in the following readings, both in the ethical concern and in the ambition to read the words on the page: I have tried to read closely and listen to what the texts themselves had to say and I have tried to be as true to the texts as possible. My basic 'methodology' – and my first counsel to all students – is to 'let the texts do the work for you' and that is what I have tried to do here. To this extent – to return to my earlier remarks on 'applying' theories – I have endeavoured as much to let Austen, Shelley, Brontë and the rest *read* Derrida, Foucault and Deleuze and Guattari as the other way round. I also happen to think that that is the right way to go about things. The exception here has been the Dickens piece for in turning to Dickens I came face to face with Steven Marcus's very accomplished oedipal reading of the 'Autobiographical Fragment' and I felt that this would make a good test, or control, for a 'deleuzian' reading: if such a reading could outflank, so to speak, and comprehend Marcus's reading – not prove it 'wrong' for Marcus's reading is what the 'Autobiographical Fragment' hankers for – then I felt that this was as good a test of Deleuze and Guattari as one could get. The reader will decide on the outcome for him- or herself.

It is with reference to my discussion of *Mansfield Park* that the provisionality implicit in the 'Partings . . .' of my title needs, possibly, to be most generously interpreted for this essay is at times speculative to the point of impertinence. It began most soberly as a re-examination of the notorious '*Lovers' Vows* episode' and of the alleged 'seriousness' of *Mansfield Park* but in the course of writing I found myself pondering issues – such as the origins of 'class-consciousness' – which can hardly be settled on the basis of a reading of one, albeit very complex, novel. Nevertheless I would like my impertinences to be allowed their little day for, in the first place, any contribution to what is a problem by no means resolved by historians themselves should not be despised on account of its narrowly 'literary' basis and, in the second, I would like to make the case that the study of literature should be far more ready to intervene in debates which not only have a significance with regard to the understanding of the past but that might also bear upon current debates and current situations.

My principal argument in the *Mansfield Park* essay is that it is not a 'defensive' novel – defending Jane Austen's class interests – but an 'aggressive' one, a determined search for a market. To achieve that, I argue, Jane Austen needed a formula of proven popular appeal and this she found in the 'jacobinism' of Kotzebue's *Lovers' Vows*. By 'stealing' the radical and popular appeal of the jacobin tradition Jane Austen managed, at one and the same time, to construct an 'ideology' that would become 'victorianism' and *made silent* – because 'their' 'speech' had been 'stolen' from them – those groups and forces – variously to be designated as 'the people', or the 'masses' – who were the more properly legitimate heirs to the jacobinical tradition. It is part of my argument that the 'Portsmouth chapters' of *Mansfield Park* which contain a whole range of heterogeneous languages and voices is the presence within the novel of a whole social sector 'beyond the pale'[21] of the dominant narrative mode of the novel as a whole. 'Portsmouth', that is, is that area of threat and 'otherness' that the ideological framework elaborated by *Mansfield Park* is designed specifically to exclude, silence, marginalize. In this sense, then, *Mansfield Park* is a 'statement' of power similar to those described by Corrigan and Sayer:

> We are registered within the state community as citizens, voters, taxpayers, ratepayers, jurors, parents, consumers, homeowners – individuals. In both aspects of this representation alternative modes of collective and individual identification (and comprehension), and the social, political and personal practices they could sustain, are denied legitimacy.[22]

What 'Portsmouth' represents, then, is that whole cluster of heterogeneity that cannot even be 'thought', not even by, indeed especially not by, the languages of 'class'. For the purposes of my book as a whole we can say that *Mansfield Park* 'produces' that area of 'unthinkability' which haunts, sadly with ever decreasing energy, the other studies – the Monster in *Frankenstein*, E.B. and the revolutionary tradition in the chapter on *Wuthering Heights*, Becky Sharp and the 'bohème' in the chapter on *Vanity Fair*, and the gangs and crowds and nomadism of the chapter on Dickens.

I know it's not fashionable to make value-judgements – given the 'scientific' pretensions of much recent theoretical work – but I have not hesitated to do so in the chapters that follow. It seems to me, for example, that Mary Shelley's *Frankenstein* is a greatly underestimated work for it addresses head-on and in the most sustained and almost breathtakingly astonishing way a whole range of problems that are germane to the understanding of our society and ourselves. The 'Monster' is the heterogeneous itself, scrambling codes, refusing classifications, shrugging off designations and identifications. If it is the ambition of 'the state' to 'mark', 'machine', 'hammer' – the words of Corrigan and Sayer – then no one is more 'marked', 'machined' and 'hammered' than is the Monster. And the violence, above all, is of language itself for only in language can the 'monstrous' itself be at once formed and execrated. What I have tried to show in my discussion of *Frankenstein* is the pain and the waste generated by a whole discursive machinery – a grammar – that is, in its very essence, despotic, patriarchal, divisive, and terrorizing. The fate of the Monster, perhaps, more than anything else in what follows illustrates graphically and forcefully what Corrigan and Sayer have to say about the 'state's' strategies of integration:

> What state activities above all regulate into silence are precisely identifications in terms of, and expressions of the experience of, differences – in other words, that which materially (as opposed to ideologically) makes us what we are. . . . Integration needs to be understood at least as much in terms of rendering the subordinate speechless – striking them dumb – as in terms of the active securing of assent. . . . It is insufficiently appreciated – including by Marxists – just how violent such 'integration' is for the 'integrated' majority . . . it is of itself a massively violent disruption of human personality, a crippling restriction of human capacity.[23]

But what the Monster also shows – herein is the 'monstrosity' – is that things might be otherwise: that there are, have been, and will be *other* social forms, *other* configurations of knowledge, *other* forms of human and personal relationships, *other* subjectivities, *other* sexualities.[24] If the notion of 'partings . . .' was appealed to rather defensively in relation to *Mansfield Park*, then here it can unembarrassedly be proclaimed on high.

For those looking for a new reading of *Wuthering Heights* I should perhaps say now that my chapter on it should perhaps be called '*Not* the *Wuthering Heights*' for there is, in fact, very little in it on the novel itself. My principal interest here has been with the person who called herself – or was called – 'Emily Brontë'. One of the angry themes running through Corrigan and Sayer's book is the way in which our society has categorized, marked, and marginalized women. In the *Frankenstein* chapter I have tried to show how one brilliant woman struggled with the labels foisted upon her, and, now in the chapter not about *Wuthering Heights*, I have tried to show how another, greater, more powerful woman transcended the petty and humiliating claustrophobia of her environment – even of her age – and achieved an intensity and reality of being that demonstrates with a force of incontestable conviction that something else is, indeed, possible. The great mystic poems I have quoted here are, if you like, the utterances of an ineffable monstrosity.

Emily's – I would prefer to say Ellis's – flight is already too hard, too frightening, too threatening for any but a few to follow and certainly any sign that it were to excite a mass exodus would be severely policed – perhaps is already policed by the grotesquely over-reverential celebration of the jejune and surrogate intensities of *Wuthering Heights*. Thackeray, too, it is the argument of the chapter on *Vanity Fair*, knew something of the allure and threat of a schizoid peregrination of intensities. Again I have used biographical material to cast light on a social crisis which I am told again and again I too lightly and too unproblematically characterize as '1848' – though I think in the *Vanity Fair* chapter I have gone some way towards providing a historical contextualization of what was, undoubtedly, a critical moment in nineteenth-century history. It was, if it was nothing else, the end of the heroic age of the bourgeoisie and it was time to take in hand and subject to more rigorous control the exuberance of its own energies and of the forces it had unleashed elsewhere. The new 'policing' is manifest in the passing of the various Factory Acts, in the professionalization of the Civil Service, the enlargement of the franchise, the beginnings of universal education and so forth. But the novel, itself, enacts its own 'policing' operations. In *Vanity Fair* it can be seen in the curtailment of contemporary references, the exclusion of modes of popular expression, the collapse of historical time, and the deployment of a new – albeit confused – moral earnestness. But it is evident most of all in the contrast established between the mercurial Becky Sharp and the spoilt, winsome and indulged Amelia Sedley. The Monster, Emily Brontë/ Ellis Bell, Becky Sharp – these are the heroic figures of an energy and a desire that refuse to be classed, gendered, grammaticalized and that offer the promise that some kind of resistance is possible. With Amelia Sedley and her infatuations with both her husband and her son all desire and energy become bound within the neurotic confines of a domestic scene structured upon a fetishized absence – not Oedipus yet, but so close, so close.

Perhaps what keeps Oedipus at bay in *Vanity Fair* is its lack of internalization, its indifference to any sustained probing of motives and psychological processes. In this sense *Vanity Fair* is, in many ways, a very superficial book – but that, as I hope my discussion of it makes clear, is not to disparage it: far from it – it is the surface, the superficial, that needs to be protected from that morbid fascination with and privileging of the 'deep', the 'inner', the 'psychological' which has so often been taken to be the 'mark' (the term itself is highly ironical) of the 'great' novelist. It is this break between surface and depth which I have tried to trace in the long essay on Dickens. The argument here – and even I am slightly aghast at it – is that 'Boz' – Dickens's pseudonym at the beginning of his career – was a 'better' writer than 'Dickens' precisely because he, 'Boz', was fascinated by the surfaces of things, by the variegated play and heterogeneity of the world about him which, to a large extent, Dickens abandons in the process of constituting himself as a 'great' novelist, turning increasingly – and being still lauded for it – to a preoccupation with inner psychological states. Dickens's 'greatness' maybe lies in the fact that he was *the* great Pied Piper of the nineteenth-century bourgeoisie in that in his work he piped out and drowned the swarming energies of the heroic period – though, like the Pied Piper, too, the price of destroying the rats was the tragic immolation of childhood as well. It is this twin process that I have tried to show taking place in my reading of his brief 'Autobiographical Fragment':

the loss of a surface of display and inscription and the morbid construction instead of an infant psychopathology. The increasing concern with
'inwardness' in the later novels is only the achievement it is so often
represented as being because we still too readily privilege 'inwardness'
as somehow 'better' than 'superficiality': it was this very privileging
that Dickens, among others, legitimized. It is another form of 'statement': 'the state' is quite happy for us to be 'inward' – 'you don't hate
Mrs Thatcher, you hate your mother' – what it can't stand is that we
take to the streets. Moreover, I don't think Dickens knew what he was
doing – or, at least, the dreadful distress of the later novels seems to me
to be the distress of a man vaguely aware that everything he is doing is
somehow wrong but he doesn't know why. The dust-heaps of *Our
Mutual Friend* are like the aftermath of a holocaust and, in so many
ways, we are still picking among the ruins.

2

Return to *Mansfield Park*

There is a certain ruefulness about the title I have given to this chapter quite apart from the political point it is intended to make and to which I shall return later. For I began this study of *Mansfield Park* several years ago, now, and my concern then was to take up yet again what are probably the two principal 'problems' raised by the text. The first was the matter of the novel's 'seriousness', the extent, that is, to which it marks a distinct break with the work that had gone before it, particularly *Pride and Prejudice.* The second was the extremely vexed question of the 'private theatricals' episode: why had Jane Austen rounded upon and so severely condemned an activity which, as we know from other sources, she had formerly so thoroughly enjoyed? In addition to addressing these two major issues it was also my intention to give rather more attention than has been generally the case to two other troublesome aspects of the novel: the first concerns the Portsmouth chapters which seem to remain so incongruously marginal to the main body of the text and the second has to do with what I have always felt to be the astounding charge of animus that surrounds the figure of Mrs

Norris. Finally, I wanted to conclude by saying something about *Mansfield Park* as an ideological institution, that is about whom it addresses and about the kinds of values it impresses upon those it addresses. It was here, in fact that the 'return to . . .' came in: why are we always returning to *Mansfield Park*? why is it a favourite 'set-text', and so on and so forth.

I am, in fact, still concerned with these issues but in the course of my own turning and returning to the book much of what I wanted to say seemed to be increasingly self-evident while, at the same time, as I became aware of the critical historical moment of *Mansfield Park* I found myself, and still find myself, grappling with problems which are more properly the province of the fully qualified historian. What these problems principally centre upon are the emergence of modern class society and class consciousness and, closely related to these, the means by which the distinctive ideology of the nineteenth-century bourgeoisie, liberal reformism, achieved its hegemonic status. These are pretty intractable matters, even for the professional historian, and I would have avoided them if I could. On the other hand it became increasingly impossible to disengage the complexities of *Mansfield Park* from at least some consideration of the wider political and social movements of its period while, at the same time, there is the flattering hope that what began as a simple textual exegesis might, in the event, contribute to a greater understanding of what is unquestionably a very critical period of nineteenth-century social history. What follows, then, may be regarded as falling into two parts, though the line between them will be anything but clear, the first consisting of a fairly straightforward 'literary' reading of the text whereas the second should be considered as a tentative and speculative excursion into a number of 'historical' hypotheses.

I will begin by considering the 'seriousness' of *Mansfield Park*.

I

The two most common explanations for the new seriousness of *Mansfield Park* are, first, biographical and, second, class situation. Possibly the most succinct summary of the biographical explanation is that furnished by Q. D. Leavis:

> In 1813 Jane Austen was in her thirty-eighth year and had gone through a great deal. She had, like her sister, lost by death the only man she could care for; she had lost her dearly loved father

and early home, and lost some of her closest friends in tragic circumstances. She had rejected on second thoughts a conspicuously eligible offer of marriage after accepting it, and had now long passed the age of twenty seven when that offer occurred – an age which in her novels is taken to mark, as she would say, a period. She must have had the sense that her real life lay in the past, and that the time had come to reconsider it.[1]

It is likely, the argument then runs, that, given this personal history and her age, Miss Austen would now be 'resigned to spinsterhood and was, inevitably, of a more serious cast of mind'[2] and it is not to be wondered at that she should critically revise the lighter ironic tone of the earlier work and set herself, instead, a more weighty ethical purpose. The letters of this period are seemingly supportive of such a hypothesis – the most frequently cited being the letter to her niece Cassandra announcing

> Now I will try to write of something else, and it shall be a complete change of subject – ordination – . . . .[3]

Furthermore, elsewhere in the letters, this change of subject and of heart seems to be connected with a changed attitude towards the Evangelical movement. Jane Austen writes to advise Fanny Knight as to how she should treat a rather serious-minded suitor:

> As for there being any objection from his goodness, from the danger of his becoming even Evangelical, I cannot admit that. I am by no means convinced that we ought not all to be Evangelicals, and am at least persuaded that they who are so from reason and feeling, must be happiest and safest. Do not be frightened from the connexion by your Brothers having most wit. Wisdom is better than wit and in the long run will certainly have the laugh on her side; and don't be frightened by the idea of his acting more strictly up to the precepts of the New Testament than others.[4]

In other words, the 'high seriousness' of *Mansfield Park*, its consistent suppression and chastisement of irony, wit, sex, pleasure, etc. is symptomatic of a profound change in Jane Austen's view of her art born of personal crisis, emotional distress and an awakening religious consciousness. Instead of the wit and spirited verve of, say, *Pride and Prejudice*, *Mansfield Park* was, to quote Marvin Mudrick, 'to be a novel vindicating the ethical foundation of Jane Austen's world'.[5]

It is at this point that we can conveniently link the biographical explanation of the novel's seriousness with the class explanation. This is to the effect that in *Mansfield Park* Jane Austen was not concerned to vindicate simply the ethical foundation of her own personal world but that of her class as a whole – the rural gentry. For reasons that will emerge later the notion of a rural class, as such, is highly problematic and it is probably more accurate to speak of Jane Austen's 'class' as a specific stratum within a much more heterogeneous gentry grouping, ranging from minor aristocratic families at the top to tenant farmers and trade-made *arrivistes* at the bottom.[6] Be that as it may, Jane Austen, the daughter of a clergyman, would have found herself situated at a particularly sensitive juncture of this formation, ideologically dominant but economically extremely vulnerable. She could not be, then, but peculiarly alert to the internal and external threats to her particular social group: the imminent collapse of the hegemonic role of the landed aristocracy and the burgeoning growth of conservative and revolutionary radicalism represented respectively by luddism and jacobinism. What *Mansfield Park* represents, then, given this context, it is argued, is a last-ditch defence of the inherited values of her group. What Fanny Price and later her sister Susan illustrate is the attempt by a gentry suffering from moral and economic decay to graft new blood onto its withered stock. It is this purging and purifying of the stock that explains the need to get rid of the irresponsible Crawfords, to teach the young Bertrams a lesson, and to make Sir Thomas face up to his shortcomings and responsibilities.

In fact I think both these explanations are almost wholly mistaken. Let us take the first one, that puts the new seriousness of *Mansfield Park* down to Jane Austen's alleged 'change of life'. It depends very largely on a highly selective use of quotations from the letters. There has already been some debate as to what the 'ordination' letter refers to – could it not just be referring to a change of topic *in the letter itself*?

> Now I will try to write of something else, and it shall be a complete change of subject – ordination – I am glad to find your enquiries have ended so well.[7]

The 'ordination' comes in very parenthetically: it reads like a nudge to a topic already well discussed rather than something entirely 'new' and, indeed, could not the enquiries have had something to do with the ordination of Henry Austen which was to take place only a couple of years later? So weak is the evidence here – as, indeed, it is in the novel as a whole – that 'ordination' or any religio-ethical theme is to figure prominently in the novel that further evidence is required. However, when we turn to the much-quoted passage on the Evangelicals we find what *immediately* runs on from it is consistently ignored:

> And now, my dear Fanny, having written so much on one side of the question, I shall turn round and entreat you not to commit yourself further, and not to think of accepting him unless you really do like him. Anything is to be preferred or endured rather than marrying without affection.[8]

and the matter is returned to again in the next letter to Fanny:

> You will think me perverse perhaps; in my last letter I was urging everything in his favour, and now I am inclining the other way; but I cannot help it; I am at present more impressed with the possible Evil that may arise to *you* from engaging yourself to him – in word or mind – than with anything else.[9]

What the letters reveal, then, when not subjected to selective quotation, is less an unequivocal endorsement of the Evangelical movement than a sensible and poised pointing-out of the risks in committing oneself to a relationship based on any values other than love. In anticipation of the argument that follows it is perhaps worth remarking here that the question as to what constitutes a 'good' marriage as opposed to a 'bad' marriage is of central importance not only to *Mansfield Park* but also to Jane Austen's earlier work, *Lady Susan*, and to Kotzebue's *Lovers' Vows*, and is discussed in all three in very similar terms.

Returning to the letters: if we, in fact, take into account all the references to *Mansfield Park*, the rather wan picture of a melancholic middle-aged spinster endeavouring to offset her youthful irreverence by a studied concern for ethical absolutes tends, increasingly, to be supplanted by another, quite different, picture. This is that of a writer who has behind her two very successful novels – the last, *Pride and Prejudice*, exceedingly so and is beginning to realize that writing might mean rather more than the amusement of a close group of friends and acquaintances. That it might require, indeed, a greater degree of professional commitment and that that commitment might bring quite considerable rewards. This new professionalism is evident in a letter to Cassandra dated 4 February 1813. Jane Austen has been talking about *Pride and Prejudice* and continues:

> The work is rather too light, and bright, and sparkling; it wants shade; it wants to be stretched out here and there with a long chapter of sense, if it could be had; if not, of solemn specious nonsense, about something unconnected with the story; an essay on writing, a critique on Walter Scott, or the history of Buonaparte, or anything that would form a contrast, and bring the reader with increased delight to the playfulness and epigrammatism of the general style.[10]

What has to be noted about this, of course, is the extent to which *Mansfield Park* can be seen as an attempt to subscribe to such a programme – not an ethical or moral programme, but a professional, structural one: what is the discussion of 'out or not out' but a piece of 'solemn specious nonsense'? For Walter Scott the novel substitutes Shakespeare, while the very laboured debate on reading and sermon writing carried on by Edmund and Henry clearly constitutes a 'long chapter of sense'. It is true that there is no history of Bonaparte, but then there is Jane Austen's well-known, indeed notorious, indifference to history. . . . We shall see. Even so, it is becoming clear that the seriousness of *Mansfield Park* is less the result of a state of mind or of class apprehension than of a studied determination to write a well-organized and well-finished book.

Allied to this new professionalism is a hard-headed business awareness. The letters of this period are almost obsessive in their concern with money and with talk of numbers of editions, of copyrights, of credits and advances; 3 July 1813:

> You will be glad to hear that every copy of *Sense and Sensibility* is sold and that it has brought me 140 pounds besides the Copyright if ever that should be of any value. – I have now written myself into 250 pounds – which only makes me long for more. I have something in hand – which I hope on the credit of *Pride and Prejudice* will sell well, tho' not half so entertaining.[11]

18 November 1814:

> You will be glad to hear that the first Edit: of M.P. is all sold. – Your Uncle Henry is rather wanting me to come to town to settle

about the second edition. . . . I am very greedy and I want to make the most of it.[12]

and in a letter of 30 November 1814 the obsession with money is registered with a note of coarseness that reminds us disconcertingly of Mary Crawford's pun on 'Rears' and 'Vices':

Thank you, but it is not settled yet whether I do hazard a 2nd. Edit. We are determined to see Egerton today, when it will probably be determined. People are more ready to borrow and praise – which cannot be wondered at; but tho' I like praise as well as anybody, I like what Edward calls Pewter too.[13]

The same note of ruthlessness and exploitative zeal is to be found again in the letter where she announces that with the appearance of *Mansfield Park* she will give up her previous practice of anonymity:

I believe that whenever the 3rd. [novel] appears I shall not even attempt to tell lies about it [the name of the authoress]. I shall rather try to make all the money than all the mystery I can out of it – People shall pay for their knowledge if I can make them.[14]

adding, rather unnecessarily it might be thought, a few lines later: 'I am trying to harden myself.'[15]

Finally, this new, eminently practical and clear-eyed attitude towards her writing is further demonstrated in the way in which she set about culling and collecting various opinions of the novel, constructing, in effect, a balance sheet of reviews. She was furious, for example, that Walter Scott did not mention *Mansfield Park* in a survey of her work published in the *Quarterly Review*.

Far from being the expression of middle-age crisis, then, what the seriousness of *Mansfield Park* manifests is the determination to produce, at all costs, a best-seller. It is this that accounts for the frequent sense of contrivance in the book, the rather arch self-consciousness of the symbolism, for example, or the little set speeches of Fanny, so embarrassing at times, her prim quotes and too pat effusions.[16] And this is the point: *Mansfield Park* is, in many ways, written against the grain. Not only is it not the expression of Jane Austen's own personal predicament, it is not even a defence of the values of her own class. The whole motivation behind the production of *Mansfield Park* is not the defence of a threatened gentry but the aggressive search for a market. This means that she must canvass and appeal to an audience far wider than that offered by her own class, to a reading public at large. To achieve this she must wean herself of her natural ideological affiliations and espouse instead those values and concerns that will strike a responsive chord in that wider 'middle sector' being brought into being at the time by industrialization and urbanization. Systematically, throughout the book, the values and attributes we would normally associate with gentry society – 'manners', 'name', 'alliance', 'accomplishment', 'grace' – are replaced by a quite different set of values: 'disposition', 'generosity', 'self-knowledge', 'humility', 'steadiness and regularity of conduct', 'principle', 'duty', 'self-denial' – that is, those values which, as 'victorianism', will constitute the very core of bourgeois ideology for the rest of the century. It is, perhaps, the major achievement of *Mansfield Park* to have broken with the system of values of a waning rural order and to have replaced it by one better suited to the rigours of an imperial and industrial age. Fanny's piety and quietism, as well as her interest in the slave trade and Lord Macartney on China, are early examples of that censorious concernedness that will serve well as an apologetics for exploitation at home and imperial expansion abroad. The question that needs to be asked now is what was it that made possible this quite considerable leap of consciousness, that allowed Jane Austen to disengage herself from the ideology of her organic roots and to forge instead what was to become the characteristic ideology of an urban and industrious – as well as industrial – middle class. It is at this point that we must turn to the absolutely crucial importance of Mrs Inchbald's translation of Kotzebue's *Lovers' Vows*.

II

Probably the single most important study dedicated to the play episode is that of Lionel Trilling.[17] Trilling, it will be remembered, is concerned to examine the play episode in relation to what he considers to be the avowed theme of the novel, that of 'ordination': the latter is taken by Trilling in its widest sense to include also the whole question of a man's 'profession'. Accordingly he argues that the play is condemned in *Mansfield Park* – and by implication so is literature itself – because it offers the opportunity for the playing of different roles, thereby threatening a loss of self and of integrity. It is Trilling's account that is to be found repeated in Tanner's Introduction to the Penguin edition of the novel:

The theatricals provide the core of the book. . . . For Mansfield
Park is a place where you must be true to your best self: the
theatre is a place where you can explore and experiment with
other selves. A person cannot live in both. . . . Even reading
offers important scope for vicarious role-playing.[18]

Other similar assessments of the play episode could be quoted but what
must be noted is that they *all* share the very values – the integrity of
the self, self-knowledge, steadiness and regularity of conduct – that we
have already shown it the very function of *Mansfield Park* to establish.
In other words, how satisfied can we be by a 'criticism' of the novel
which brings to it no more than the very system of values which it itself
constructs?

An alternative account and interpretation of the play episode, much
more historically informed than Trilling's, is that offered by Marilyn
Butler. Butler's argument is that *Lovers' Vows* must be condemned
because it represents a potentially revolutionary ideology:

its message is the goodness of man, the legitimacy of his claims to
equality, and the sanctity of his instincts as a guide to conduct. . . . There could be no doubt in the minds of Jane Austen
and most of her readers that the name of Kotzebue was synony-
mous with everything most sinister in the German Literature of
the period. A sanguine believer in the fundamental goodness and
innocence of human nature, the apostle of intuition over conven-
tions, indeed of sexual liberty over every type of restraint, he is a
one sided propagandist for every position which the anti-jacobin
novel abhors. Unless the modern reader feels, like Fanny, the
anarchic connotations of the whole play – rather than like Edmund
and Mary, the daring of individual speeches – he is in no position
to understand its significance in relation to Mansfield Park and its
owner, Sir Thomas.[19]

William Reitzal, who was perhaps the first to note the political threat of
Lovers' Vows, quotes a contemporary review of the play when it was
performed in Bath in Cobbett's virulently anti-jacobin *Porcupine and
Anti-Gallican Monitor*:

On Saturday evening was performed. . . . the anglicised German
play of *Lovers' Vows*. We have ever beheld, with regret, the
avidity with which imported nonsense is attended to, while the

truly admirable productions of native genius are thrown to moulder on the shelf of forgetfulness. *Lovers' Vows*, the natural son of Kotzebue, is not among the least objectionable dramas of German notoriety. It is the universal aim of German authors of the present day, to exhibit the brightest examples of virtue among the lowest classes of society; while the higher orders, by their folly and profligacy, are held up to contempt and detestation. This is fully exemplified in *Lovers' Vows*.[20]

The suggestion, then, is that *Lovers' Vows*, with its rabid jacobinical egalitarianism and popular-democratic appeal, was a shrewd target for the moral earnestness of *Mansfield Park*. The argument, as far as it goes, is convincing and a further observation by Butler provides a salutary adjustment of Trilling's account:

> In touching one another or making love to one another on the stage these four (Edmund, Mary, Henry and Maria) are not adopting a pose, but are, on the contrary, expressing their real feelings. The impropriety lies in the fact that they are not acting, but are finding an indirect means to gratify desires which are illicit and should have been contained. The unbridled passions revealed by the play acting are part of the uninhibited selfishness which it has been the purpose of the sequence to bring out. The point is underlined by the casting, for the actors play exaggerated versions of themselves. . . . The stage roles . . . imply not insincerity but liberation.[21]

Nevertheless, what seems to me to be quite extraordinary in all the discussions that concern the play episode is that the most obvious point of all is consistently overlooked: the way in which *Lovers' Vows* and its dramatis personae *fit Mansfield Park* and its characters. When I first read *Mansfield Park* it always bothered me that Jane Austen should have been so lucky or so clever as to find a play that so perfectly answered all that she could have required of it. Once the matter is given a moment's thought, however, it must surely become quite obvious that that is not what happened at all. Given the fact that *Lovers' Vows* was a real historical play, antecedent to *Mansfield Park*, possibly seen by Jane Austen at Bath and certainly intimately known by her, is it not far more likely that rather than the characters of *Lovers' Vows* being exaggerated versions of those in *Mansfield Park* it is the other way round: *Mansfield Park* derives *its* characters – and, as I shall argue later, many of its principal themes and concerns – from *Lovers' Vows*. At this point we must turn to Q. D. Leavis's brilliant, albeit controversial, 'archaeological' account of the process of composition of *Mansfield Park*.[22]

Mrs Leavis's basic thesis, which can here be briefly summarized only, is that *Mansfield Park*, finally written between 1811 and 1813, was a revised and amplified version of an early epistolary novel, *Lady Susan*, written about 1797–9 but of which there remains only a fair copy of 1805. Between *Lady Susan* and *Mansfield Park* Mrs Leavis postulates an 'ur-*Mansfield Park*' written in epistolary form in 1809: her basic argument here is that the calendar used in *Mansfield Park* is that of 1809 and that it was Jane Austen's custom to draw upon the contemporary calendar. The 'ur-epistolary' version of *Mansfield Park* is also supposed to explain the 'dimmed and distant effect of much of the novel, the impression it gives of low spirits in its presentation'.[23]

The story of *Lady Susan* is briefly as follows: Lady Susan is an attractive and vivacious widow of thirty-five who, at the beginning of the story, has been obliged to leave the house where she has been a guest and where her flirtation with her host has seriously threatened the tranquillity of his marriage. She removes, then, to a country house, Churchill, where she at once sets about seducing the much younger and initially hostile Reginald de Courcy. In spite of the resistance he puts up and of the disapproval of everyone around them she quickly succeeds. Her triumph is thwarted however by the unexpected arrival of her very quiet and totally dominated daughter Frederica whom she is trying to marry off to an imbecilic but wealthy suitor, Sir James Martin. By her very simplicity Frederica finally wins the love of Reginald, once his infatuation with Lady Susan has been broken by irrefutable proof of her infidelities, while Lady Susan herself must settle for Sir James.

It is Mrs Leavis's argument that *Mansfield Park* can be seen as an elaborate and amplified development of *Lady Susan*, the result of a number of shifts and permutations – a kind of 'dreamworking' of displacements, reversals, splittings and condensations – of the earlier novel. The seductive and amoral Lady Susan, for example, splits into Henry and Mary Crawford while Reginald evolves into Edmund. Sir James Martin, in turn, might be regarded as foreshadowing both Rushworth and Yates. The most striking change, of course, affects

Frederica who from being the very peripheral figure in *Lady Susan* becomes the very central figure of Fanny in *Mansfield Park*.

Clearly, however, *Mansfield Park* is a much bigger and more complex book than *Lady Susan* and the transition from the one to the other must have been a lengthy process. It is for this reason that Mrs Leavis postulates an 'ur-*Mansfield Park*', probably written in 1809 in letter form, the residual traces of which might be the letters that figure so prominently in the last part of the novel. Unfortunately there is no evidence that any such intermediate text ever existed – as Mrs Leavis's detractors have been too ready to point out. On the other hand, and this is the thesis I would like to put forward, there was a text of 1808–9 which might well have served as the intermediary between *Lady Susan* and *Mansfield Park* and that was the second edition of Mrs Inchbald's translation of *Lovers' Vows*.

The first edition of Mrs Inchbald's translation had appeared in 1799, that is at about the time Jane Austen was writing *Lady Susan* if we accept Mrs Leavis's dating of that text. Again we must briefly summarize the plot. It begins with Frederic, the illegitimate offspring of his mother, Agatha, and Baron Wildenhaim, who had seduced her as an orphan in his parental home, returning home and finding his mother in abject poverty. At the same time the Baron, who had married a wealthy woman who has since died, also returns to the district with his daughter Amelia and her tutor Anhalt, a clergyman. With them comes also Amelia's foppish suitor, Count Cassel. The play contains two more or less parallel plots: on the one hand Amelia must make her father understand that she detests Cassel and will only marry Anhalt: she succeeds all the more easily because the Baron is full of regret at his past conduct and abandonment of his true love for Agatha; at the same time Frederic has been caught attempting an armed robbery on the person of the Baron and is thrown into prison. Here he finally manages, with the help of Anhalt, to make his true identity known to the Baron and the latter, after some gentle persuasion, agrees to marry Agatha and make Frederic his legitimate heir.

Considering the three texts it is already possible to show how the 'dreamwork' might have operated, albeit in a somewhat mechanical way. There is, for example, the major change in status of the Frederica of *Lady Susan* who becomes the Fanny Price of *Mansfield Park*: could this not have been mediated by the centrality of Frederic in *Lovers' Vows*, Frederic who might in turn, by splitting, have yielded both

Fanny and her brother William, the adventurous youth? Reginald, on the other hand, evolves into Edmund by a process of condensation, accruing to himself both the characteristics of a brother from Frederic and of tutor/clergyman from Anhalt. Count Cassell, in turn, might be seen as the mediating figure between Sir James Martin and Rushworth (stupid), Yates (foppish idler) and Henry Crawford (unsuitable suitor). But Henry, in turn, partakes of characteristics of both the Baron (successful seducer) and Cassell, while Agatha's seduction by and later marriage to the Baron, the heir of the house, is reworked in its ambiguity in Maria's seduction by Henry (disapproval) and Fanny's marriage to Edmund (approval). There is much, too, of the Baron in Sir Thomas himself: the remorse at his mistakes, the regret at his education not having been all that it might have been, his coming to the conclusion that wealth and status might be less valuable than a good heart and strong principle. Clearly there are limits to the legitimacy of such an analysis: that there is, indeed, an unaccounted-for residue in the Agatha/Baron; Maria/Henry : Fanny/Edmund displacements might explain the need for Julia whose elopement with and subsequent marriage to Yates most clearly follows the Baron/Agatha scheme.

Whether such a tight pattern of interlinkings can be demonstrated or not is, in the end, not the essential thing. What any close reading of *Mansfield Park* reveals beyond any shadow of doubt is that Jane Austen was thoroughly steeped in *Lovers' Vows*. There are many verbal echoes, like the references to the two long speeches on good and bad marriages in Act III, Scene 2 (which, as we have noted earlier, echo many of the sentiments we have seen Jane Austen discussing in correspondence with her niece). Or there is the precise irony that at the very moment of Sir Thomas's return it is likely that what would have been heard from the stage would have been the Cottager's

> We regretted his absence much, and his arrival has caused great joy.[24]

More important, however, than these specific echoes and allusions is the fact that practically all the major themes of *Mansfield Park* are to be found in *Lovers' Vows*: first and foremost, of course, is the question of the importance of marriage, of the need to marry for love rather than for convenience or connection; but there is also the theme of education and what are the consequences if it is mishandled or misdirected; again, the role and responsibilities of the clergyman are also brought under close scrutiny as well as what is closely related to these, the importance of conscience as a guide to conduct. But the play was not just Kotzebue's: Mrs Inchbald is at pains in her Preface to the translation to make it clear that she has frequently found it necessary to tone down some of the excesses of the original for an English audience and it may well have been from Mrs Inchbald herself that two other major features of *Mansfield Park* derive. The first is a matter of tone: that of a certain prurience with regard to sexual behaviour. Mrs Inchbald comments, for example, on her treatment of Amelia:

> The part of Amelia has been a very particular object of my solicitude and alteration: the same situations which the author gave her, remain, but almost all the dialogue of the character I have changed: the forward and unequivocal manner, in which she announces her affection to her lover, in the original, would have been revolting to an English audience.[25]

The second, curiously enough, is the very question which has so frequently formed the ground of any discussion of *Mansfield Park*: that of the relative effectiveness of the stage or pulpit as agents of moral reform. Observing that 'the pulpit has not had eloquence to eradicate the crime of seduction', Mrs Inchbald goes on to propose that 'the stage may be allowed an humble endeavour to prevent its most fatal effects'.[26]

Let us try for a moment to summarize the argument so far. I have taken issue with the orthodox accounts that would attribute the 'seriousness' of *Mansfield Park* either to Jane Austen's personal predicament – emotional distress, middle age, religious inclinations – or to an ambition to defend and refurbish the values of her class. What I have concerned myself with instead is the way in which a writer with a new 'greedy' and 'hardened' (her words, remember) consciousness of the potential rewards for her craft set about writing a book which would appeal to and attract a wider reading public. In order to achieve this end it was necessary, first, that she should wean herself of her own class – ideological inclinations and provide herself instead with a formula with a proven popular appeal. That formula was provided, it has been the burden of the foregoing to establish, by the sensationalist pieties of a notoriously jacobinical text, *Lovers' Vows*. *Lovers' Vows* serves as the transforming matrix between *Lady Susan* and *Mansfield Park*, as the midwife to Jane Austen's delivery from her own class allegiances.

What made *Mansfield Park* possible, and what allowed Jane Austen to emerge as a major ideologue, not of the gentry but of the new middle classes, was the appropriation and containment of the popular appeal of egalitarian jacobinism. It was a ploy that was fraught with risks for there was always the danger that the radical, even revolutionary, heritage of this purloined discourse might suddenly erupt into life again. It is this, I think, that explains the virulence with which *Lovers' Vows* is condemned in *Mansfield Park*: it is condemned, not because it is an area of false consciousness, nor simply because it has a revolutionary message, but because it was so desperately *needed*. Put more generally and perhaps too crudely: the new urban and industrial 'middling' classes were able to forge for themselves an identity and a consciousness only by modelling themselves upon and appropriating to themselves – after due deodorization – the popular democratic mobilizations of the revolutionary jacobinism of the 'people'. The animus with which *Lovers' Vows* is condemned is due to that bad faith that is endemic to an ideological consciousness that must at one and the same time acknowledge but disavow its debt to the revolutionary tradition.

The question that must now be asked is just how and why jacobinical mobilizations generally, and *Lovers' Vows* in particular, became free for appropriation by a class whose interests should have been profoundly alien to them? Some clue as to what happened may be gleaned from glancing briefly at the career of William Cobbett. We have already seen Cobbett's virulently anti-jacobin *Anti-Gallican Monitor* savaging *Lovers' Vows* in an early review. In 1804, however, we hear of Cobbett himself using jacobinical arguments against the Tory government of Pitt.[27] In 1802 Cobbett had lamented the election of the patrician Radical Sir James Burdett; in 1804, however, the same Cobbett was actively supporting him.[28] What had happened? Believe it or not: Napoleon Bonaparte! – that one element in the programme for a novel that Jane Austen drew up in 1813 still not accounted for.

In 1802 Napoleon had made himself First Consul for Life and in 1804 he had accepted the Crown as hereditary Emperor: from being the figurehead of revolutionary republicanism he had become the epitome of tyranny and repression. Napoleon's defection from the revolutionary cause freed and made available jacobin arguments for, in the first instance, appropriation by a patriotic war effort – in 1808 a former secretary of the London Corresponding Society, John Bone, could bring out a journal supporting the war against France while at the same time pressing many old jacobin demands[29] – and, in the second instance, protest against reactionary and oppressive government at home. In other words, jacobinism as a mobilizing popular democratic discourse was severed from its revolutionary sources and used instead to construct an ideology of liberal reformism.

III

Few things are more difficult to establish than the processes by means of which modern class society and class consciousness emerged at the beginning of the nineteenth century. Both 'left' and 'right' historians[30] are agreed, however, that the crucial period was the second decade of the century, that is, between the luddist disturbances of 1811–12 and the Peterloo Massacre in 1819 with, in between, the severe economic crisis following upon the end of the Napoleonic wars in 1816. Again, both left and right historians are agreed that one of the principal preconditions for the emergence of modern class society and consciousness was the startlingly sudden and complete collapse of the paternalist traditions of the eighteenth century in the face of the new free-for-all market forces of *laissez-faire* economics. What this 'abdication on the part of the governors', or this 'abrogation of paternalist legislation' entailed was the creation of a massive power vacuum at the very moment when the new crises – the 'boom-slump' cycles of industrial capitalism – were creating intolerable hardships for the mass of the population. 'In this situation,' writes John Foster, 'the infusion of "Jacobinism" into the lower orders was almost inevitable.'[31] For a few years, from 1811 to 1819, the possibility of a violent revolution in England was greater than at almost any other time and was contained, with ever increasing difficulty, by the resort to force alone – over 12,000 troops were tied down in the north and midlands in 1811–12. 'In 1816,' writes E. P. Thompson, 'the English people were held down by force.'[32] Instead of a revolution, however, what emerged was modern class society and the redirection of energies in the direction of parliamentary reform. The question that needs to be raised is whether this emergence of class society was not the means by which revolution was frustrated rather than its pre-condition – and whether or not the continuing acceptance of the classic model of class society and the class struggle is not still a barrier to the development of a viable alternative to capitalism.

We still haven't examined just 'how' class consciousness developed. There are three principal theories with which I will concern myself here. The first is that of E. P. Thompson whose massive *The Making of the English Working Class* makes moving and exhilarating reading. For Thompson the emergence of working-class consciousness was the result of a long and painful learning process gained in the bitter struggles against the intolerable excesses of the new era of industrial capitalism. The heroes of this struggle are men like Despard and Brandreth and its culmination is at Peterloo. The problem with Thompson's account is that it too often seems like wish-fulfilment. His treatment of Despard and Brandreth is characteristic: he deduces from the fact that neither of them offered effective defences to the charges brought against them or implicated others by way of mitigation that this is evidence of an underground tradition of professional revolutionaries. Much as one might wish this to have been true, indeed might still wish it to be true, to present this as evidence for the fact is, to say the least, to be rather less than convincing. Even by his own account the Pentridge rising was a complete mess and it is deluding oneself to then conclude, as Thompson does:

> We may see the Pentridge rising as one of the first attempts in history to mount a wholly proletarian insurrection, without any middle class support.[33]

This is merely assertive as is, again, his claim after quoting a description of the Peterloo massacre:

> There is no term for this but class war.[34]

The danger of such a starry-eyed view of the emergence of the working class and working-class consciousness is perhaps clearer to us today in the wake of the scenes witnessed during the 1984–5 Miners' Strike in the context of which Thompson's triumphal conclusion to his account of Peterloo seems incredibly naive:

> But never since Peterloo has authority dared to use equal force against a peaceful British crowd.[35]

The second hypothesis as to how class consciousness developed in the early nineteenth century is that proposed by John Foster in his *Class Struggle and the Industrial Revolution*. This is, frankly, for all its meticulous research, a dangerously doctrinaire approach to a very

difficult subject. Foster's principal thesis is that a working-class consciousness was first developed by a political vanguard and then used to
gain mass support. The schematism of the proposal may be gauged
from the following note:

> At the risk of oversimplifying, two stages may be distinguished in
> the process by which the proletarian vanguard is able to achieve
> mass realization of its ideas: first, the securing of mass leadership
> itself (and thus access to labour as a whole), and second, the *use* of
> that position to convince people of the need for a total change in
> the social system.[36]

As with Thompson one often gets the impression that Foster is *willing*
his evidence to confirm his theory (see, for example, his frequent resort
to a nervous 'clearly' or 'it should now be clear' or 'it should also be
obvious', pp. 48 and 72, op. cit.). Nevertheless Foster believes that he
has established that such a vanguard did exist in Oldham in the late
1830s and early 1840s and that it managed, in fact, to demonstrate 'the
intellectual bankruptcy of the existing order'![37] It also, claims Foster,
won some measure of mass support. Which makes the question that
has to be asked in the end all the more poignant:

> Which finally brings us to the most crucial question of all . . . :
> why, if the movement was so effective in mobilizing mass
> support, it ultimately collapsed so completely.[38]

One answer, of course, in spite of Foster's touching optimism –

> Compared with later proletarian movements this primitive
> English working class is remarkable for the long-sustained level
> [of] its mobilisation. (It should be remembered that even Lenin's
> revolutions required the external stimulus of war.)[39]

– is may be that the whole thing never happened in the first place. But,
if we allow that it did, it is interesting to learn what are Foster's
explanations for its collapse in the late 1840s. Briefly his argument is
that the movement was the victim of its own success: its very gathering
of itself as a potentially revolutionary mass alerted the bourgeoisie to
the peril they were in and they set about at once adopting a policy of
'liberalization', the conceding, that is, of many of the demands of the
threatening proletariat, specifically, argues Foster, the passing of the
Ten Hours Bill and the offer of Universal Household Suffrage.[40] For

Foster this was a major tactical victory by the bourgeoisie and far more responsible for restabilization after 1848 than either economic revival or law and order. What the bourgeoisie had achieved by this strategy, argues Foster, is the 'appropriation' of 'the two major slogans of the working class movement'.[41] Now what I find questionable about this explanation for the failure of the 1840s – the appropriation by the middle classes of the mobilizing slogans of the masses – is that it is thirty years too late, for it is precisely that appropriation that we have seen happening in *Mansfield Park*. And when I say *Mansfield Park* what I am really saying, of course, is that this process was already going on in the early decades of the century, indeed effectively so, to the extent that revolution was prevented. In fact I am claiming even more than that: that is that the new middling classes in their very hetero-geneity could establish for themselves a coherent or, if not coherent at least cohesive, ideological identity *in the first place* only by taking to themselves the universalistic claims and mobilizations of the jacobin tradition. Bourgeois ideology, in its very origins – and here one recalls Proudhon's dictum with regard to property – was *theft*.

It is in the credit that I wish to give to the formative influence of the jacobin tradition that I differ from the third of the major theorists of the emergence of class consciousness, Harold Perkin. In his *Origins of Modern English Society* he summarizes at one stage what he calls 'the Moral Revolution, that profound change in the national character which accompanied the Industrial Revolution':

> Between 1780 and 1850 the English ceased to be one of the most aggressive, brutal, rowdy, outspoken, riotous, cruel and blood-thirsty nations in the world and became one of the most inhibited, polite, orderly, tender-minded, prudish and hypocritical. The transformation diminished cruelty to animals, criminals, lunatics, and children (in that order); suppressed many cruel sports and games, such as bull-baiting and cock-fighting, as well as innocent amusements, including many fairs and wakes; rid the penal code of about two hundred capital offences, abolished transportation, and cleaned up the prisons; turned Sunday into a day of prayer for some and mortification for all; 'bowdlerised' Shakespeare, Gibbon and other 'obscene' classics, inhibited every kind of literature save that suitable for family reading, and almost gave the death-blow to the English stage; and generally removed from the language,

except in official publications and medical literature, all words calculated to bring a blush to the cheek of the young person. [42]

For Perkin the principal agent of this change was 'sectarian religion':

> Reluctant to be born, the new class society needed a midwife to help it into existence. It found one in the unexpected form of sectarian religion.
>
> The role of sectarian religion was three fold: to give expression to emancipation from the dependency system before it hardened into overt class antagonism; to provide the means, or at least the model, of class organization; and, not so much by passive teaching of patience as by active example of the benefits of non-violent organization, to influence class conflict in the direction of non-violence, and so to administer an analgesic against the pains of labour. [43]

Perkin's argument has a certain comforting plausibility – derived, in part, I suspect, from keeping the explanation within a specifically 'English' context (and in this he is very similar to Thompson whom he is otherwise at such pains to criticize) in that he speaks of 'the traditional puritanism of the English middle ranks'[44] – but, firstly, even in Perkin's own account the Dissent and Evangelical movements seem to have promoted divisiveness and factionalism rather than unity and, secondly, it is never demonstrated that the sectarian tradition could command the kind of universalistic appeal that class consciousness would require. It was this that jacobinical mobilizations offered. Moreover, if we read through again Perkin's account of the 'Moral Revolution' which is supposed to have taken place between 1780 and 1850 (and this is a very generous allocation of dates) it is striking the extent to which that shift is encapsulated, as it were, in *Mansfield Park*, a shift facilitated as I have insistently argued by the resort to a notoriously jacobin model. Fanny Price, to bring the charges once again, is 'inhibited, polite, orderly, tender-minded, prudish and hypocritical'; she is kind to animals (worrying about overworking her old pony); interested in the slave trade; reads only books suitable for family reading; disapproves of acting and is easily made to blush by *risqué*, not to mention coarse, language.

Let me try to bring this rather long and, I suppose, very 'unliterary' section to an end. What I am arguing is that in so far as it is a question of *mechanisms* all three of the theories I have criticized here have something to be said for them. Thompson is right that there was a 'revolutionary' origin to class consciousness; Foster is right that class consciousness involved a process of 'appropriation'; Perkin is right in that class consciousness needed a viable mobilizing force on which to model itself. What all three fail to recognize is that, respectively, the 'revolutionary' source was in jacobinism, the 'appropriation' was the appropriation of jacobinism, and that the viable mobilizing model was, again, jacobinism. There is one other very complex point that I would like to make now. This is that in appropriating to itself, in order to constitute itself, the radical and popular mobilizations of jacobinism, the middle class while establishing itself as a class in fact established itself as *the* class and *that* 'class' becomes the model according to which the other strata of society are required to conform. It is an incredible play of mirrors: the emergent middle class in all its heterogeneity 'borrows' from the jacobinical traditions of the people the mobilizations that allow it an ideological identity as a homogeneous and universal 'class' and then, with astonishing effrontery, offers 'class' as the only possibility of cohesion to those very groupings whose radical and revolutionary possibilities they have deprived of utterance.

Let us turn to the Portsmouth chapters of *Mansfield Park*.

IV

The Portsmouth episode really is a very strange piece of work for, looked at carefully, it seems to consist of a whole rag-bag of modes of writing quite eccentric to the dominant mode of the novel as a whole. There is, first, as has often been noted, a reversion to an epistolary mode not used by Jane Austen since *Lady Susan*. But what is striking about this device is that it is in the letters that we begin to hear something like an authentic voice. This is particularly true of Edmund's letters. Up to now he has all too often sounded stuffy and given to pompous little set speeches. In his letters, on the other hand, we get a sense of a real intelligence and sensitivity at work, a sense of a real sentient human being caught in the toils of doubt and anguish and indecision:

> My dear Fanny,
>
> Excuse me that I have not written before. Crawford told me that you were wishing to hear from me, but I found it impossible to write from London, and persuaded myself that you would understand my silence. – Could I have sent a few happy lines, they should not have been wanting, but nothing of that nature was ever

in my power. – I am returned to Mansfield in a less assured state than when I left it. My hopes are much weaker. – You are probably aware of this already. – So fond of you as Miss Crawford is . . . you have my thoughts exactly as they rise, my dear Fanny; perhaps they are sometimes contradictory, but it will not be a less faithful picture of my mind. Having once begun, it is a pleasure to me to tell you all I feel. I cannot give her up. . . . Were it a decided thing, an actual refusal, I hope I should know how to bear it, and how to endeavour to weaken her hold on my heart – and in the course of a few years – but I am writing nonsense – were I refused, I must bear it; and till I am, I can never cease to try for her. (pp. 411–13)

What there is here, in the quick changes of pace and mood, the darts of shifting possibilities is something very like what later comes to be described as 'a stream of consciousness'. Mary's letters, too, reveal the sides of her character which she has managed to keep from us in the rest of the book: I think our sympathy goes from her for the first time when she betrays her suppressed glee at the possibility that Tom might die and leave the way clear for Edmund to inherit the estate. Even Lady Bertram's letters show this change from mere posing to real urgency of feeling. Her early letters on Tom's illness are still slightly artificial – 'It was a sort of playing at being frightened' (p. 417) the text remarks.

Then a letter which she had previously been preparing for Fanny, was finished in a different style, in the language of real feeling and alarm; then she wrote as she might have spoken. 'He is just come, my dear Fanny, and is taken up stairs; and I am so shocked to see him. I am sure he has been very ill. Poor Tom, I am quite grieved for him, and very much frightened, and so is Sir Thomas.' (p. 417)

But this new note is not just found in the letters. Consider the following:

The sun was yet an hour and a half above the horizon. She felt she had, indeed, been three months there; and the sun's rays falling strongly into the parlour, instead of cheering, made her still more melancholy; for sun-shine appeared to her a totally different thing in a town and in the country. Here, its power was only a glare, a stifling, sickly glare, serving but to bring forward stains and dirt that might otherwise have slept. There was neither health nor gaiety in sun-shine in a town. She sat in a blaze of oppressive heat, in a cloud of moving dust; and her eyes could only wander from the walls marked by her father's head, to the table cut and knotched by her brothers, where stood the tea-board never thoroughly cleaned, the cups and saucers wiped in streaks; the milk a mixture of motes floating in a thin blue, and the bread and butter growing every minute more greasy than even Rebecca's hands had first produced it. (pp. 427–8)

This is a quite extraordinary piece of writing, quite unlike anything else to be found in Jane Austen's work. There is a sensibility here to the worked and living textures of the small family room that we do not find again in fiction until Mrs Gaskell or D. H. Lawrence or even Orwell – so close is the sensibility to revulsion. I think it would be wrong to regard this scene as mediated through Fanny's educated sensibility for even though there is a revulsion here there is also a familiarity, a sympathetic knowingness, a closeness that Fanny could not possibly have known. I think it is found again in the description of Mrs Price's 'slow bustle':

> Her days were spent in a kind of slow bustle; always busy without getting on, always behind and lamenting it, without altering her ways; wishing to be an economist, without contrivance or regularity, dissatisfied with her servants, without skill to make them better, and without helping, or reprimanding, or indulging them, without any power of engaging their respect. (p. 382)

In fact Jane Austen herself goes some way to suggesting that the animus of the condemnation of Mrs Price's mismanagement is rather more than Fanny's own:

> She might scruple to make use of the words, but she must and did feel that her mother was a partial, ill-judging parent, a dawdle, a slattern. (p. 383, my emphasis)

These are pretty strong terms. It is almost as if, in the Portsmouth chapters, the restraint and the control of the rest of the book no longer prevail, allowing fluctuations of mood and consciousness and intensities of feeling to well through where they have earlier been held in check.

It is this, perhaps, that explains the extremely odd incident of 'little Mary' and her knife (pp. 378–9). Little Mary, we are told, had died just after Fanny had first gone to Mansfield and Mrs Price tells us how, on her death-bed, she had left the knife to Susan:

Poor Mary little thought it would be such a bone of contention when she gave it me to keep only two hours before she died. Poor little soul! she could but just speak to be heard, and she said so prettily, 'Let sister Susan have my knife, mamma, when I am dead and buried.' – Poor little dear! she was so fond of it Fanny, that she would have it by her bed, all through her illness. It was the gift of her good godmother, old Mrs Admiral Maxwell, only six weeks before she was taken to her death.

This, again, is not a very Jane Austenish kind of writing: it is more like the kind of sentimental death-bed scene of Dickens at his most maudlin. But the disturbance is not just stylistic. Why this sudden introduction into the story of a 'little Mary' whose death is supposed to have occurred at the beginning of the novel and to have affected Fanny a great deal but which was not recorded at the time? And why should we be told that this Mary had been the favoured god-child of 'old Mrs Admiral Maxwell'? Could the explanation not be that here Jane Austen is trying to have her cake and eat it? Perhaps the greatest sacrifice that had to be made so that the new moral earnestness of *Mansfield Park* should prevail was the defeat and banishment of Mary Crawford and she, it will be remembered, had been the favourite of her aunt, a Mrs Admiral Crawford, whose death, early in the book, was the immediate reason for departing from her uncle's house. The coincidences are too striking. The story of 'little Mary' allows Jane Austen to mourn, albeit briefly, that sacrifice of all gaiety that made *Mansfield Park* possible. Moreover the 'little Mary' is closely identified with Susan and, again, it is possible that there is here the return of yet another piece of repressed material – of that merry widow, Lady Susan, whom we have argued to be the origin of both the Crawfords.

What the eccentricity and heterogeneity of the Portsmouth chapters demonstrate, then, is that there are large areas of consciousness and sensibility that cannot be accommodated within the dominant narrative mode of *Mansfield Park* as a whole. Portsmouth, we are told again and again, is a place of noise and disorder, of confusion and mismanagement. Here lurks the unthinkable and the unspeakable, here is the return of repressed wishes and the vague apprehensions of the menace of poverty. And this is the point: it is Portsmouth that represents the threat to Mansfield and its values, not *Lovers' Vows*. I cannot emphasize this too strongly: the threat comes not from the gauche imposturing of an amateur theatre but from a welter of forces set free by a shift in the mode of production.

What Portsmouth shows is that there remained a whole social strata that lay beyond the pale of Mansfield and where its ideological writ did not run and with which its 'system of narration'[45] could not cope. Portsmouth, we have to remember, was, at this period, a major port and naval installation and, as such, far more like a modern industrial town than, say, Oldham, which, as we have seen, was the major focus of a study such as Foster's. And it would be in a town like Portsmouth where the consequences of a major shift in the structure of the social formation are most likely to have been in evidence.[46] And it is here, in the Price household, the small shops, the Sunday promenade, the alehouse fellowship, that we find that stratum of the social formation which historians have found so difficult to designate – the 'uneasy class' according to E. G. Wakefield; the 'disqualified' according to John Stuart Mill; the 'middling class' according to a more recent writer, R. S. Neale. Perhaps the most accurate name for this group, no longer conceivable of as the 'populace' and not yet identifiable as a petite bourgeoisie, was that by which they were addressed by the Philosophical Radicals of the time: 'the people'. In one way it is possible to see this extremely unstable and amorphous mass as that flotsam left 'free' by the receding tide of paternalist surveillance and legislation – that 'abdication on the part of the governors' we have mentioned earlier. But it is also possible, I would like to argue here, to see that mass, in its very heterogeneity and lack of identity, as the victims of another deprivation, that of those mass mobilizations and populist claims afforded, briefly, by revolutionary jacobinism. In other words, when jacobinism as a strategy of mass mobilization became available for appropriation by a programme of liberal reform – as we have described above – it left those very areas of the populace to whom it was originally designed to appeal speechless, literally without words. This is why the Portsmouth section of *Mansfield Park* is such a medley of styles: there is, quite simply, no language for it.

And yet, as we have seen, it is in this area where no one language prevails that we begin to hear a number of languages, all extrinsic to the dominant mode of the novel, which sometimes ring false (the death of little Mary) and sometimes ring true (the description of the heat in the Price house, Edmund's letter). This is precisely the problem that this area represents: its total unpredictability, its constant presentation of alternatives, its gamut of moods and positions, its volatility. It is this that makes it dangerous, a perpetual threat to any equilibrium that might be established elsewhere. For if, on the one hand, characteristic products of such a double deprivation as I have described are the foul-mouthed, spirit smelling, idle, lounging Price and his hopelessly inadequate wife, there are others, too, such as William and Susan whose intelligence and energy enable them to see the corruption that surrounds them and who refuse to accept the frustrations of their condition and who will seek to change it.

It is a group, then, that cannot be safely ignored and much of nineteenth-century history can be seen as a series of manœuvres on the part of the state to humour, divert, accommodate, and concede demands emanating from it. The Portsmouth episode shows us some of the favourite strategies. There is first the adroitness with which the power bloc spots the more talented members of this group and quickly incorporates them within its own privileged domain: it is this that happens to Susan, 'rescued' from her oppressive environment and transported to the parklands of Mansfield. It is also what happens to William, and his successful career in the navy reminds us just how, at this period, the 'senior service' is about to become a powerful symbol of national pride and self-confidence. The passionate obsession with the *Thrush* is preparing the ground for the jingoism which will become such an escape valve for populist sentiment later in the century. Thirdly there are the palliative consolations of alcohol and the alehouse, the licensing of the latter at this period ensuring that it changed from a locus of potential subversion to a means of state supervision. Fourthly, we are shown the role of the Press: the gossip column which carries the story of Maria's adultery is just an early example of that sensationalist press that will mouth back to the 'people' the proprieties, rendered prurient in the process, which they, themselves, in the form of 'respectability', have done so much to foster in the first place.[47] (Here I would have liked to develop a long note on the bewilderment that this strategy causes, when those groups that are potentially radical are harangued in the very terms it has been their achievement to dignify, when they are abused by, even mocked by, their own language first stolen from and then turned against them: the example that comes to mind at once is the notion of the 'working miner'. It leaves 'real' 'working miners' bereft of words.)

Finally, there is literature itself. While in Portsmouth, we recall,

Fanny takes out a subscription to a circulating library so that she can initiate Susan into the joys of reading that have meant so much to her. One of the books, we might conjecture in a kind of *nouveau roman* way, might have been *Mansfield Park* itself. For *Mansfield Park*, uncritically, or even critically, read in wilful ignorance of its provenance or its ideological effects, is a powerful ideological institution. It was, as we have seen, designed to be so. As long as 'criticism' of it remains within the very values it did so much to establish it will continue to act as such an institution – again we may recall its canonical position in 'the great tradition'.

The trouble is, however, that *Mansfield Park* bears too many marks of the labour that brought it into being, of that massive effort that entailed first and foremost that Jane Austen break with the inherited values of her own social group and construct, instead, a work that would appeal instead to a market constituted by a new and quite distinct reading public whose tastes and requirements were so alien to her own. To have achieved this was, as we have seen, a massive act of management, motivated, in part, by 'greed', entailing a deliberate 'hardening' of herself, the sacrifice of much that was happiest in herself, and the opportunistic exploitation of the populist formulae afforded by a jacobinical melodrama. It was, in a way, a terrible act of self-alienation. It is this, I think, that explains the animus that invests the figure of Mrs Norris. For if, at the ideological level, what *Mansfield Park* enshrines is Fanny Price, then, at the level of its production what the book required was the grasping, selfish, calculated insensitivity of a Mrs Norris. With the creation of Mrs Norris what Jane Austen allowed herself was the luxury of a scapegoat upon which she could discharge all the rage provoked by the sense of meanness and betrayal with which she herself had become complicit in the course of writing the book. For if *Mansfield Park* was the result of a massive act of 'management' then it required a Mrs Norris to manage it. If that is so then it is more than likely that Mrs Norris's greatest crime was not her hatred of Fanny, nor her infatuation with Maria, but her assumption of the role of stage-manager for the production of *Lovers' Vows*. For all else she might have been forgiven, but not for that, for at that point she is touching the sorest point of the whole book, the guilty secret of what made it, itself, possible.

3

Frankenstein: the making of a monster

Much of what follows is heavily indebted to Jacques Derrida's *Of Grammatology*, particularly the opening chapters and the essay dedicated to Rousseau – 'That dangerous supplement'.[1] I shall be engaged, that is, in what it is fashionable to describe as an exercise in 'deconstruction'. What such an exercise involves, as I understand it, is the strategic deployment of a number of seemingly oppositional categories – here, for example 'body'/'mind', 'writing'/'speech', 'female'/'male', 'articulation'/'meaning', 'repetition'/'origin' – in order to 'deconstruct' such categories, even to 'deconstruct' the notion of 'category' itself.

In case anyone should fear that we are concerned here merely with rather esoteric philosophical or logical, as opposed to, say, 'real human', problems it might be as well that I begin at once by saying that much of the astonishing intelligence and complexity of *Frankenstein* derives from the lived intensities of the domestic and political contexts in which it was composed. To understand the significance of the former we need to imagine what it must have been like for a young girl like

Mary Shelley, while suffering all the traumas of awakened sexuality, the birth and death of her first child, the birth of a second child, and the tragic death of Shelley's first wife by suicide, to come to terms with the almost insufferable intellectual precocity of Shelley and his circle of friends and acquaintances. As far as the significance of the political context is concerned it is important to remember that the years 1815 to 1819 marked, to use the phrase of E. P. Thompson, 'the heroic age of popular radicalism':[2] from Waterloo in 1814 to Peterloo in 1819 the threat of revolutionary insurrection was greater than at any other time between 1789 and 1832.

I

Mary, of course, adored Shelley and his early death ensured that her infatuation would never be subjected to the test of time and maturity. It is only intermittently and fleetingly that we get a glimpse in her letters and *Journal* of potential sources of irritation and grounds for criticism – in her evident impatience with Shelley's flirtations with her half-sister Claire, or in a mild reproach like the following:

> How you reason and philosophize about love – do you know if I had been asked I could not give one reason in its favour – yet I have as great opinion as you concerning its exaltedness and love very tenderly to prove my theory.[3]

It's a tiny breach here, worth, perhaps, a pout, but it is not difficult to imagine how that rub between an incorrigible cerebralism and sensuous warmth might become a smart and then a terrible wound. Perhaps an indication of how grave the difference might have become might be found if we briefly compare Shelley's 1817 Preface to *Frankenstein* with Mary's Introduction to the 1831 edition. Shelley, in the assumed role of the author, writes of the intentions behind the novel:

> my chief concern in this respect has been limited to the avoiding of the enervating effects of the novels of the present day, and to the exhibition of the amiableness of domestic affection, and the excellence of universal virtue. (p. 58)[4]

Now, apart from its breathtaking disingenuousness, given the experience afforded by any reading of the story, there is no reason for not thinking that this represents what Shelley really thought the story was about. What is more it is thoroughly consonant with the views he has on the function of literature set out in his *Defence of Poetry* two years later. Here Shelley propounds the quintessentially romantic notion of the nature of poetic inspiration and its moral effects. 'Poetry', he writes, 'is indeed something divine',[5] and poets are the 'hierophants of an unapprehended inspiration'[6] whose task is the creation of new materials of knowledge and the improvement of the moral nature of man by enlarging and replenishing the imagination, 'the great instrument of moral good'.[7] The whole process, from divine inspiration to moral effect, is wholly idealist, taking place in thought alone, completely unmediated, and hence untainted, by any material consideration or practice. It is because, for Shelley, language alone is capable of this totally unmediated, indeed transparent, act of expression and communication that poetry is preferred before all the other arts:

> For language is arbitrarily produced by the imagination and has relation to thoughts alone; but all other materials, instruments, and conditions of art have relations among each other which limit and interpose between conception and expression. The former is a mirror which reflects, the latter is a cloud which enfeebles the light of which both are mediums of communication.[8]

It is wholly consistent with such a theological conception of the poetic process that such mundane and practical features of language as 'the copiousness of lexicography and the distinctions of grammar' are, compared to 'original language near its source', 'merely the catalogue and the form of the creation of poetry'.[9] That is, compared with the pure immediacy of thought to itself, the actual practice of writing itself is no more than a contemptible supplement, purely ancillary. Finally, and of a piece with all the rest of the *Defence*, there is no place at all in Shelley's conception of the role of the artist for anything that smacks of determined effort and conscious decision:

> Poetry is not like reasoning, a power to be exerted according to the determination of the will. A man cannot say, 'I will compose poetry.' The greatest poet even cannot say it . . . I appeal to the great poets of the present day, whether it be not an error to assert that the finest passages of poetry are produced by labour and study.[10]

What we find when we turn to Mary Shelley's account, in the 1831 Introduction, of the process of production of *Frankenstein* and the effect she designed it to have is an 'aesthetic' which, in all major points, seems to be diametrically opposed to that of Shelley's *Defence*. Whereas Shelley had proclaimed that no one could simply sit down and decide to write, Mary Shelley seems to be at pains to make it clear that her tale was the product of deliberate and conscious decision. In contrast to Shelley's grandiloquence – just as in her attitude to love – Mary Shelley's approach to her writing is unpretentious and unaffected. She is practical, down to earth, 'formalistic' we might say today, even materialist. Not for her the myth of divine inspiration:

> Invention, it must be humbly admitted, does not consist in creating out of void, but out of chaos; the materials must, in the first place, be afforded: it can give form to dark, shapeless substances, but cannot bring into being the substance itself. (p. 54)

Earlier she has described herself as a 'close imitator' and much of her Introduction is taken up with recounting the particular and specific circumstances, narratives and events, that contributed to the original idea of the novel. Compared with Shelley's profoundly ideological myth of the divine status of poetic inspiration Mary's concern is with the real processes and conditions of literary production, with what she happily terms the 'machinery' of a story.

She differs from Shelley, too, in her conception of the nature of the aesthetic effect. Whereas Shelley spoke of an unmediated address to the imagination as a moral agent Mary speaks instead of a direct affront to the bodily nervous system, a kind of physiological shock:

> I busied my self *to think of story* – a story to rival those which had excited us to this task. One which would speak to the mysterious fears of our nature and awaken thrilling horror – one to make the reader dread to turn round, to curdle the blood, and quicken the beatings of the heart. (p. 53)

Before we too readily dismiss this as 'gothic' commonplace we would do well to remember that in its search for the thrilling *frisson* the 'gothic' was the last 'aesthetic' in the proper sense of the term – that is as an address to the senses unmediated by thought – before the term was pilfered to construct a vapid, and *an*-aesthetic, ideology of 'taste' – such, in fact, as that propagated by Shelley's *Defence of Poetry*.

The differences between the Preface and the Introduction are well-nigh irreconcilable: the pout has become a fully worked out and consistent statement of irreducible difference – pretty petulance has become suppressed rage. You don't have to be a very attentive listener to hear the turbulence beneath the following:

> My husband, however, was from the first very anxious that I should prove myself worthy of my parentage and enrol myself on the page of fame. He was forever inciting me to obtain literary reputation, which even on my own part I cared for then, though since I have become infinitely indifferent to it. At this time he desired that I should write, not so much with the idea that I could produce anything worthy of notice, but that he might himself judge how far I possessed the promise of better things hereafter. Still I did nothing. Travelling, and the cares of a family, occupied my time; and study, in the way of reading or improving my ideas in communication with his far more cultivated mind, was all of literary employment that engaged my attention. (p. 52)

and, again, later:

> At first I thought but of a few pages – of a short tale, but Shelley urged me to develope the idea at greater length. I certainly did not owe the suggestion of one incident, nor scarcely of one train of feeling, to my husband, and yet but for his incitement it would never have taken the form in which it is presented to the world. From this declaration I must except the preface. As far as I can recollect, it was entirely written by him. (p. 56)

It is not difficult to feel the pain here caused by that endless cajoling to live up to your parents' name and achievements, to prove yourself fit mental companion for your brilliant husband, to appreciate properly the privilege of being in communication with his 'far more cultivated mind'. And then, when you have done something, to see him being given all the credit for it, or the suggestion that you owe it all to him. The exquisiteness of the pain is no way better conveyed than in that repeated use of the verb 'incite' – 'inciting', 'incitement': it suggests a peculiar perversity in the process, a perversity against which one's whole being, flesh and soul, should rebel.

II

The theme of rebellion, or more properly mutiny, figures prominently, of course, in the Walton story that frames the Frankenstein narrative itself. Here it is the refusal of the sailors unreasonably to risk their lives in support of Walton's foolhardy determination to reach the Pole. It is again, as with Mary's defence of her writing compared with Shelley's enthusiastic posturings, the refusal of those materially engaged in a real practice to remain uncritically subservient before the mercurial ravings of a dewy-eyed idealist. For all the evidence is that, not to put too fine a point on it, Walton is a bit 'wet', the product of privilege, indulgence and 'feminine fosterage' (p. 64). Moreover, from his own account of it, there is something inherently perverse about his own ambition:

> I try in vain to be persuaded that the pole is the seat of frost and desolation; it ever presents itself to my imagination as the region of beauty and delight. There, Margaret, the sun is forever visible, its broad disk just skirting the horizon and diffusing a perpetual splendour. There – for with your leave, my sister, I will put some trust in preceding navigators – there snow and frost are banished; and sailing over a calm sea, we may be wafted to a land surpassing in wonders and in beauty every region hitherto discovered on the habitable globe. Its productions and features may be without example, as the phaenomena of the heavenly bodies undoubtedly are in those undiscovered solitudes. (p. 59)

The Pole Walton searches for is a complete myth, wilfully pursued in spite of all evidence to the contrary. It is a myth of innocence, of purity, of originality, the search for 'a land never before imprinted by the foot of man' (p. 270), whose 'productions and features may be without example' (p. 269). What the Pole promises is a unique, perfect, unmediated, undifferentiated, absolutely singular, centre. In all this it is very much like the poetic faculty of Shelley's *Defence*: ineffably original, uniquely perfect, and compared with which all that comes after is a taint, a blemish, a fall, secondary and supplemental. Just as Shelley expresses impatience with 'the copiousness of lexicography and the distinctions of grammar' compared to 'original language near its source', so Walton despises writing as a means of communicating feeling:

I shall commit my thoughts to paper, it is true; but that is a poor medium for the communication of feeling. (p. 63)

The undisguised scorn for the complexities of writing, the impatience expressed at its inadequacy, is the other side of the celebration of the voice, of so called 'living speech', as a transparent medium for the expression of thought and feeling. Voice, like Walton's Pole, is thought of having never suffered the indignity of being 'imprinted', of being essentially uncontaminated, ideal, uncluttered by matter. What the celebration of the voice and the search for the Pole are at one with, moreover, is a privileging of the self before otherness, of identity before difference. The above quotation continues:

I desire the company of a man who could sympathise with me, whose eyes would reply to mine. You may deem me romantic, my dear sister, but I bitterly feel the want of a friend. I have no one near me, gentle yet courageous, possessed of a cultivated as well as of a capacious mind, whose tastes are like my own, to approve or amend my plans. (ibid.)

What is suggested here, and it confirms our previous impression of Walton, is a radical narcissism, a debilitating obsession with the self, where the only relationship possible is one of identity and identification, not one of otherness and difference.

It is here that we might summarize the drift of the argument so far. It is simply this: Shelley's privileging of the imaginative faculty, the celebration of the immediacy to thought of the voice, the search for a pristine Pole, the obsession with self and identity are all symptomatic of a profound failure to appreciate and credit those practices and institutions that make such immaculates possible: the imagination requires the material support of a body – an aesthetic is physiological before it is 'spiritual'; the voice needs, first, the material support of air – later, in fact, Frankenstein reminds us that a 'loud voice' might produce 'a concussion of air sufficient to draw destruction upon the head of the speaker' in the shape of an avalanche (p. 139) – but also, so that it might be intelligible, the systematic articulation of signs that constitute a language; the pursuit of the Pole is made possible only by the labour of the sailors who man the ship; finally, the self itself is only a composite made possible by the many not-selves of the body, labour and language. The self is not an original identity, but the produced effect, mobile rather than static, nomadic rather than fixed, of fabulous plays of differences.

It is Frankenstein's principal tragedy that from first to last he is caught in the idealist web. Like his much later demonic avatar, Kurtz of *Heart of Darkness*, he is introduced to us by Walton primarily as a *voice*. He is described early as having

> a facility of expression and a voice whose varied intonations are soul-subduing music. (p. 74)

and Walton is quickly captivated by his 'full-toned voice' (p. 75). His last act is his harangue to the rebellious crew:

> He spoke with a voice so modulated to the different feelings expressed in his speech, with an eye so full of lofty design and heroism, that can you wonder that these men were moved? (p. 253)

Perhaps the idealism that lies behind this belief in the voice is nowhere better illustrated than in noting the process by means of which Frankenstein 'discovers' the guilt of the Monster:

> No sooner did that idea cross my imagination than I became convinced of its truth. . . . The mere presence of the idea was an irresistible proof of the fact. (p. 119)

This is, of course, pure Cartesianism. Frankenstein is often regarded as a kind of prototype of the modern scientist and I suppose it is possible to find some evidence for such an interpretation. My own view, however, is that Frankenstein is less a harbinger of what is to come than a rather sad, even backward, child of the Enlightenment. His principal intellectual disciplines, for example, other than alchemy, are chemistry and mathematics, those two most pre-eminently Enlightenment sciences, and he accepts uncritically M. Krempe's conception of what the scientific task should entail – 'to give new names and arrange in correct classifications' (p. 93). Moreover the extent to which Frankenstein shares the prejudices of the Enlightenment becomes even clearer if, while still remaining with the theme of language, we compare him with his friend Clerval.

It is usual to accept Frankenstein's contrast between himself and Clerval in terms of a contrast between someone interested in 'the physical secrets of the world' and someone interested in 'the moral relations of things' (p. 82). This would make Frankenstein the practical scientist while Clerval would remain no more than some kind of effete intellectual. But there is an almost Kierkegaardian irony at work here, for what a close reading of the text reveals is that, caught in an ideology that privileges voice and meaning before writing and articulation, Frankenstein totally fails to understand Clerval's strategic location, not in the realm of ideas, but in a colonial power structure:

> His design was to visit India, in the belief that he had in his knowledge of its various languages, and in the views he had taken of its society, the means of materially assisting the progress of European colonization and trade. (p. 199)

It is true that Frankenstein sees in Clerval here an 'image of [his] former self' (ibid.) but we should not let this further instance of narcissistic identification deceive us. Frankenstein just cannot conceive that Clerval's project is radically different from his own – not to mention Walton's – working within an epistemological domain quite beyond his comprehension, in fact *unthinkable* by him. This is evident in the way Frankenstein attempts to distinguish his approach to the 'works of Orientalists' from Clerval's:

> I did not, like him, attempt a critical knowledge of their dialects, for I did not contemplate making any other use of them than temporary amusement. I read merely to understand their meaning, and they well repaid my labours. (p. 112)

For Frankenstein the essence of language is its meaning, its thought-content or truth, and to that the 'critical knowledge of . . . dialects', that is the 'copiousness of lexicography and the distinctions of grammar' disdained in the *Defence*, is purely supplementary. For Frankenstein language has a grammar only because it has a meaning. For Clerval, evidently, language has meaning only because it has a grammar.[11] It is not he who speaks most eloquently or most truthfully that has power, but he who successfully occupies those locations within language and the structures of power *from which one speaks* in the first place.

III

Perhaps the most notorious criticism ever made of *Frankenstein* is that of Mario Praz who complains that the novel 'has a fundamental

weakness' – viz. Mary Shelley's refusal to tell us exactly how the
Monster was made![12] In a way, I suppose, he has a point, but then I
wonder what he expected. On the other hand, however, I would want
to argue the exact opposite: the novel is absolutely obsessed with how a
Monster is made and in the making of the Monster Mary Shelley has
depicted with disturbing effectiveness just what 'monstrosity' is.

This is achieved by the contrast Mary Shelley establishes between
the way in which the Monster is educated and the actual process of its
creation. The former is contrived by means of the Monster's long
sojourn with the De Lacey family, while the latter is the morbid
preoccupation of the young Frankenstein in a solitary chamber in
Ingolstadt.

It has not been sufficiently noticed, as far as I am aware, that the De
Lacey story is set up as a kind of ideal mirror image of the main story
itself. The blind and old De Lacey reminds us very much of the rather
asexual – or, if anything, rather maternal – figure of Frankenstein's
own father, while the relationship between Felix and Agatha is not
unlike that between Frankenstein and Elizabeth, his foster sister. This
leaves Safie, the beautiful Arabian, and her father, a stereotypically
'wicked Turk': to the extent that they are the origin and cause of Felix's
preoccupations and sorrows they are to Felix what the Monster is to
Frankenstein. That 'two' should be required to supply the role of 'one',
in this aseptic version of the main story, is something that will become
clearer later.

Compared to the 'workshop of filthy creation' (p. 98) where the
Monster is actually made, the whole De Lacey episode, apart from its
savage denouement, is a pastoral idyll, a romantic interlude of heroes
and fair ladies, pledged honour and broken faith, dark villainy and
deeply plighted troth. It is in this context of contrived, and slightly
faded, gentility that the Monster struggles to educate itself. What its
education consists of is basically language, history and literature, all
within a framework of essentially Enlightenment thinking. But it is an
education that needs to be critically examined. In many ways, the
syllabus, if we may call it that – and the reading list of Volney,
Plutarch, Goethe and Milton (plus the Bible and Shakespeare, of
course) would have been familiar to many of the autodidacts of this
period[13] – is wholly unexceptionable: but is it suitable for a Monster?
This is all very much grammar school stuff and wouldn't it be better
off in a comprehensive school or even on a Youth Opportunity

Programme? Here we have to be very careful for the only account we have of the education is from the Monster itself and because it *is* the Monster's education it is very difficult for it to know whether it is good for it or not. It cannot know otherwise than what it knows. The Monster can hardly stand outside itself. The adequacy or inadequacy of the Monster's education can only be gauged by examining it athwart, as it were, the Monster's own account of it.

Suspicion is aroused, however, from the very beginning by the very conditions under which the Monster has to labour to learn anything at all. For what the Monster is allowed is no more than the overhearing of the domestic chatter of a group of fallen aristocrats. It is a case of the underprivileged being grateful for the scraps tossed by privilege – that this has been a characteristic feature of much bourgeois education is perhaps worth noting. Be that as it may, perhaps it is because of the suspicions triggered by such an inauspicious educational environment that we feel inclined to pay rather more than a passing scrutiny to what follows. Let us take the Monster's acquisition of language:

> By degrees I made a discovery of still greater moment. I found that these people possessed a method of communicating their experience and feelings to one another by articulate sounds. I perceived that the words they spoke sometimes produced pleasure or pain, smiles or sadness, in the minds and countenances of the hearers. This was indeed a godlike science, and I ardently desired to become acquainted with it. But I was baffled in every attempt I made for this purpose. Their pronunciation was quick, and the words they uttered, not having any apparent connexion with visible objects, I was unable to discover any clue by which I could unravel the mystery of their reference. By great application, however, and after having remained during the space of several revolutions of the moon in my hovel, I discovered the names that were given to some of the most familiar objects of discourse; I learned and applied the words, 'fire,' 'milk,' 'bread,' and 'wood.' I learned also the names of the cottagers themselves. The youth and his companion had each of them several names, but the old man had only one, which was 'father.' The girl was called 'sister' or 'Agatha', and the youth 'Felix,' 'brother,' or 'son.' I cannot describe the delight I felt when I learned the ideas appropriated to each of these sounds and was able to pronounce them. I distinguished several

other words without being able as yet to understand or apply them, such as 'good,' 'dearest,' 'unhappy.' (pp. 153–4)

This is an extraordinarily complex paragraph but, fortunately, the point I wish to make can be clarified by quoting another, briefer passage, that follows closely after:

> This reading had puzzled me extremely at first, but by degrees I discovered that he uttered many of the same sounds when he read as when he talked. I conjectured, therefore, that he found on the paper signs for speech which he understood, and I ardently longed to comprehend these also; but how was that possible when I did not even understand the sounds for which they stood as signs? (p. 155)

What the Monster seems to be dimly aware of, and confused by, is that there are here *two* radically opposed theories of language. One is that words express ideas, the other is that words are articulations of sounds. For the one theory language is the expression of thought, for the other thought is an effect of language. Some of the confusion between the two views is to be detected in the Monster's phrase concerning 'the ideas appropriated to each of these sounds': the question of priority is fudged, though the bias is towards sound.

Let us put it another way: the Monster evidently *thinks* that language is a question of nomenclature, classification and reference, but what, and how, in fact it *learns* is by way of sounds, effects, moods and practice. What it first notes are not meanings, but sounds and effects producing pleasure or pain, smiles or sadness, not truths or knowledges. Even when, after several months, the Monster learns how to apply the words 'fire', 'milk', 'bread' and 'wood', this, despite what it may think, is not the mastering of the names of things, but the discovery of a primitive grammar: 'fire' is linked to 'wood', and 'bread' is linked to 'milk' first by practice and then by metonymy – both a matter of contiguity – so that we have 'fire-wood' and 'bread-and-milk'. Neither belong to a class, or are susceptible of decomposition (except artificially and a posteriori): it would be a bit like trying to analyse the taste of 'tea-first-thing-in-the-morning' or 'tea-out-of-an-enamelled-mug-with-sweetened-milk' as opposed to, say, distinguishing between China tea and Indian tea. It cannot be done: these things are uncategorizable, they resist categorization, they are as much an experience as a classification, an event as much as a name. In a sense that most people will think trivializing but which I mean very seriously indeed it is precisely here in the production of indefinable and incalculable effects that language does, indeed, become a 'godlike science'.

This, too, hopefully, will become clearer as we continue. The Monster next, it says, 'learned also the names of the cottagers themselves'. In the end, of course, it *is* their 'names' that it learns, but is that what it learns first? The boy and the girl, as the Monster observes, have 'several names' – 'sister' or 'Agatha', 'Felix', 'brother' or 'son': but are these 'names'? The question is even more pertinent when we take into account that both 'Felix' and 'Agatha' are adjectives, 'happy' and 'good', before they are 'names'. So that, for example, there's no reason why Felix shouldn't say 'I feel Agatha-ish' nor Agatha say 'I feel Felix-ish'. Isn't the point being made that, for the Monster, to begin with at least, it was a question of indifference as to whether the youth is 'named' – the Monster not yet having the concept 'name' – 'Felix' or 'youth' or 'son', or whether the girl is 'named' 'Agatha' or 'sister' – come to that, what would the distinctions of 'youth' and 'girl' mean either? In other words, as far as the Monster is concerned, 'Felix', 'Agatha', 'son', 'brother', 'sister', do not serve to constitute a hierarchic identity of address, viz:

Youth
Son
Felix

but a dispersed repertory of roles, of moods and affects, capable of any number of arbitrary couplings and connections, so that 'Felix' will be sometimes just 'Felix'/'son', but, at others he might be 'Felix'/'son'/ 'brother', or just 'brother'/'son' – or even, 'Agatha'/'brother'/'son' or 'sister'/'brother'/'Felix'/'Agatha'/'daughter'/'son'. It is what I have called elsewhere the 'Keegan effect':[14] the ability to occupy several seemingly incompatible positions at once, a harlequin dispersal of identity before the final 'taking' of gender, vital state, and descent. It is this that is established, here, with the single name of the Father. With the establishment of the figure of the Father specific, exclusive identities are possible and 'names' proper emerge: but 'naming' is much more the arrest of language than the conditions of its possibility.

The common-sense view that language is a matter of 'naming' rather than acquiring a grammar is at one with the privileging of the voice before articulation we have discussed above and is here, in the De Lacey episode, further underpinned by the ideological notion of the 'divinity' of music and song – De Lacey's guitar playing produces, we are told, 'divine' sounds, while Safie's singing is described as 'entrancingly beautiful' or as 'wondrous' sounds (p. 160) – compared with the monotony of reading (pp. 150–1), and by the role played by translation in the teaching of language. Learning a foreign language inevitably, to begin with, encourages the notion that there is some common, ideal, referent for two words 'meaning the same' in different languages. It is only later that it becomes clear that these common 'ideals' do not exist and that language learning is much more concerned with the differential values and articulations internal to each language itself. The Monster may be forgiven for sharing the common prejudice in this matter in view of the fact that its own learning of language is greatly aided by his being able to overhear Felix's teaching Safie his own language, French, as a 'foreign' language.

Despite thus appearing to privilege the purity of song and the pedagogical efficacy of translation the text again and again slips in the odd burr to remind us that no matter how 'divine' the harmonies of song might seem, human, meaningful utterance, the art of language, begins, not in the head, but in the suppleness of the vocal organs:

> My organs were indeed harsh, but supple; and although my voice was very unlike the soft music of their tones yet I pronounced such words as I understood with tolerable ease. (pp. 156–7)

Even the divine Safie must resort to 'articulate sounds' (p. 159) when she wishes to make herself understood. Or again, we are reminded that no matter how extensive one's vocabulary might or might not be, the acquisition of a foreign language begins not with the translation of 'ideas' but with the 'frequent recurrence of some sound' (p. 159).

Once it has mastered language the Monster's education can proceed apace:

> While I improved in speech, I also learned the science of letters as it was taught to the stranger, and this opened before me a wide field for wonder and delight.
> The book from which Felix instructed Safie was Volney's *Ruins of Empires*. I should not have understood the purport of this book had not Felix, in reading it, given very minute explanations. He had chosen this work, he said, because the declamatory style was

framed in imitation of the Eastern authors. Through this work I obtained a cursory knowledge of history and a view of the several empires at present existing in the world; it gave me an insight into the manners, governments, and religions of the different nations of the earth. I heard of the slothful Asiatics, of the stupendous genius and mental activity of the Grecians, of the wars and wonderful virtue of the early Romans – of their subsequent degenerating – of the decline of that mighty empire, of chivalry, Christianity, and kings. I heard of the discovery of the American hemisphere and wept with Safie over the hapless fate of its original inhabitants. . . . I heard of the division of property, of immense wealth and squalid poverty; of rank, descent and noble blood. . . .

Other lessons were impressed upon me even more deeply. I heard of the differences of sexes, and the birth and growth of children; how the father doated on the smiles of the infant, and the lively sallies of the older child; how all the life and cares of the mother were wrapped up in the precious charge; how the mind of youth expanded and gained knowledge; of brother, sister, and all the various relationships which bind one human being to another in mutual bonds. (pp. 160–2)

It is not difficult from our post-liberal vantage point to detect the ideological bias of this programme though I suspect that not so long ago it would have appeared fairly unexceptionable. It consists principally of establishing a pretty rigorous set of simple and, as far as possible, homologous polar classifications, ranging from gender – the 'differences of sexes' – through social classes – 'I heard of the division of property, of immense wealth and squalid poverty' – to historical and racial characteristics – 'I heard of the slothful Asiatics, of the stupendous genius and mental activity of the Grecians.' We mustn't let ourselves be deceived by that pious reference to 'the division of property': 'immense wealth' and 'squalid poverty' are taxonomic categories only, not indices of a nascent class consciousness. It's worth comparing that easy coupling of the epithet 'squalid' with the pressure of syntax when the Monster describes how it finally discovered what the De Laceys were suffering from:

it was poverty, and they suffered that evil in a very distressing degree. (p. 153)

There is the insistence of an experience here whereas that 'squalid' serves to deodorize rather than reinforce the concept of poverty.

But, again, we need to pay careful attention, for what can be seen in this account of the Monster's education is the imminent clouding or breakdown of these seemingly transparent and innocuous categories. It starts off confidently enough:

> I heard of the slothful Asiatics, of the stupendous genius and mental activity of the Grecians . . .

Fine, fine: 'slothful Asiatics' (i.e. 'them'), 'stupendous Grecians' (i.e. 'us'), no problem. On to Rome ('us', *ergo* 'good') and the Barbarians ('them' *ergo* 'bad') – but that's not what happens. It's almost as if the lesson hasn't been quite learned: the labels don't stick, there is a fumbling, this is not what I am supposed to be saying, a collapse into a mumble:

> . . . of the wars and wonderful virtue of the early Romans – [here's the fumble, what's happened to the Barbarians? D.M.] of their subsequent degenerating [what's this degenerating *from within*? D.M.] – of the decline of that mighty empire, of chivalry, [here's the mumble, D.M.] Christianity and kings.

Some degree of poise is regained in the following sentence:

> I heard of the discovery of the American hemisphere and wept with Safie over the hapless fate of its original inhabitants.

But this is pretty flatulent compared to the vigour of the 'slothful Asiatics', 'stupendous Grecians', 'wonderful virtue' used above. The whole thing has run out of steam, partly no doubt because the facile categorizing of 'us, good' and 'them, bad' no longer holds true, but also because categorizing itself has become difficult – 'hapless' and 'original' precisely avoid any specification – and all that's left is a vague sentimentalism as an alibi for confusion.

But where categorizing most signally fails is with respect to the Monster. The classifications of gender, society and history just do not apply to it, any more than the spurious identities proffered to it later by the reading of Plutarch, Goethe and Milton. After all its education the Monster is still left with the question: 'What was I?' and the only answer it is able to formulate, the only one available to it, is that it is a 'Monster'. But what is a 'Monster'? And this is the point: *The Monster*

is a Monster, is monstrous, because it escapes classification, because it
scrambles codes, confounds rules, causes administrative chaos. It is
this that makes it catastrophic. The Monster is not 'in itself' monstrous, there is no inherent monstrousness; monstrousness is that
which is prescribed and proscribed by the facile categorizings of the
social and cultural order. The Monster is all that a society refuses to
name, refuses even to make nameable, not just because its very
heterogeneity, mobility, and power is a threat to that society but, much
more importantly, it is the very flux of energy that made society
possible in the first place and as such offers the terrible promise that
other societies are possible, other knowledges, other histories, other
sexualities.

What disturbed the history lesson was the discovery that history
does not proceed by a simple logical dialectic, Grecians versus Asiatics,
Romans versus Barbarians, but by 'degeneration' *within.* It is the
discovery that the 'simple' is not 'pure' but 'impure', flawed, divided,
double, corruptible. Interestingly, the history rehearsed by Volney's
Ruins of Empires has already been referred to earlier in the novel,
prompted by Frankenstein's ruminations of what had been the fatal
flaw in his own scientific project:

> If the study to which you apply yourself has a tendency to
> weaken your affections and to destroy your taste for those simple
> pleasures in which no alloy can possibly mix, then that study is
> certainly unlawful, that is to say, not befitting the human mind. If
> this rule were observed; if no man allowed any pursuit whatso-
> ever to interfere with the tranquillity of domestic affections,
> Greece would not have been enslaved, Caesar would have spared
> his country, America would have been discovered more gradually,
> and the empires of Mexico and Peru had not been destroyed.
> (p. 99)

What this commendation of innocence, of 'simple pleasures', actually
entails is not just the avoidance of the violence of history, but of any
history at all. It is the refusal to recognize that there is no such thing as
the 'simple': that all is always 'alloy', 'unlawful' – it is just possible, in a
Horn Tooke kind of way, to derive 'alloy' from the French *'a-loi'*,
suggesting 'beyond' or 'outside of the law' – 'not befitting the human
mind'. History, alas, like desire, is the unthinkable, a matter of
contingencies not of categories, of migrations and accidents,

catastrophes and discontinuities, always and everywhere exorbitant with respect to thought and the law.

IV

And isn't it this that makes the Monster so frightening – that it is a gigantic hulk of heterogeneity, a terrible alloy of living-dead flesh, ungendered, ubiquitous, indescribable?:

> How can I describe my emotions at this catastrophe or how delineate the wretch whom with such infinite pains and care I had endeavoured to form? His limbs were in proportion, and I had selected his features as beautiful. Beautiful! Great God! His yellow skin scarcely covered the work of muscles and arteries beneath; his hair was of a lustrous black, and flowing; his teeth of a pearly whiteness; but these luxuriances only formed a more horrid contrast with his watery eyes, that seemed almost of the same colour as the dun-white sockets in which they were set, his shrivelled complexion and straight black lips. (p. 101)

In the novel itself the Monster is assumed to be male, but in what I have written so far I have tried to keep the question of gender open by referring to it as 'it'. For the Monster resists, or rather transcends, gender designations: here the lustrous black hair and pearly white teeth suggest 'feminine' attributes, contrasted with the straight black lips and the prominent musculature, which suggest predominantly 'masculine' traits. It is not enough, though it was long overdue, to argue that the Monster is Mary Shelley's 'monstrous Eve':[15] what the Monster radically questions is the adequacy of the notion of gender itself. The Monster 'is' 'male' and 'female' and all other genders too, just as it 'is' 'alive' and 'dead', 'parent' and 'child'. The Monster thus presents the appalling prospect of embodying the three major familial neuroses:

> the phobic person can no longer be sure whether he is parent or child; the obsessed person, whether he is alive or dead; the hysterical person whether he is man or woman.[16]

The Monster, that is, refuses to accommodate itself to the cosy disjunctions of the family; it exceeds them on all sides. Worse: the Monster confounds also the distinctions between pursuer and pursued, between master and servant, between nature and culture, deficiency and excess, guilt and innocence, promise and refusal. What the Monster challenges, above all – and we shall turn to this again later – at a specific historical moment, are the easy taxonomies of Enlightenment thought: the eruption of all that it itself can no longer think consigns the achievement of the philosophy of the Enlightenment to being henceforth no more than ideology.

So much for the Monster constituted, but what can we learn by looking at the process of his production:

> These thoughts supported my spirits, while I pursued my under-taking with unremitting ardour. My cheek had grown pale with study and my person had become emaciated with confinement. Sometimes on the very brink of certainty, I failed; yet still I clung to the hope which the next day or night might realize. One secret which I alone possessed was the hope to which I had dedicated myself; and the moon gazed on my midnight labours, while, with unrelaxed and breathless eagerness, I pursued nature to her hiding places. Who shall conceive the horrors of my secret toil as I dabbled among unhallowed damps of the grave or tortured the living animal to animate the lifeless clay? My limbs now tremble, and my eyes swim with the remembrance; but then a resistless and almost frantic impulse urged me forward; I seemed to have lost all soul or sensation but for this one pursuit. It was indeed but a passing trance, that only made me feel with renewed acuteness so soon as, the unnatural stimulus ceasing to operate, I had returned to my old habits. I collected bones from charnel-houses and disturbed, with profane fingers, the tremendous secrets of the human frame. In a solitary chamber, or rather cell, at the top of the house and separated from all the other apartments by a gallery and staircase, I kept my workshop of filthy creation: my eye-balls were starting from their sockets in attending to the details of my employment. The dissecting room and the slaughter-house fur-nished many of my materials; and often did my human frame turn with loathing from my occupation, whilst, still urged on by an eagerness which perpetually increased, I brought my work near to a conclusion. (p. 98)

Ellen Moers has argued persuasively that '*Frankenstein* is a birth myth'[17] and that it owes much of its power to Mary Shelley's experience of the birth and death of her baby daughter. For Moers what constitutes the distinctive originality of Mary Shelley's tale is that it conveys some of the revulsion felt by a mother in the immediate aftermath of birth and in this the novel offers a counterweight to the more prevalent myth of birth as a happy event – exemplified by, to cite the example used by Ellen Moers, Amelia Sedley's delivery of the young George in *Vanity Fair*.

I am afraid that, as with Sandra Gilbert and Susan Gubar's proposal that the Monster represents Mary Shelley's 'Eve', I do not think this is a sufficiently radical reappraisal of the text. Ms Moers quotes the description of the finished Monster that I have used earlier but she makes no reference to the long account of the actual process of making the Monster I have just quoted. Now whatever this process is it does not seem to me to represent 'birth'. Firstly, it is regarded as an act of 'filthy creation' (elsewhere it is referred to as a 'filthy secret'), a 'passing trance' effected by an 'unnatural stimulus'. Secondly, this process is accompanied by both eagerness and delay, procrastination and haste, and the overall mood is one of guilty addiction. Thirdly, the effects on Frankenstein are to render his cheeks pale and emaciated while a particular strain is put on his eyes – 'my eyeballs were starting from their sockets'. Finally, the whole thing takes place in tremendous secrecy and isolation.

It seems to me that the one human activity that comes to mind at once as partaking of all the above features is that of masturbation – the secrecy, the haste, the furtiveness, the delay, the guilt, the addiction – plus the supposed symptoms of paleness, emaciation and eye-strain. Moreover, other aspects of the process, taken as a whole, would seem to support this hypothesis. Firstly it begins, in effect, when Frankenstein is 13 with his discovery of Cornelius Agrippa (p. 83): that is, it begins in adolescence and corresponds with the normal period of sexual rediscovery. For Frankenstein it is made more difficult by the dismissive (prohibitive) reaction of his father – 'Ah! Cornelius Agrippa! My dear Victor, do not waste your time on this; it is sad trash.' (ibid.) – and the further reading of Cornelius Agrippa, Paracelsus and Albertus Magna could only have been pursued guiltily in the face of parental disapproval. The prohibition, that is, turns the alchemical texts into something like pornography, a forbidden knowledge and pleasure. This first period lasts precisely two years, from 13 to 15, when the discovery of electricity arouses interests in other areas. Nevertheless,

and this may be the second corroborative point, Frankenstein returns
to the alchemical texts when, just after the death of his mother, he takes
up his studies at Ingolstadt – i.e. at moments of deprivation and
loneliness he returns to his 'alchemical' texts as a guilty and surrogate
consolation.

Now this is not something I particularly want to pursue – it's a bit
like discussing, if not Lady Macbeth's children, then her menstrual
cycle – but a hang-up about masturbation would not contradict, rather
it would go some way to explain, much of what we have already sensed
as the disturbed psychology of the tale. It would fit, for example, what
we have seen of Walton's libidinal weakness and thinly disguised
homosexual narcissism. It would explain, also, the rather less than
full-blooded sexual relationships of the novel: Frankenstein's father's
paternalistic adoption of a child wife, the self-effacement of Walton's
ship's master before a rival, the very asexual – quasi-incestuous –
relationship of Frankenstein with Elizabeth and his failure to consummate his marriage with her. It would account, also, for the terrible
confusion in Frankenstein's mind as to whether he is innocent or
guilty: his problem is that he feels guilty because he is innocent – the
neurasthenic dread he feels comes not from what he's done but from
what he has not done.

At this point it is probably necessary to ask the question that Mary
Shelley herself anticipates in her Introduction – 'How [she], then a
young girl, came to think of and to dilate upon so very hideous an idea?'
(p. 51). Again at a level of analysis I think it would be pointless to
pursue, it is possible to speculate as to what Mary Shelley had
discovered or intuited with respect to Shelley's own sexual proclivities
or the deeper significance of the flamboyant 'machismo' of a man
like Byron. Certainly it is not difficult to understand how a highly
intelligent and warmly sensuous young girl might become extremely
impatient at, and increasingly sceptical of, the flagrant egotism and
self-absorption of practically all the men around her – Godwin,
Shelley, Peacock, Byron, Jefferson.

Be that as it may, what I think is required is that we should consider
the 'problem' of masturbation as symptomatic of a much wider 'crisis'
– though that masturbation should be either a 'problem' or a 'crisis' is
precisely what the problem or crisis is in the first place. For what
masturbation is is the solace and confusion of a particular ideological fix
which might loosely be denominated 'idealism' but only in the sense

that this embraces that privileging of thought, voice, self, innocence, purity, logical categories – that series that has emerged in the course of our discussion – before that other series of body, writing, other, desire, alloy, heterogeneity which is *not* the 'polar opposite' of the first series but the condition of its possibility. In other words, what masturbation confronts us with is the impossibility of the 'purely' 'imaginary' and the absolute irreducibility of the supplementary body. Masturbation is the introduction of difference into the very essence of the delusion of self-sufficiency. The Argentine writer Cortázar's joke that masturbation observes all the classic unities of time, place, and action is, in fact, the very opposite of the case: it *fractures* them. Instead of the security of identity masturbation offers the threat of a dispersal: not merely that in masturbation we become both active subject and passive object, but also male and female, aggressor and victim, absent and present, prized and disdained, indulged and chastized – all at once. In masturbation inscriptions of gender, generation and vital state become unfixed to allow instead a momentary play of difference.

What the Monster represents, then, is the claim of terrible desires denied and disavowed by a society that privileges the claims of the ideal, insists on a severe sexual coding, and disdains all difference. At one level it is the outrage of Mary's body and soul at the crass cerebralism and insensitivity of Shelley's 'idealism'. At another level it is Frankenstein's refusal to come to terms with his own sexuality. Over and against the 'penetrative' intensities of Shelley, Walton, and Frankenstein – and the metaphor is unequivocally phallic – the Monster presents the risk and the joy of a distributive dispersal, of polyvalent discriminations, of migratory boundaries. The Monster's preferred metaphor for acquiring knowledge is that of an 'opening' (p. 260). This is how it describes how the world 'first opened upon [it]':

> No distinct ideas occupied my mind; all was confused. . . . I began to distinguish my sensations . . . to perceive the boundaries. . . . My sensations had by this time become distinct . . . I distinguished the insect from the herb, and by degrees, one herb from another. . . . How strange, I thought, that the same cause should produce such opposite effects! (p. 145)

This is a mode of knowing completely inconceivable to the logical mind for it is essentially nomadic, a tracing of surfaces, a migration along boundaries *between*. The Monster's characteristic location is the hut or the clearing, fittingly 'no-man's' lands. The tracery of the Monster's scars are not the mark of shame, or of deficiency, but hieroglyphs containing the secrets of unimaginable pleasures. It is this, perhaps, that explains the link established by Mary Shelley between the Monster and the book –

I bid my hideous progeny go forth and prosper. (p. 56)

and, hence, between masturbation and writing – sensed, perhaps, by Shelley, in his fear of the 'enervating effects of the novels of the present day' (p. 58): both testify to the irreducibility of a difference inconceivable to thought. It is in this being the 'unthinkable' that the Monster most clearly announces its modernity. For if, according to Foucault, De Sade marks the demise of libertinage to the extent that he takes to its limit the compatibility of desire and the possibility of its being represented, then Mary Shelley should be credited with having launched upon the world the monstrosity of a desire that resists and overflows representation on all sides.

V

Mary Shelley, Mary Shelley. Yes, it's pretty infuriating. But Mary did like her name – all of it: Mary Wollstonecraft Godwin Shelley. Few women can have been so constrained by descent and alliance, both being as much bonds of intellect as bonds of blood. Mary was trapped by 'her' names, by the names by which she was known and in which, as far as we know, she seemed to rejoice. But we have already suggested that the constant reminder of who her parents had been and who her husband was must have been a source of some irritation to her. And there is evidence of this elsewhere. Perhaps the sweetest letter in her correspondence is an early one to Thomas Jefferson Hogg with whom, at the time (the time, incidentally, of *Frankenstein* and the death of her first baby) she was enjoying a mildly (some argue that it was more than mild) flirtatious affair. She writes:

Dear Jefferson,
        It would have required more than mortal fortitude (and such the Pecksie does not boast of) to have resisted the sight of Green fields and yew trees & have jogged up to London again – when your letters arrived Shelley's distich was truly applicable

On her hind paws the Dormouse stood
In a wild and mingled mood
Of Maieshness & Pecksietude

. . . . .

Well Jefferson take care of yourself and be good – the Pecksie
will soon be back all the better for her Dormouseish jaunt &
remember nothing take away from my Maieshness

For Maie girls are Maie girls
Wherever they're found
In Air or in Water
    or in the ground

Now think of me very kindly while I am away & receive me
kindly when I come back or I will be no more

Your affectionate Dormouse[18]

Here is a delightful shrugging off of Mary Wollstonecraft Godwin
Shelley and a marvellous release of skittishness, of 'wild and mingled
mood', 'Of Maieshness and Pecksietude'. These are not names but
moods, not identifications but impersonal and prepersonal states of
being – not even human but 'Dormouseish' – joyous and irresponsible.
It's the moment when Felix can be 'Agatha-ish' again. Interestingly, at
the date of Mary's flirtation with Hogg, Hogg himself was using and
being generally addressed by a nickname, Alexy, taken from a novel he
had just written. Moreover yet another member of what was at this
time an intensely closed group, Jane Clairmont, Mary's step-sister,
was driving everyone insane by changing her name almost daily: from
Jane to, first, Clara, then Clary, then to Clare and finally to Claire. Of
course none of these little strategies is particularly radical but they
do suggest an underlying resistance to being named, classed, even
gendered.

So far we have kept discussion pretty close to the text and the
domestic milieu. But the problem of 'naming' was perhaps the most
critical *political* problem of the period. The years 1816 to 1819 were
years of acute political unrest beginning with the Spafields riots of
December 1816 and culminating in the Peterloo massacre of August
1819. In between were the March of the Blanketeers, the Ardwick
Conspiracy and the Pentridge Rising of 1817 which was to result in the

execution of Jeremiah Brandreth and two of his fellow 'mutineers', Turner and Ludlam. It was also a period of massive repression on the part of the authorities, with the suppression of habeas corpus in 1817 and the passing of the Six Acts in 1819.[19] The basic political imperative of the period, as far as the forces of 'law and order' were concerned, was to stem and contain the massive tide of popular unrest brought on by the collapse of traditional industries, the post-war depression and the spread of revolutionary propaganda. But before anything else, the very nature of the threat had to be *named*. And therein lay the rub.

The question posed by Hazlitt in 1818 – 'What is the people?' – to a very large extent remained, and remains, unanswered. The nature of the problem is well indicated by E. P. Thompson:

> We have spoken of the *artisan* culture of the Twenties. It is the most accurate term to hand, and yet it is no more than approximate. We have seen that *'petit-bourgeois'* (with its usual pejorative associations) will not do; while to speak of 'working class' culture would be premature. But by artisan we should understand a milieu which touched the London shipwrights and Manchester factory operatives at one side and the degraded artisans, the outworkers, at the other. To Cobbett these comprised the 'journeymen and labourers', or, more briefly, 'the people'.[20]

In a sense it is the same problem that we touched upon towards the end of our discussion of *Mansfield Park*: what is this variegated and heterogeneous mass that resists designation? that remains disconcertingly 'without' or 'across' or 'between' all available modes of categorization?

To many, of course, it was the 'mob' or, more luridly, the 'Monster'. And in this sense, as has been noted many times before, it is possible to see *Frankenstein* as a kind of anti-jacobinical tract with the Monster representing all that the social order most deeply feared and apprehended. Moreover, with the creation of the Monster what Mary Shelley provided all established authorities with was a fearsome stereotype of subversion and unrest which could be rapidly deployed whenever there was any threat to the status quo.[21]

For Thompson, on the other hand, what is of interest is the way in which this 'mob' or 'Monster' will emerge as a 'class', partly through the pressures of political confrontation, as at Peterloo, and partly through the development of programmes of self-help and self-education. As far as the latter is concerned Thompson speaks of the great impact that works of the Enlightenment – and he mentions Volney as a particularly popular writer – must have had on the minds of men increasingly suspicious of and dissatisfied by the homilies and tracts fobbed off on them by the established order.

Well, yes, but: the 'but' is prompted by what we have seen happening in *Frankenstein*. For there we have seen the Monster being given a pretty thorough education in Enlightenment thought, in Volney in particular, only to find that that thought and its ideals do not apply to it: not only do the De Laceys give it very short shrift indeed when it throws itself on their mercy but, and this is what is perhaps more important, the very *categories* of Enlightenment thought itself are totally unable to accommodate it. For what the Monster 'represents' is that which exceeds representation on all sides, that confounds categories and scrambles codes, that refuses to be *classed*. It is this that is troubling, that perhaps those very notions for which the 'working class' is indebted to the Enlightenment, above all the notion of 'class' itself, are not those best designed to accommodate and give legitimacy to those myriad and heterogeneous experiences and aspirations and groupings that are its own. Rather the possibility must be entertained that these seemingly 'enlightening' notions are none other than the most cynical imposition of a mode of thought which makes any alternative to itself impossible, literally 'unthinkable', monstrous. In other words, what seemed so much like the possibility of escape, was, in fact, a capitulation, a capitulation to a mode of thought that privileged categorization and division, classification and conflict, representation and monstrosity at the expense of heterogeneity and sharing, migration and festival, repetition and transcendence – that mode of thought that serves only one class, the bourgeois class, and the capitalist economic formation.

It is not that the 'monstrous' or the alien cannot be accommodated altogether. This is what the story of Safie shows. Safie is as much an outsider as is the Monster, coming, as she does, from an alien race and culture. But her accommodation is achieved only by means of a number of strategies and compromises. First, she is idealized as a 'sweet Arabian', virtually transformed into an 'oriental princess'; secondly, she is given a Christian mother which goes some way to giving her honorary European status; thirdly, she is shorn of any problematic features, of any embarrassing awkwardnesses. This is achieved by virtually splitting her in two: while Safie is allowed to embody all that might be accommodated in the alien, it is on her father, an archetypal 'wicked Turk', that has been loaded all that might be feared and execrated. It is this that explains why, in this idealized reworking of the main theme of the story, *two* are required to take the place of *one*: if Safie and her father were a unit, that is if the complexity and difference and intractability of the orient were truly represented, it would be 'monstrous' too – definitely not to be let in.

But therein lies the hope: if the 'monstrous' is that which cannot be accommodated by a society wedded to 'class' then it may mean that in pondering afresh what this monstrosity actually is we shall find some clue as to what might be the alternatives available to us.

VI

We might begin by recapitulating what have been those forces and potentialities that have accumulated around the figure of the Monster in the course of what has been written so far. Early on, for example, before the Monster made its appearance but in anticipation of that event, we considered those material practices and instituted plays of difference – the body, labour and language – that made possible all those ideal constructs such as an immaterial speech, the search for a chimerical Pole, or the immediacy of thought to itself (see above, pp. 49–50). What these practices and differences fractured were all the consolations of a self-sufficient identity and the self-evidence of the 'cogito' (p. 50). With that fracture the security and transparence of the systems of classification characteristic of Enlightenment thought – of which Frankenstein is a last avatar – fell into disarray, consigned henceforth to be no more than an ideology such as that embraced and mouthed by the De Lacey family in their protected pastoral asylum. It is this that the massive heterogeneity of the Monster and its resistance to all categorization most disturbingly threatens. For the Monster confounds all classifications and identifications: it is alive and dead, male and female, master and slave, pursued and pursuer, parent and child – all at once. Rather than allowing itself to be located in a system of classification what the Monster embodies is a radical dispersal of roles and states and a nomadic roaming across and between them. The Monster is always ahead or behind, always elsewhere, ever in a condition of migratory adjacency. Moreover the tracery of these migrations, like the scars on its body, are not the investments of limits but the openings of boundaries, the splitting of ever new laminations, the establishment of ever fresh surfaces. The Monster's wounds are not the evidence of a history but the sensitized possibility of a beginning. Or, rather, it is because there has been a history that there can be a beginning – just as there can be identity because there is difference, or thought because there is language. One does not begin with the punctuality of a birth but the reappropriation of a scattered genesis. One begins, that is, with repetition.

Earlier, when we were considering how the Monster was 'made' we looked at, first, the education it received at the hands of the De Lacey family and, secondly, at the secretive processes of its physical constitution in Ingolstadt. What we omitted to make any reference to at all is what was probably the most decisive experience of all: that is the Monster's discovery of Frankenstein's detailed journal of the four months preceding its creation. What the discovery and perusal of this journal allows the Monster is a reading of its own coming into existence; it allows it, that is, the dubious luxury of reliving, of repeating as in a kind of primal therapy, the trauma of its own constitution. What the journal reveals is that the Monster had not been born but made, that its originality was essentially derivative, that it was an unholy amalgam of heterogeneous and discrepant materials, that its uniqueness was supplementary and subsequent to a bewildering diversity. Worse: the Monster discovers that it has been old before it has been young, dead before it has been alive, worm-ridden before it has been fashioned. On all sides, then, what the Monster finds is that it is not contemporary with itself, that it is radically divided, that it has always been anticipated, provided with a body that is not its own, the product of a process of production that is indifferent to it, and allowed to speak only a language that cannot accommodate it. But perhaps it is in this very moment when the Monster discovers its negative relationship with all that constitutes it – life, labour and language – that the true nature of its monstrosity becomes clear. It is that with the very dispersal of its genesis, the indifference of its origins, the multiplicity of its histories, a certain choice becomes possible. It is to allow the dispersed, the indifferent, the multiple to return.

But perhaps it is not enough to talk of a 'return'. In the course of his extraordinarily elegant account of the eclipse of Enlightenment thought and the emergence of a 'thought' that might be termed 'modern' Michel Foucault announces with almost breath-taking nonchalance:

> Before the end of the eighteenth century *man* did not exist – any more than the potency of life, the fecundity of labour, or the historical density of language. He is quite a recent creature, which the demiurge of knowledge fabricated with its own hands less than two hundred years ago: but he has grown old so quickly that it has been too easy to imagine that he had been waiting for thousands of years in the darkness for that moment of illumination in which he would be finally known.[22]

It is Foucault's principal thesis that with the demise of Enlightenment thought based, as it was, on the self-evidence of the 'cogito' and the transparency of representation to itself, what emerged in its place was an order of knowledge based upon the problematic status of 'man' himself as a labouring, living, speaking creature. Knowledge is no longer the deployment of categories in a space of representations – 'to give new names and arrange in connected classifications' (p. 308) to quote M. Krempe again – but the laborious dwelling on what it means to have a history (and be subject to time), a body (and feel need), and a language (and to experience desire) which confound as much as constitute the securities they afford and deny.

In the light of Foucault's work it is now possible to see – and it is our shame not to have seen it before – what has been Mary Shelley's most remarkable achievement, even though it is thrust before us on almost every page of the novel: that is the invention of 'man'. There is not place here to rehearse in detail Foucault's account of that configuration of knowledge that centres on the emergence of 'man' but even if we take the most general headings of his discussion it is not difficult to see to what extent the problematic he describes is anticipated and illustrated by *Frankenstein*.

The first characteristic of modern thought that Foucault describes is what he calls the 'analytic of finitude', that is that man finds himself irredeemably confronted by the finiteness of his condition, deprived of any hope of transcendent salvation. For the first time man finds himself the lone subject and object of his own history. It is man who lives, speaks and labours but in all these processes he finds himself in a condition of necessarily subjacent density, in an irreducible anteriority, a living being, an instrument of production, a vehicle for words which exist before him. All these contents that his knowledge reveals to him as exterior to himself, and older than his own birth, anticipate him, overhang him with their solidity, and traverse him as though he were merely an object of nature, a face doomed to be erased in the course of history.[23]

This is precisely the experience that must have been the Monster's in its perusal of Frankenstein's notes: that far from being the sovereign subject of its own fate it was dependent on and subject to a process of labour, a body, and a language not its own. Paradoxically, however – and here I simplify Foucault's argument drastically – this discovery of finitude becomes the very ground of modern knowledge. In a curiously secular version of the Pascalian wager, since there is nothing to lose, for all is lost, there is everything to gain by slowly beginning again the accumulation of a knowledge which will never be but limited but might well be endless.

The second characteristic of modern thought that Foucault describes is what he calls the 'empirical and the transcendental'. This, in a sense, complements what has been described in the discussion of the 'analytic of finitude' for if that provides a knowledge based upon the finitude of the body, that is an empirical accumulation of facts, it is necessary to articulate that knowledge upon the inherited wisdom of culture. It is necessary, that is, to articulate a painfully emerging knowledge on the achieved and constituted knowledges of the past, to articulate what might be described as the *nature* of knowledge – its anatomo-physiological conditions – upon a *history* of knowledge – those 'sedimented significations' which become the raw material of ideology. Caught between the two, a knowledge of a positivist type on the one hand and an eschatology on the other, man finds himself both reduced and promised. This, painfully and immediately, is the experience of the Monster, caught between the anatomo-physiological discoveries of its body and the sclerotic doxology of the De Laceys. It is the principal dilemma that the Monster faces throughout the book: that its experience never conforms with what it has been taught, that its body and the discoveries of its senses are denied and travestied by the language and the history that are available to it.

This takes us to the third feature of modern thought announced by

Foucault: the contemporaneity of the 'cogito' and the unthought. He writes:

> Man and the unthought are, at the archeological level, contemporaries.[24]

Earlier he has explained this by a series of questions that might well have been prompted by considering the fate of the Monster:

> How can man *be* that life whose web, pulsations, and buried energy constantly exceed the experience that he is immediately given of them? How can he *be* that labour whose laws and demands are imposed upon him like some alien system? How can he be the subject of a language that for thousands of years has been formed without him. . . ?[25]

The Monster, the produced effect of a labour, a body and a language not its own, is never in the place that they would assign it, and the place in which it finds itself is not reducible to the available co-ordinates of labour, life and language. Anomalous and exorbitant with respect to all that would define it the Monster is the very figure of the unknown that haunts modern thought. This must be understood properly: the unthought is not something waiting in the shadows to be brought to light at some later date. The unthought that haunts the modern world is that that is the very condition of its knowledge. The basic paradigm of modern thought is not that of question and answer but the elaboration of 'problems' – the problem of gender, the problem of age, the problem of meaning, the problem of identity. It is that paradigm announced in the Monster's cry:

> What did this mean? Who was I? What was I? Whence did I come? What was my destination? These questions continually recurred, but I was unable to solve them. (p. 170)

In no more telling way does the Monster announce its modernity than in its perpetually posing such problems: am I alive or dead, male or female, parent or child, natural or artificial, victim or assailant. . . . Our tragedy is that we consider ourselves safe in possessing an answer to such questions.

Finally, Foucault speaks of 'the retreat and return of the origin'. Finding himself everywhere anticipated, invested by a myriad determinants, forestalled and pre-empted by all that precedes him, man cannot comfort himself with the punctuality of a birth or the innocence of a simple origin. But it is the very heterogeneity, indifference and asynchronousness of the chronologies that invest him that allows man to disperse himself amongst different times and different histories. In this sense the 'origin', or even 'origins' is that ecstatic choice made possible by the very plethora of geneses available to him. Man can become the locus where the old can be as contemporary as the new, where the already embraces the not yet, and where transcendence is made possible by repetition. By this reversal man no longer exists 'in' time but becomes, rather, the very field where many different times might mingle – the times of plants and of rocks, the times of beasts of prey and their victims, the times of individuals and crowds, of dynasties and exiles, of many births and many deaths. It is such a commingling of times, all indifferent and alien, that the Monster endures and enjoys: it is both of the past and of the future, a part of nature as well as the product of science, fossil as well as sentient, master as well as slave, dead as well as alive. Given this predicament, volatile in the extreme, neither the Monster nor man should resign it or himself to being the passive victim of a history that bears down upon him, but should be prepared to rejoice in the fact that it is in him that many histories are possible. In this sense the Monster is not that on which history has left its scar, but the very wound from which time can flow. It is this that is the experience of the Monster: not that it takes place in a beginning, but that a beginning takes place in it:

> Soon a gentle light stole over the heavens and gave me a sensation of pleasure. I started up and beheld a radiant form rise from among the trees. I gazed with a kind of wonder. It moved slowly, but it enlightened my path, and I again went out in search of berries. (p. 145)

What the Monster is, then, is 'man' as he emerged as the foundation of knowledge at the beginning of the nineteenth century and it is that that makes it monstrous for in many ways we have still not come to terms with that creation. The Monster is the body we still fear, the conjugation of sexualities we would deny, the lawlessness we disguise from ourselves, the histories that are available to us, the beginnings we flee like the plague. The Monster threatens our pathetic little identities, the bland securities of our answers, the crassness of our accommo- dations; it fractures the claustrophobic closure of our calendar, and it offers the hope of unspeakable ecstasies.

4

Wuthering Heights: the unacceptable texts

Several years ago I gave a paper at the Sociology of Literature Conference held at the University of Essex entitled '*Wuthering Heights* – the unacceptable text' which was subsequently published in the *Proceedings*[1] of that conference. My concern at that time was to show to what extent *Wuthering Heights* could be seen as what Pierre Macherey and Etienne Balibar have termed an 'ideological operator'[2] – that is an 'acceptable' text that works to provide ideologically anodyne identifications (we can all identify ourselves with the great passion of Heathcliff and Cathy), aesthetically reconcilable contradictions (rather than the irreconcilable contradictions of the 'real' world), and a 'literate' language which itself posits a certain normative discourse that both pre-empts the possibilities of more analytical or abstract thought and marginalizes regional and more 'vulgar' alternatives (as Nelly Dean's commonsensical narrative both mediates the passions unleashed by the story and supplants the regional dialect of Joseph). By way of further illustration of my argument I went on to show how, consistently, throughout the text literacy, literature, books, culture, education serve to suppress desire (Lockwood's use of a 'pyramid of books' to shut out the cry of the waif Cathy), to underwrite legitimacy (Hareton learning to read his own name), to provide a culturalist gloss to the roughage of history (Hareton and Catherine's costly picture book – referred to as an 'accepted text' incidentally – contrasted with Joseph's bible strewn with banknotes, those twin motors of capitalist accumulation).

It was at this point – where a close reading of the text revealed a disturbing self-consciousness of its own strategies of accommodation, where it began to 'lay bare' its devices – that I invoked the notion of the novel's 'unacceptability'. Behind the façade or, better, within the interstices of the 'acceptable' text was to be found an 'unacceptable' text, 'unacceptable' because it exposed the very mechanisms by means of which bourgeois ideology sought to disguise and resolve the contradictions of its own predicament, that predicament which can be briefly, if inadequately, characterized as '1848'.

Such, very much compressed, was the burden of my earlier paper. It was highly formalistic, much under the influence of Pierre Macherey's distinction between a text's 'ideological project' and its 'real conditions of production' and clearly, if not simplistically, indebted to the Freudian conception of the relationship between 'latent' and 'manifest' texts. In the end it remained no more than a quite clever (I still think) piece of 'literary criticism' which had left the work with, if anything, only greater autonomy and authority. Above all I felt that the notion of the 'unacceptable' text was no more than gestural. Or, put another way, I felt that I had begun to ask the right questions but that the answers themselves lacked conviction, lacked, in a way, the materiality that the phrase 'real conditions of production' leads one to expect. It is this materiality that I hope to supply in what follows.

I think it might help if at this point I put down some methodological markers as to what I am doing. I have already mentioned Pierre Macherey twice, once in reference to the notion of the text as an 'ideological operator', and again with reference to his distinction between a text's 'ideological project' and its 'real conditions of production'. The latter distinction comes from his earlier work, *Towards a Theory of Literary Production* while the former comes from his 'Presentation', with Etienne Balibar, to Renée Balibar's *Les Français fictifs*. The point is that between the book and the 'Presentation' there is a remarkable shift of position, though as far as I know it has never been overtly acknowledged. *Towards a Theory of Literary Production* is a highly formalistic text, even idealist, more at home in a Kantian tradition than within the Marxist–Leninist tradition it avowedly espouses. The 'Presentation' to Renée Balibar's work, on the other hand, is a much more materialist approach to the function of literature as an ideological institution and practice, particularly with regard to its place in the educational apparatus or, and it is with this that Renée Balibar is particularly concerned – and with which I shall be particularly concerned in what follows – the place of the educational apparatus in literature, not as a theme, but as a detectable and determinative effect. Perhaps the most provocative illustration of Renée Balibar's thesis is her study of Camus' *The Outsider* where, refusing to be seduced into an 'existentialist' interpretation of the peculiarly laconic style of the book, she traces each chapter back to early school exercises undertaken in conjunction with Maquet, Flot and Roy's *Cours de langue française*, the official text book for Camus' primary education in Algeria. Here are to be found set topics such as 'description of objects', 'the lazy man', 'description of an animal', 'Sunday', 'description of a landscape' which might serve as chapter titles for many of the episodes of *The Outsider*.[3] This is far from the formalism and theoretical sophistication of *Towards a Theory of Literary Production*: indeed it could hardly be more uncompromisingly empirical. But if we are to take the notion of the 'real conditions of literary production' seriously, then, surely, it is just such an exercise that we must engage in. Balibar's work is, in some ways, outrageous: it is outrageous because it is so naïve, so preposterous, so crude – but it is also outrageous that it hasn't been done before. I think what I am going to say about Emily Brontë is also outrageous: it is outrageous because it is very naïve, obvious, crude, and it is also outrageous because, as far as I know, it has not been said before: indeed, on the contrary there almost seems to have been a wilful determination not to say it. It is my belief that the clue to any understanding of the 'real conditions of production' of *Wuthering Heights*, or of Emily Brontë's later poems, or of the last years of her life is to be found in the school exercises, the set texts, the intellectual challenge offered to Emily Brontë during the ten months she spent with her sister Charlotte at the Pensionnat de Jeunes Filles in the Rue d'Isabelle in Brussels under the supervision of M. Constantin Héger.

There is a curious episode in *Wuthering Heights* that must have struck many readers as rather 'odd' but which, as far as I know, has not received the attention that it deserves. Nelly is recounting an incident that had occurred to her on one of her many visits to the Heights:

> One time, I passed the old gate, going out of my way, on a journey to Gimmerton. It was about the period that my narrative has reached – a bright frosty afternoon; the ground bare and the road hard and dry. I came to a stone where the highway branches off on to the moor at your left hand; a rough sand-pillar, with the letters W.H. cut on its north side, on the east, G., and on the south-west, T.G. It serves as guide-post to the Grange, and Heights, and village.
>
> The sun shone yellow on its grey head, reminding me of summer; I cannot say why, but all at once, a gush of child's sensations flowed into my heart. Hindley and I held it a favourite spot twenty years before.
>
> I gazed long at the weather-worn block; and stooping down perceived a hole near the bottom still full of snail-shells and pebbles, which we were very fond of storing there with more perishable things – and, as fresh as reality, it appeared that I beheld my early playmate seated on the withered turf, his dark, square head bent forward, and his little hand scooping out the earth with a piece of slate.
>
> 'Poor Hindley!' I exclaimed involuntarily. I started – my bodily eye was cheated into a momentary belief that the child lifted its face and stared straight into mine! It vanished in a twinkling; but, immediately, I felt an irresistible yearning to be at the Heights. (p. 147)[4]

Much might be said about this incident. First it should be noted that it marks a distinct break in the narrative, a break that is also a disturbance because for the first time it implicates Nelly Dean in the emotional web of the story in a way in which her otherwise 'homely' and rather dispassionate narrative does not. Secondly it is an incident that centres upon a signpost marked by initials – W.H., G., T.G. – that are not correlated here 'respectively' with what they denote – Heights, village, Grange – but with 'Grange, and Heights, and village'. This slippage, we shall see, is important.

But what is most striking and disturbing about this episode is that in the juxtapositioning of the hole full of snail-shells and pebbles and the hallucinatory glimpse of a child's face from twenty years before there is a conflation of the two most traumatic moments of the story as a whole: Lockwood's nightmare glimpse of Cathy at the window – notice the detail of the probing 'little hand' in both episodes – *though with the gender of the subjects reversed*; and the painful glimpse of a childhood crime revealed at the height of Cathy's delirium during her illness: she has plucked a lapwing's feather from her pillow –

> and this – I should know it among a thousand – it's a lapwing's. Bonny bird; wheeling over our heads in the middle of the moor. It wanted to get to its nest, for the clouds touched the swells, and it felt rain coming. This feather was picked up from the heath, the bird was not shot – we saw its nest in the winter, full of little skeletons [cf. the snail-shells in the Nelly episode. D.M.]. Heathcliff set a trap over it, and the old ones dare not come. I made him promise he'd never shoot a lapwing after that, and he didn't. Yes, here are more! Did he shoot my lapwings, Nelly? Are they red, any of them? Let me look. (p. 160)

The mixture here of prurience and fascination, of guilt and thrill, together with the powerful sexual innuendo of the imagery, suggests a complicity between Cathy and Heathcliff far more traumatic than anything otherwise revealed by the narrative as a whole. It is, indeed, a rent in the text.

The strange hiatus, then, of Nelly's experience at the signpost, the faltering, in a sense, of her narrative control, allows the irruption into the text of questions concerning signposting, gender, and sexuality.

Cathy's delirium, Lockwood's nightmare and Nelly's hallucination that brings them together reach far into Emily Brontë's past and almost certainly mark moments of traumatic crisis. The first of these, that which centres on the lapwing skeletons and the snail-shells, is probably too nebulous, painful and buried for us to locate with any kind of precision, though it is worth noting that a trace of it is to be found in Emily Brontë's poetry:

> Why do I hate that lone green dell?
> Buried in moors and mountains wild,
> That is a spot I had loved too well
> Had I but seen it when a child.

There are bones whitening there in the summer's heat,
But it is not for that, and none can tell;
None but one can the secret repeat
Why I hate that lone green dell.[5]

The second traumatic crisis – that concerning a disturbance of gender and a thrusting hand – can be located with more confidence. It occurred when Emily was about ten years of age and is recounted, as follows, by Winifred Gérin:

> On a certain Oakapple day in those early years, a performance was decided on of Charles II's escape from Worcester, and Emily, because the tallest and darkest of that predominantly fair family, was chosen to play the chief part. Exiled monarchs were to feature conspicuously in her Gondal chronicles and she had no difficulty in identifying herself with such a harrassed but heroic character. Outside Mr. Brontë's parlour window grew a double cherry tree, and in default of an oak in that sparse ground the cherry tree was fixed on for the exile's hiding place. The tree was in full blossom and afforded luxurious shelter for a hunted monarch. To Emily's long legs the ascent presented no problems, especially as the high branches were on a level with Papa's bedroom windows. Papa was obviously away for the day, on one of his long parochial tours, and it must also have coincided with one of Miss Branwell's rare absences from home on a round of calls. Heaven generally favours the bold, the little Brontës had read, and they were prepared to sustain the roles of hunters and hunted all day, until the sinister sound of rending wood brought the branch on which Emily was sitting crashing to the ground. Her own agility saved her from harm, but there was an ugly gash in the tree-trunk necessitating a hurried consultation with Tabby. A bag of soot was fetched from across the lane at John Brown's stone-mason's yard and applied to the gash; but though invention was strong in the children their sense of truth was apparently stronger, and when Mr. Brontë came home he was given a full account of what happened. What his reactions were have remained unrecorded.[6]

I don't think it is too difficult to sense the horror of this episode. Emily, always a tomboy, has assumed a masculine role almost as though by right – her colouring and height – and has clambered up her father's favourite tree whose topmost branches brushed the windows of his bedroom: the climb is a powerful and reckless act of aspiration, even usurpation – not merely of a masculine role, but of the very place of the father himself. Then comes the sickening tearing of the branch, the rending open of a ghastly wound, the frenzied attempts to staunch the damage, the bitter shame and abjection of confession. Mr Brontë's reactions may well have remained unrecorded but it is surely not too difficult to imagine their tenor and effect. There would have been upbraiding of the reckless tomboy, the asseverations to the effect that 'girls do not climb trees', the counselling of a more lady-like comportment in the future. In short, at a most critical and vulnerable age, Emily finds herself subjected to all the rigour of what Lacan has called the 'Symbolic Order': that is that socially sanctioned order of gender allocation that finally thwarts all imaginary identifications with their accompanying illusions of freedom of choice and omnipotence. The monarch of this little civil war, like Charles II in that greater one, must be exiled: Emily must henceforth be feminine. It will be nearly twenty years before her exiled and orphaned soul will again seek entry with the tapping of a branch on a casement.

Emily's life during this period must have been deeply divided, if not to say schizophrenic, if by that we understand what Deleuze and Guattari mean when they characterize this condition in their *Anti-Oedipus*[7] on which I shall be drawing freely in what follows. Reading the biographies of not only her, but of other members of the family – particularly those of Charlotte and Branwell[8] – one gains the impression of an almost deliberate conspiracy afoot (albeit an unconscious one) on the part of the family to maintain Emily in a feminine role. Apart from a brief period teaching in Halifax in 1837 Emily spends all her time at home and as both her aunt, Miss Branwell, and the old housekeeper, Tabitha, get older it is on Emily's shoulders that the running of the house devolves. It is from this period that may date the well-known image of her:

> When at home, she took the principal part of the cooking on herself, and did all the household ironing; after Tabby grew old and infirm, it was Emily who made all the bread for the family; and any one passing by the kitchen door, might have seen her studying German out of an open book, propped up before her, as she kneaded the dough; but no study, however interesting, interfered with the goodness of the bread, which was always light and excellent.[9]

This is from Mrs Gaskell's *Life of Charlotte Brontë* and, indeed, Charlotte often seems to be excessively anxious to ascribe 'femininity' to Emily:

> When Charlotte planned to open a school with her sisters' help, she told M. Héger: 'Emily does not care much for teaching but she would look after the housekeeping and, although something of a recluse, she is too kind hearted not to do all she could for the well-being of the children. She is very generous by nature.'[10]

Charlotte's tendency to totally misunderstand her sister is, of course, quite notorious[11] but at times the misunderstanding seems to be compounded by an almost wilful determination to construct an image wholly inconsistent with that to be derived from other sources. Perhaps some clue as to why this should have been so may emerge from what follows.

Apart from Charlotte, Emily's relationship with the other members of her family also enjoined upon her a 'womanly' role: 'wife' as well as daughter to her widowed father; 'wife' and 'mother' as well as sister to her wretched brother Branwell. Finally, there is some evidence that the emergence into prominence at this period of the young Princess Victoria who was only nine months younger than Emily and with whom she was inclined to identify herself also played its part in reconciling Emily to a quintessentially feminine role – though she was probably not unique in succumbing to such an identification – cf. the Princess Di look-alikes today.

Bound, then, in her daily life to a severely administered femininity it is not surprising that Emily's real affective life went underground, into the construction of the so-called Gondal legend. Here, in a world of passionate intensities, the imperious Augusta Geraldine Almeda (A.G.A.) can be seen as a miraculous compensation for the frustrations Emily must have felt at her pastry board. A.G.A.'s life consists of an endless stream of loves and betrayals, of conquests and defeats, of murders and seductions. She loves and loses, through treachery or death, a whole series of noble, tragic lovers: Alexander, Lord of Elbe; Lord Alfred of Aspin Castle; Julius Brenzaida; Fernando de Samara – and, in turn, meets her own death at the hands of the dark and moody and enigmatic Douglas. There is no space here to give even a summary account of the whole saga which centres primarily on the rivalry of two turbulent states, Gondal and Gaaldine. In the first place the difficulties attendant upon any attempt to establish the facts of the narrative are enormous – as attested to by the person best qualified to do so, Fanny Ratchford, whose *The Brontës' Web of Childhood* is the most ambitious bid to unravel the story to date:

> Only a small per cent of the poems carry headings, and the few headings we have are made up of initials which raise as many problems as they solve. Varying sets of initials appear for the same character, corresponding to given name, family name, and titles. For example, the heroine of the epic enjoys six certain designations, probably more: Augusta Geraldine Almeda, A.G.A., Rosina of Alcona, A.S., 'Sidonia's deity', and Gondal's Queen. Julius Brenzaida, Prince of Angora, King of Almedore, and Emperor of Gondal, is known by all his titles and their abbreviations. Worse still, several characters in the Gondal drama have the same initials, while family names are applied to all of the blood. A.S. stands in one place for Alexander S., Lord of Elbe; on another for Lord Alfred S. of Aspin Castle; again for Lord Alfred's daughter Angelica; and still again for A.G.A. when she was the wife of Lord Alfred. G.S. in one poem is a boy, in another, a woman. The family names Exina and Gleneden appear both with and without distinguishing first initials for the several members of these families. The climax of puzzlement is reached in a poem representing a conversation between a girl named Ierne and her father, headed 'I.M. to I.G.'[12]

There are other problems too: many of the poems were revised many times and often it is impossible to date the essential core of the poem; or, again, a number of the poems begin with an intensely personal tone which then modulates into the tone of a Gondal person and in several poems there is clearly a conjugation of personae.

Faced by such intractable problems one is surely led to question whether Mrs Ratchford's endeavours, admirable and ingenious as they are, are not radically misguided. The mistake is to have even sought for a coherent scheme: *the poems and their titles are not the epiphenomena of a lost narrative – they are an aggregative ensemble 'anterior to' and resistant of narrative appropriation.* Consider the titles given to the poems by Emily herself:

> A.G.A.   to A.E.;   A.G.A.   to A.S.;   A.S. to G.S.;   D.G.C. to J.A.;   E.W. to A.G.A.;   E.G. to M.R.;   M.G.   for the U.S.;   I.M. to I.G., etc., etc.[13]

What the titles remind us of, thus written out, is an elementary and arbitrary connective code where everything might connect with everything else – like dominoes pieced together by a child without reference to the number of the dots. What does it matter with such a code if A.S. refers sometimes to Alexander, Lord of Elbe and at others to Lord Alfred of Aspin Castle, or whether A.G.A. and Rosina of Alcona refer to the same person or to different persons? The pleasure is in the making of connections, any connections, with blithe disregard for the rules of selection and exclusion, for the identifications that narrative requires. It is, in other words, the mode of a wilfulness and perversity that eludes the strictures and structures of the Symbolic Order. Thus, over and against the imperative 'be feminine' what the Gondal material manifests is the revelry of endless connections and miraculous conjugations: here one can be male and/or female, boy and/or girl, father and/or daughter, mother and/or son *all at once*. Instead of the exclusive disjunctions, the either/or of the Symbolic Order, in Gondal there prevail the conjunctive syntheses, or rather, the affirmative disjunctions and diverse intensities of the schizoid condition:

> The schizophrenic is dead or alive, not both at once, but each of the two as the terminal point of a distance over which he glides. He is parent or child, not both, but the one at the end of the other, like the two ends of a stick in a non-decomposable space.[14]

A.G.A. not only has the reversibility of a palindrome, but the names themselves – Augusta, Geraldine – are indices of an imperious androgyny.

Ironically, but fittingly, Mrs Ratchford gets closer to the truth of the matter where she fails: she lists the Gondal poems 'unplaced in the story pattern':

A. Poems of unidentified events.
B. Poems in the A.G.A. tone.
C. Poems of war, imprisonment, and exile.
D. Poems of death and parting.
E. Poems of memory and remorse.
F. Poems of courage and defiance.
G. Poems pertaining to Gondalian institutions: The Unique Society and the Palace of Instruction.
H. Poems, probably pertaining to Douglas, suggestive of Heathcliff in *Wuthering Heights*.[15]

The Gondal poems are precisely not about 'identified' events: it is identity that they are an escape from. They are about 'tone', 'war, imprisonment, and exile', 'death and parting', 'memory and remorse', 'courage and defiance': that is about pre-personal or trans-personal moods available to nomadic and impersonal occupation. A.G.A., Rosina of Alcona, Julius Brenzaida, Alexander, Lord of Elbe *do not designate identities but are the co-ordinates of capriciously scanned affective fields*: they offer the intensities of being able to say 'I feel/I do not feel like a man', 'I feel/do not feel like a woman', 'I feel/do not feel like a queen', 'I feel/do not feel like a slave' – *all at the same time*:

> I am God I was not god I am a clown of God; I am Apis. I am an Egyptian. I am a red Indian. I am a Negro. I am a Chinaman. I am a Japanese. I am a foreigner, a stranger. I am a sea bird. I am a land bird. I am the tree of Tolstoy. I am the roots of Tolstoy. . . . I am husband and wife in one. I love my wife. I love my husband.[16]

There is probably a more technical term for this phenomenon but the closest I have come to designating it is as the 'Keegan effect' – the reference is to the footballer who seems to be on every part of the pitch at the same time! Here one is not a single subject but an assemblage of singularities – hence the unplacing of 'poems pertaining to Gondalian institutions': for the notion of a 'Unique Society' closely conveys the paradox of collective/correlative singularities which narrative cannot scan while the 'Palace of Instruction' reminds us of the commingling of discrete delights and admonishments that is the inherent thrill of such a volatile condition. That is the problem, this schizoid peregrination of intensities is highly volatile: it is always likely to break down into the manic-depressive anxiety that provides its essential motor. It is this that explains 'Douglas': he is no harbinger of Heathcliff – to suggest that is to engage in the crudest kind of retrospective reductionism: what 'Douglas' denotes, if anything, is the depressive 'low' that ever haunts the miraculous and manic 'high' of A.G.A.

In a long poem written between 1841 and 1844 A.G.A. is finally slain by Douglas. At about the same time Emily Brontë set about rearranging her poems into two books, one containing the poems of the Gondal cycle, the other containing her other verses. It is as if Emily, in taking stock of her production so far, is preparing to close the Gondalian chapter of her experience and its rather adolescent imbroglios and to face head-on the sterner implications of the forces that

assailed her. It is in the second volume that we begin to find the great
mystical poems which, for me, represent her finest work as a writer:

> O thy bright eyes must answer now,
> When Reason, with a scornful brow,
> Is mocking at my overthrow;
> O thy sweet tongue must plead for me
> And tell why I have chosen thee!
>
> Stern Reason is to judgement come
> Arrayed in all her forms of gloom:
> Wilt thou my advocate be dumb?
> No, radiant angel, speak and say
> Why I did cast the world away;
>
> Why I have persevered to shun
> The common paths that others run;
> And on a strange road journeyed on
> Heedless alike of Wealth and Power –
> Of Glory's wreath and Pleasure's flower.
>
> These once indeed seemed Beings divine,
> And perchance heard vows of mine
> And saw my offerings on their shrine –
> But, careless gifts are seldom prized,
> And mine were worthily despised;
>
> So with a ready heart I swore
> To seek their altar-stone no more,
> And gave my spirit to adore
> Thee, ever present, phantom thing –
> My slave, my comrade, and my King!
>
> A slave because I rule thee still;
> Incline thee to my changeful will
> And make thy influence good or ill –
> A comrade, for by day and night
> Thou art my intimate delight –
>
> My darling pain that wounds and sears
> And wrings a blessing out from tears
> By deadening me to real cares;
> And yet, a king – though prudence well
> Have taught thy subject to rebel

And am I wrong to worship where
Faith cannot doubt nor Hope despair
Since my own soul can grant my prayer?
Speak, God of Visions, plead for me
And tell why I have chosen thee![17]

Or, again:

'Enough of Thought, Philosopher;
Too long hast thou been dreaming
Unlightened, in this chamber drear
While summer's sun is beaming –
Space sweeping soul, what sad refrain
Concludes thy musing once again?

'O for the time when I shall sleep
Without identity,
And never care how rain may steep
Or snow may cover me!

'No promised heaven, these wild Desires
Could all or half fulfil;
No threatened Hell, with quenchless fires,
Subdue this quenchless will!'

– So said I, and still say the same;
– Still to my Death will say –
Three Gods within this little frame
Are warring night and day.

Heaven could not hold them all, and yet
They all are held in me
And must be mine till I forget
My present entity.

O for the time when in my breast
Their struggles will be o'er;
O for the day when I shall rest,
And never suffer more!

'I saw a Spirit standing, Man,
Where thou dost stand – an hour ago;
And round his feet, three rivers ran
Of equal depth and equal flow –

'A Golden stream, and one like blood,
And one like Sapphire, seemed to be,
And where they joined their triple flood
It tumbled in an inky sea. . . .'[18]

These are, I think, amongst the finest poems in the language. The affective intensities of the Gondal poems are here taken in hand and embraced with passionate but celibate mastery.

The transcendent and yet materialist metaphysic of these poems has been frequently cited, of course, as foreshadowing the poignant dream of Cathy – her distress at finding herself in heaven:

I was only going to say that heaven did not seem to be my home; and I broke my heart with weeping to come back to earth; and the angels were so angry that they flung me out, into the middle of the heath on the top of Wuthering Heights, where I woke sobbing for joy. (pp. 120–1)

and, later, the passionate quasi-mystical longings of Heathcliff:

And yet I cannot continue in this condition! – I have to remind myself to breathe – almost to remind my heart to beat! And it is like bending back a stiff spring . . . it is by compulsion, that I do the slightest act, not prompted by one thought, and by compulsion, that I notice anything alive or dead, which is not associated with one universal idea. . . . I have a single wish, and my whole being and faculties are yearning to attain it. They have yearned towards it so long, and so unwaveringly, that I am convinced it will be reached – and soon – because it has devoured my existence – I am swallowed in the anticipation of its fulfilment. (p. 354)

The connections are, indeed, obvious but to see the poems as some kind of trial run for the novel is to make the mistake we accused Mrs Ratchford of earlier: what is remarkable about the poems is that they are so much *better* than the passages quoted from the novel, so much more complex and achieved. The consistent mistake of so many students of Emily Brontë is to look for the 'genesis of *Wuthering Heights*', to quote the title of Martha Visick's little book,[19] in the poetry. But the question that still has to be asked is what enabled Emily Brontë not only to break out of the stranglehold of Haworth and its insistence on her 'femininity', but also to soar beyond the manic-depressive and essentially adolescent world of the Gondal poems and write some of the great mystical poems of the language and what some would argue to be its greatest novel? How, in other words, did she manage to break with the frustrations of the domestic scene and attain the epicenic conviction of the visionary?

In 1842 Emily and Charlotte Brontë spent nine months in Brussels studying under M. Constantin Héger. The impact Héger made on Charlotte's life and work is well known and at least one commentator has remarked that English literature is already sufficiently in the Belgian professor's debt. On the other hand, as I remarked earlier, there seems to have been an almost wilful refusal to consider that Héger's impact on Emily was, if anything, even more important and decisive than it was on her sister. Winifred Gérin writes, for example, as far as her schooling in Brussels was concerned, 'she might never have been abroad – her writings contain no trace of the experience'.[20] Because there is so little evidence available it is, indeed, difficult to establish exactly what happened in Brussels but the very fragmentary evidence that we do have suggests an extremely involved and powerful drama.

There is, first of all, Mrs Gaskell's account of Héger's opinion of both the girls:

> He seems to have rated Emily's genius as something even higher than Charlotte's; and her [that is Mme Héger's] estimation of their relative powers was the same. Emily had a head for logic, and a capability of argument, unusual in a man, and rare indeed in a woman, according to M. Héger. Impairing the force of this gift, was her stubborn tenacity of will, which rendered her obtuse to all reasoning where her own wishes, or her own sense of right, was concerned. 'She should have been a man – a great navigator', said M. Héger in speaking of her. 'Her powerful reason would have deduced new spheres of discovery from the knowledge of the old; and her strong, imperious will would never have been daunted by opposition or difficulty; never have given way but with life.' And yet, moreover, her faculty of imagination was such that, if she had written a history, her view of scenes and characters would have been so vivid, and so powerfully expressed, and supported by such a show of argument, that it would have dominated over the reader, whatever might have been his previous opinions, or his cooler

perceptions of its truth. But she appeared egotistical and exacting compared to Charlotte, who was always unselfish (this is M. Héger's testimony); and in the anxiety of the elder to make her younger sister contented, she allowed her to exercise a kind of unconscious tyranny over her.[21]

Emily, Charlotte records in her letters, did not 'draw well' with Héger and there is much evidence in Mrs Gaskell's account of the Brussels stay that her relationship with Héger was, to say the least, stimulating, if not abrasive. Even so it is clear from the above account that Héger thought highly of her, and that before he had the evidence of *Wuthering Heights* before him. Moreover, what is striking is how this egotistical and tyrannical Emily differs from the selfless bread-maker of Haworth. But the most suggestive evidence of a different Emily emerging in Brussels comes from the French exercises she prepared for Héger.[22]

There are seven of them that have come down to us and they are titled as follows: 'Le Chat'; 'Portrait: le Roi Harold avant la Bataille de Hastings'; 'Lettre: Ma chère Maman'; 'L'Amour filial'; 'Lettre d'un frère à un frère'; 'Le Papillon' and 'Le Palais de la Mort'. They are a remarkable series of documents. One interesting question they raise is how much French Emily knew before going to Brussels: if very little, then the standard she achieved under Héger in such a short time argues strongly for the efficiency of his teaching methods and her application and intelligence. Mrs Gaskell, for example, in comparing Charlotte and Emily's performance of the same exercise judges that Emily's is far the superior. Even so, another commentator, Herbert Dingle, cautions us against placing too much confidence in the French work:

> The French essays, for example, can by no means be accepted at their face value, for, when writing in a foreign language of which one is not completely master, what one says may be at least partly determined by what one is able, and not what one wishes, to say.[23]

In fact, I think this eminently sensible point of view is almost the complete opposite of the truth – as anyone who has struggled with a foreign language will testify to. The very unfamiliarity of the foreign language frees one from the inhibitions and taboos of one's own language. Things can be said in a foreign language that one would never dare to say in one's own: the very unfamiliarity a boon rather than a handicap.

There is no room here to offer a detailed summary of all the exercises and we will have to be content with brief notes and extracts. The first exercise, 'Le Chat', consists of an elaboration on the parallels to be drawn between cat and human behaviour. A cat is more like a human than a dog, for a dog is too good, whereas a cat shows all the attributes of 'hypocrisy, cruelty, ingratitude' and if it is argued that only evil people have these qualities,

> je réponds que . . . cette classe renferme tout le monde.[24]

Again, in reply to a 'dame délicate' who would defend the human race, Emily reminds her of the conduct of her husband when hunting:

> Ainsi, lorsqu'il a couru un animal à son dernier soupir, il le tire des gueules des chiens, et le réserve pour souffrir encore deux ou trois fois la même infliction, terminant finalement en la mort.[25]

An even more withering indictment of human conduct is to be found in the fourth exercise, entitled 'L'Amour filial'. Its tenor may be gauged by quoting the first paragraph:

> 'Tu honoreras ton père et ta mère si tu veux vivre.' C'est par un tel commandement que Dieu nous donne une connaissance de la bassesse de notre race, de ce qu'elle parait à ses yeux, pour remplir le plus doux, le plus saint de tous les devoirs – il lui faut une menace; c'est par peur qu'il faut forcer la maniacque à bénir elle-même. Dans cette commandement est caché un reproche plus amer qu'aucune accusation ouverte ne püisse renfermer, une charge contre nous, d'aveuglement entier ou d'ingratitude infernale.[26]

While most animals, she continues, manifest naturally a close bond between parents and offspring, it is the human race only that requires the thundering command: 'Honorez vos parents ou vous mourrez!'

The fifth exercise, 'Lettre d'un frère a un frère', consists of the sad letter of a man who has left home years before after a quarrel with his brother and who, now, after much wandering and suffering, is seeking to return to effect a reconciliation. The outcast tells how he had approached the house the evening before:

> Pendant je contemplais par la lumière douteuse du feu, les tableaux sur les murs, les rangs de livres au dessous et tous les objets familiers que m'entouraient, quelque-chose se remuait

dans la chambre. C'était un grand chien qui s'éleva d'un coin et s'approchait pour examiner l'étranger, il ne trouva pas un étranger, il me reconnut et il témoigna sa reconnaissance par des caresses les plus expressives; mais moi, je le repoussai, parcequ'il était le vôtre. Pardonnez, Edouard, à ce dernier acte du tyran qui avait usurpé si longtemps la place de la nature dans mon sein. [27]

The sixth and seventh exercises carry this tragic and disenchanted view of the universe further. In 'Le Papillon' Emily imagines herself in a forest watching the creatures sing and play when she is suddenly struck by the huge cycle of death and destruction that seems to characterize the very essence of the universe:

La nature est un problème inexplicable, elle existe sur un principe de destruction; il faut que tout être soit l'instrument infatigable de mort aux autres, ou qu'il cesse de vivre lui-même . . . en ce moment l'univers me parraisait une vaste machine construite seulement pour la mal . . . 'Le monde aurai dû être détruit,' je dis, 'écrasé comme j'écrase ce reptile qui n'a rien fait pendant sa vie que rendre tout ce qu'il touche aussi dégoutant que lui-même.'[28]

It is true that there follows the sight of a butterfly emerging from its chrysalis and that this offers Emily some hope that beyond the cycle of death and destruction there may be some more glorious alternative (but see below).

Even if there is this redemptive hope in the sixth exercise, it is gone from the seventh. Here, in 'Le Palais de la Mort', Death is presented as interviewing new candidates to help Old Age who is finding that humanity has grown too numerous for him to handle alone. A whole series of aspirants appear – Anger, Vengeance, Envy, Treachery, Famine, Plague and so on. But the successful applicant is Intemperance because while all the others would have succumbed one after another to the work of Civilization, Intemperance alone would thrive and prosper with it.

Now, while it is true that in some of Emily's earlier poems there is evidence of disillusionment and a tragic view of the world – one recalls the stanza

'Twas grief enough to think mankind
All hollow, servile, insincere;
But worse to trust to my own mind
And find the same corruption there. [29]

– and that the Gondal poems are full of a kind of swashbuckling violence and betrayal, there is nothing of the sustained, almost vindictive,
misanthropy of the French exercises. The vocabulary and the thought
obsessively circles around themes of hypocrisy, ingratitude, treachery,
destruction – the word 'écraser' appears often – and the mood is hard
and unforgiving. The world appears as a malicious farce where beings
torture beings, where filial love reeks of curses, where jealousy
supplants love and where Civilization itself colludes with Death. It is a
vision of a 'poor forked humanity' that, indeed, reminds us of *Lear*.

I would not want to argue too urgently for a direct influence of these
French pieces on *Wuthering Heights* but surely some connections
suggest themselves. There is the image of the hunter torturing his prey
for the mere pleasure of it which recalls the disturbing strain of sadism
that runs right through the novel. Or, again, in the cynical indictment
of the whole farce of filial love is there not a trace of that rage against
domesticity figured in Heathcliff's disruptive effect on his introduction
to the Heights or in the glimpse of the young Edgar and Isabella tearing
a puppy in half? Furthermore, in the 'Lettre d'un frère à un frère' do we
not have a curious anticipation not only of the Cain-like wanderings of
Heathcliff but also a kind of early draft of Lockwood's first visit to the
Heights: his taking in of the furnishings, his consciousness of the fire
in the hearth, his glance at the shelves of books and his entanglement
with the dogs? And, finally, in the last exercise, is there not a wicked
calling into question of all the proprieties and niceties, the literacy and
the conciliations, that *Wuthering Heights* seemingly promotes but at
one and the same time damns by the standard of the intensities that
have been sacrificed and the deliberate confusion of 'culture' and
'devastation' (pp. 336 and 347) towards the end of the novel.

More generally and perhaps more speculatively it might also be
argued that much of the world vision of the French pieces and even
some of their vocabulary are used by or in reference to Heathcliff.
Compare the following, for example, with the language of 'Le
Papillon':

'I seek no revenge on you,' replied Heathcliff less vehemently.
'That's not the plan – The tyrant grinds down his slaves – and they
don't turn against him, they crush those beneath them. You are
welcome to torture me to death for your amusement, only allow
me to amuse myself a little in the same style – and refrain from

insult as much as you are able. Having levelled my palace, don't erect a hovel and complacently admire your own charity in giving me that for a home.' (p. 151)

or:

'I have no pity! I have no pity! The more the worms writhe, the more I yearn to crush out their entrails! It is a moral teething, and I grind with greater energy, in proportion to the increase of pain.' (p. 189)

or Cathy's description of him to Isabella:

'He's not a rough diamond – a pearl-containing oyster of a rustic; he's a fierce, pitiless, wolfish man. I never say to him let this or that enemy alone, because it would be ungenerous or cruel to harm them, I say – "let them alone, because I should hate them to be wronged": and he'd crush you, like a sparrow's egg, Isabella, if he found you a troublesome charge.' (p. 141)

or Nelly's description of the way Heathcliff looks at the infatuated Isabella:

And he stared hard at the object of discourse, as one might do at a strange repulsive animal, a centipede from the Indies, for instance, which curiosity leads one to examine in spite of the aversion it raises. (p. 144)

Elsewhere, of course, there are Heathcliff's outbursts against 'duty and Humanity' (p. 185) and against 'kindness' (p. 306) which recall the impatience with sentimentality and cant in the French work.

In other words, the French exercises evince a dramatic and qualitative change of consciousness from that displayed in the poems of the Gondal cycle. Instead of the romantic and aristocratic fantasies of a siren woman and her countless paramours there is a ruthless and dispassionate insight into the horror at the heart of nature and of human relationships. It is in some ways like a shift from a construction of the world in feudal terms to a perception of it as a seething cauldron of contradictions and competition, a struggle for survival where the weak go to the wall – the world, perhaps, of capitalism. But it is another point that I wish to make here: the break with the Gondal cycle and the asylum of a foreign language can be seen as having allowed Emily Brontë to make contact again with her own deepest intuitions and perceptions. The prohibitions inflicted on her on that Oakapple Day long ago, the great constraining yoke of the Symbolic Order, have been, if not lifted, then greatly lightened. What Emily Brontë was allowed to discover in Brussels was that as far as her deepest self was concerned it was the Symbolic Order itself that had been an Imaginary Capture: it was from this dreadful double bind that she had been released by the intervention of a second 'Symbolic Father' quite different from the conservative, parochial and partly blind parson of Haworth: the innovative, cosmopolitan, mercurial M. Constantin Héger.

We have already called attention to Héger's estimate of Emily's character and intelligence and the somewhat abrasive nature of their relationship. It is not difficult to imagine just how much this kind of intense exchange must have stimulated Emily – how different from having to look after a father going blind or a brother addicted to alcohol and opium. Perhaps, too, Héger's impact on her, or what facilitated the transference (which in turn gave him such authority) was made all the more possible by a most curious coincidence. We have seen how the heroine of the Gondal cycle – Augusta Geraldine Almeda – frequently figures as A.G.A.: if one pronounces those letters very quickly as a word one gets something very much like Héger as pronounced in French – éjé! Be that as it may, we do know that A.G.A. was killed off between 1841 and 1844, that is at the very period that Emily got to know Héger.

It is almost impossible to reconstruct in detail Héger's relationship with Emily but there are a few tantalizing clues. So far we have looked at five of the seven exercises Emily did for him. There are two more. The third is the 'Lettre: Ma chère maman'. There is already a terrible irony here for Emily's mother died when she was very small and it is no surprise that it is by far the least interesting of her exercises. But at the close there is a small marginal comment by M. Héger:

> N.B. Aucune marque de souvenir pr papa – c'est une faute. C. Héger[30]

This again is ironic in the light of the thesis I am putting forward here: it is precisely the father that Emily is trying to forget at this period. But it is the actual scene of the correction that I think we should try to envisage: the small smile that goes with this correction, the little 'tut' of rebuke, perhaps a little paternal waggle of the finger. What Héger is doing here is reminding the girl of her father but also of himself as father/maître/master.

Finally there is the second exercise: 'Portrait: Le Roi Harold avant la Bataille de Hastings'. I have argued above that the French exercises can be seen as an abandonment of the romantic and feudal world of the Gondal legend. In a sense the portrait of Harold on the eve of Hastings would seem to contradict that claim. But what the exercise marks is precisely the death of that heroic world and Emily presents Harold as stoically and indifferently confronting his fate:

> Il est intérieurement convaincu qu'aucun pouvoir mortel ne l'abbatera. La Mort, seule, peut emporter la victoire de ses armes, et Harold est prêt à s'incliner devant elle, parceque la touche de cette main est au héros comme le geolier qui lui rendait la liberté, serait à l'esclave.[31]

It is easy to understand what Emily is saying but Héger evidently picked up the slight contradiction of being freed by a gaoler – in fact a kind of 'double bind' which itself is further revelatory of Emily's state of mind at this time – or at least felt that the idea could be better expressed, and he offers a marginal alternative:

> Le coup de l'épée que tue un héros sur le champ de bataille n'est (que le) coup de baguette dont le maître frappe son esclave pour l'affrancher.[32]

It is a significant and evocative note for what it expresses is precisely the role I have argued Héger plays in relation to Emily: it is he who is the 'maître' who in touching Emily with his power (and it is difficult to ignore the sexual innuendo in the homophony of 'baguette' and 'braguette') has effectively freed her from the inhibitions and constraints that have formerly imprisoned her.

At some length, I have argued, then, that far from leaving no mark on Emily's life her experience in Brussels was absolutely crucial. Thanks to the licence afforded by the free play with a foreign language and thanks to the eruption into her life of a teacher of authority and genius who recognized her real strength, Emily could disengage herself from the taboos of her family and society and enter again into the sovereign possession of her own true being.

But it was not only from herself that Emily had been separated on that Oakapple day: it was also, in a sense, from history too. It was to this too that she regained access through Héger. We know something of Héger's teaching methods and the syllabus he set for Emily and Charlotte. One of his favourite techniques for teaching French was to have them read a passage from a distinguished French author and then have them compose a similar piece. The model he set for Emily's 'Portrait: le Roi Harold' was 'Mirabeau orateur' taken from Hugo's 'Sur Mirabeau'.[33]

One of the great sports of literary criticism and scholarship must be the search for the origins of Heathcliff. Practically every major writer of the romantic tradition has at one time or another been put forward as a possible 'source' of the enigmatic hero of *Wuthering Heights*: Scott, Byron, Coleridge, Hoffman, etc., etc. But what is quite extraordinary is that, as far as I know, no attention whatever has been given to the series of texts with which we absolutely *know* Emily Brontë to have been closely engaged during her stay in Brussels. Hugo's 'Sur Mirabeau' is possibly the most important and a reading of it must leave one with very little doubt that Emily's debt to it is considerable.

What fascinates Hugo are the dramatic changes of fortune and the multiple contradictions of Mirabeau's career. He opens the essay by reconstructing a conversation between Mirabeau's father and uncle in 1781: again that significant date: *Wuthering Heights* begins in 1801 but is at once concerned with events of twenty years before. The problem discussed by Mirabeau's father and uncle is what they should do with the young Mirabeau who is described by them as an 'homme avorté', a 'créature disloquée', as a wastrel and profligate who is a threat to domestic and social propriety. The father confesses his complete inability to master his son and is seeking to get the uncle to assume responsibility for him: there is already here, perhaps, the seed of Heathcliff's orphanage and foster-upbringing. By 1791, however, this recalcitrant and wayward figure is being acclaimed as a national hero and on his death in that year he is afforded the supreme accolade of being laid to rest in the newly constructed Pantheon. By way of creating dramatic effect Hugo, at one point, concentrates the vicissitudes of Mirabeau's career into three days – every epithet in the following is footnoted by Hugo:

> Ainsi, jusqu'au 1er avril 1791, Mirabeau est *un gueux, un extra-vagante, un scélérat, un assassin, un fou, un orateur du second ordre, un homme médiocre, un homme mort, un homme enterré,*

> *un monstrueux bavard, hué, sifflé, conspué plus encore qu'ap-*
> *plaudi;* Lambesc propose pour lui les *galères*, Marat la *potence*. Il
> meurt le 2 avril. Le 3, on invente pour lui le Panthéon.[34]

The portrait of Mirabeau is built by other contrasts too. Hugo con-
ceives of his life having been dominated by two great passions: the first
for his mistress, Sophie, and the second, his commitment to the
revolution. He adds:

> Ne vous étonnez donc pas que pour la maîtresse il brise tous les
> liens domestiques, que pour la révolution il brise tous les liens
> sociaux.[35]

Does not this remind us at once of the great divide of Heathcliff's life:
his passion for Cathy for which he is prepared to violate all domestic
ties and the later ruthless pursuit of retributive vengeance which makes
havoc of the social order?

Between 1789 and 1791 – a space of three years: remember the
three-year absence of Heathcliff – Mirabeau dominated the revolutionary assembly and, again, Hugo sees the whole drama in terms of
violent contrasts. Between, for example, the genius of Mirabeau and
the mere talent of men like Banarve: the impact of the former on the
assembly, he says, was like a tempest; that of the other was received
only with smiles[36] and one recalls at once the famous essay on
Wuthering Heights by David Cecil in terms of the contrast between
children of the storm and children of the calm.[37] Moreover, if, on the
one hand, Mirabeau was the one man who had the temerity to defy
Louis XVI, it was he also who resisted the anarchist threat to the
Convention led by Robespierre. Mirabeau, that is, was a colossus who
bestrode two epochs and this was both his triumph and his tragedy:

> Il y avait dans la révolution française du passé et de l'avenir.
> Mirabeau n'était que le présent. . . . Sous Mirabeau, ni la monar-
> chie ni la république n'étaint possibles. La monarchie l'excluait
> par sa hiérarchie, la république par son niveau. Mirabeau est un
> homme qui passe dans une époque qui prépare. . . . Son père . . .
> disait de lui: Cet homme n'est ni la fin ni le commencement d'un
> homme. Il avait raison. 'Cet homme' était la fin d'une société et le
> commencement d'une autre.[38]

Mirabeau was the great catalyst of the revolution and when his seminal
task had been achieved, Hugo claims, '[il] est mort à propos'.[39]

Again and again, surely, we are reminded of the dazzling trajectory of Heathcliff's life and death: like Mirabeau, a man of no beginnings and no ends, who bestrides the Heights and Grange like a giant, a catalyst of change and relationships in spite of himself, and who, like Mirabeau, at the end may be seen to be dying on purpose. It remains only to quote the specific set piece on 'Mirabeau orateur' set by Héger:

> Il était orateur parce qu'il avait souffert, parce qui'il avait failli, parce qu'il avait été, bien jeune encore et dans l'âge où s'épanouissent toutes les ouvertures du coeur, repoussé, moqué, humilié, méprisé, diffamé, chassé, spolié, interdit, exilé, emprisonné, condamné; parce que, comme le peuple de 1789 dont il était le plus complet symbole, il avait été tenu en minorité et en tutelle beaucoup au delà de l'âge de raison; parce que la paternité avait été dure pour lui comme la royauté pour le peuple; parce que, comme le peuple, il avait été mal élevé; parce que, comme au peuple, une mauvaise éducation lui avait fait croître un vice sur la racine de chaque vertu. Il était orateur, parce que, grace aux larges issues ouvertes par les ébranlements de 1789, il avait enfin pu extraverser dans la société tous ses bouillonements intérieurs si longtemps comprimés dans la famille; parce que, brusque, inégal, violent, vicieux, cynique, sublime, diffus, incohérent, plus rempli d'instincts encore que de pensées, les pieds souillés, la tête rayonnante, il était tout semblable aux années ardentes dans lesquelles il a resplendi et dont chaque jour passait marque au front par sa parole.[40]

Emily's French exercise may have been on Harold before Hastings, but it is Heathcliff that is being heralded here.

Hugo's essay does not end with the death of Mirabeau for he goes on to ask why there are no more Mirabeaus at the time that he is writing (1834) and then proceeds to sketch an answer:

> Dans les moments comme celui où nous sommes, le parti de l'avenir se divise en deux classes, les hommes de révolution, les hommes de progrès. Ce sont les hommes de révolution qui déchirent la vieille terre politique, creusent le sillon, jettent la semence; mais leur temps est court. Aux hommes de progrès appartiennent la lente et laborieuse culture des principes, l'étude des saisons propices à la greffe du telle ou telle idée, le travail au

> jour le jour, l'arrosement de la jeune plante, l'engrais du sol, la
> récolte pour tous.[41]

He goes on for some time to argue that after the ferment of revolution
there is required a time of peace and consolidation, when progress and
reform must replace destruction and extirpation. The essay, then,
modulates from a fervent celebration of the revolutionary demagogue
towards the counselling of patience and steady labour. It is, of course,
the same pattern that we find in *Wuthering Heights* where the passions
unleashed by Cathy and Heathcliff become contained and domesticated
in the quieter love of Catherine and Hareton.

Mirabeau was not the only historical and revolutionary figure
introduced to the Brontës by Héger:

> Take Cromwell, for example. He [Héger] would read Bossuet's
> description of him in the 'Oraison Funèbre de la Reine
> d'Angleterre,' and show how in this he was considered entirely
> from the religious point of view, as an instrument in the hands of
> God, pre-ordained to do His work. Then he would make them read
> Guizot, and see how, in his view, Cromwell was endowed with the
> utmost power of free will, but governed by no higher motive than
> expediency; while Carlyle regarded him as a character regulated
> by a strong and conscientious desire to do the will of the Lord.
> Then he would desire them to remember that Royalist and
> Commonwealth men had each their different views of the great
> Protector. And from these conflicting characters he would require
> them to sift and collect the elements of truth, and try to unite
> them into a perfect whole.[42]

Lengthy though some of them are I think it is worthwhile looking at
the passages from Bossuet, Guizot and Carlyle in some detail. First
from Bossuet:

> Un homme s'est rencontré d'une profondeur d'esprit incroyable,
> hyopocrite raffiné autant qu'habile politique, capable de tout
> entreprendre et de tout cacher, également actif et infatigable dans
> la paix et dans la guerre, qui ne laissait rien à la fortune de ce qu'il
> pouvait lui ôter par conseil et par prévoyance; mais au reste si
> vigilant et si prêt à tout, qu'il n'a jamais manqué les occasions
> qu'elle lui a présentées; enfin un de ces esprits remuants et
> audacieux, qui semblent être nés pour changer le monde. Que le

sort de tels esprits est hasardeux, et qu'il en paraît dans l'histoire à qui leur audace a été funeste! Mais aussi que ne font-ils pas, quand il plaît à Dieu de s'en servir? Il fut donné à celui-ci de tromper les peuples, et de prévaloir contre les rois. Car, comme il eut aperçu que, dans ce mélange infini de sectes, qui n'avaient plus de règles, le plaisir de dogmatiser sans être repris ni contraint par aucune autorité ecclésiastique ni séculière, était le charme qui possédait les esprits, il sut si bien les concilier par là, qu'il fit un corps redoutable de cet assemblage monstrueux. Quand une fois on a trouvé le moyen de prendre la multitude par l'appât de la liberté, elle suit en aveugle, pourvu qu'elle en entende seulement le nom. Ceux-ci, occupés du premier objet qui les avait transportés, allaient toujours, sans regarder qu'ils allaient à la servitude; et leur subtil conducteur, qui, en combattant, en dogmatisant, en mêlant mille personnages divers, en faisant le docteur et le prophète, aussi bien que le soldat et le capitaine, vit qu'il avait tellement enchanté le monde, qu'il était régardé de toute l'armée un chef envoyé de Dieu pour la protection de l'indépendance, commença à s'apercevoir qu'il pouvait encore les pousser plus loin. Je ne vous racontera pas la suite trop fortunée de ses entreprises, ni ses fameuses victoires dont la vertu était indignée, ni cette longue tranquillité qui a étonné l'univers. C'était le conseil de Dieu d'instruire les rois à ne point quitter son Eglise. Il voulait découvrir, par un grand exemple, tout ce que peut l'hérésie; combien elle est naturellement indocile et indépendante, combien fatale à la royauté et à toute autorité légitime. Au reste, quand ce grand Dieu a choisi quelqu'un pour être l'instrument de ses desseins, rien n'en arrête le cours.[43]

There is already much material here that could have gone into the make-up of Heathcliff: the accomplished hypocrite, the ruthless opportunist knowing exactly when to seize his chance, the cynical leading by the nose those who have fallen into his power, the restless energy and vigilance of a man seemingly destined to shake the world. There is also in him something of Bossuet's notion of Cromwell as some kind of avenging angel, an instrument in the hands of the Lord, sent into the world to punish some unexpiated sin, some ancestral crime of long ago.

The next piece we can look at is from Guizot:

Cromwell mourut dans la plénitude de son pouvoir et de sa grandeur. Il avait réussi au delá de toute attente, bien plus que n'a réussi aucun autre des hommes qui, par leur génie, se sont élevés, comme lui, au rang suprême, car il avait tenté et accompli, avec un égal succès, les desseins les plus contraires. Pendant dix-huit ans, toujours en scène et toujours vainqueur, il avait tour à tour jeté le désordre et rétabli l'ordre, fait et châtié la révolution, renversé et relevé le gouvernement dans son pays. A chaque moment, dans chaque situation, il démêlait avec une sagacité admirable les passions et les intérêts dominants, pour en faire des instruments de sa propre domination, peu soucieux de se démentir pourvu qu'il triomphât d'accord avec l'instinct public, et donnant pour réponse aux incohérences de sa conduite l'unité ascendante de son pouvoir. Exemple unique peut-être que le même homme ait gouverné les évènements les plus opposés et suffi aux plus diverses destinées. Et dans le course de cette carrière si forte et si changeante, incessamment en butte à toute sorte d'ennemis et de complots, Cromwell eut de plus cette faveur du sort que jamais sa vie ne fût effectivement attaquée; le souverain contre lequel était écrit le pamphlet, 'Tuer n'est pas assassiner', ne se vit jamais en face d'un assassin. Le monde n'a point connu d'exemple de succès à la fois si constants et si contraires, ni d'une fortune si invariablement heureuse au milieu de tant de luttes et de périls.

Pourtant, Cromwell mourut triste. Triste, non seulement de mourir, mais aussi, et surtout, de mourir sans avoir atteint son véritable et dernier but. Quel que fût son égoïsme, il avait l'âme trop grande pour que la plus haute fortune, mais purement personelle et éphémère, comme lui-même ici-bas, suffît à le satisfaire. Las des ruines qu'il avait faites, il avait à coeur de rendre à son pays un gouvernement régulier et stable, le seul gouvernement qui lui convînt, la monarchie avec le Parlement. Et en même temps ambitieux au delà du tombeau, par cette soif de la durée qui est le sceau de la grandeur, il aspirait à laisser son nom et sa race en possession de l'empire dans l'avenir. Il échoua dans l'un et l'autre dessein: ses attentats lui avaient créé des obstacles que ni son prudent génie ni sa persévérante volonté ne purent surmonter; et comblé, pour son propre compte, de pouvoir et de gloire, il mourut déçu dans ses plus intimes espérances, ne laissant après lui, pour lui succéder, que les deux ennemis qu'il avait ardemment combattus, l'anarchie et les Stuart.[44]

Again it is not difficult to see how this material might have contributed to the fashioning of Heathcliff: the contrarieties of his career, his propensities for creating chaos as well as order, his total domination of all who cross his path, his absolute unassailability, the sheer triumph of his will. And yet the ultimate frustration of all his designs, the almost mocking collapse of all his plans as his son disappoints him; as, against his very will, he cares for Hareton; as the eyes of the younger Catherine torment him with the trace of the elder's; as, at the very moment of success, when all power lies in his hands, his very *raison d'être* seems to abandon him and at his death the very forces that he has combated with such venom, Hareton and the young Cathy, are left to inherit all that he has achieved.

Finally, we can look at Carlyle's piece:

> Poor Cromwell, – great Cromwell! The inarticulate Prophet; Prophet who could not speak. Rude, confused, struggling to utter himself, with his savage depth, with his wild sincerity; and he looked so strange, among the elegant Euphemisms, dainty little Falklands, didactic Chillingworths, diplomatic Clarendons! Consider him. An outer hull of chaotic confusion, visions of the Devil, nervous dreams, almost semi-madness; and yet such a clear determinate man's-energy working in the heart of that. A kind of chaotic man. The ray as of pure starlight and fire, working in such an element of boundless hypochondria, unformed black of darkness! And yet withal this hypochondria, what was it but the very greatness of the man? The depth and tenderness of his wild affections: the quality of sympathy he had with things – the quantity of insight he would get into the heart of things, the mastery he would yet get over things: this was his hypochondria. The man's misery, as man's misery always does, comes of his greatness. Samuel Johnson too is that kind of man. Sorrow-stricken, half-distracted; the wide element of mournful black enveloping him, – wide as the world. It is the character of a prophetic man; a man with his whole soul seeing, and struggling to see.[45]

Here the similarities with Heathcliff are less precise – though there are striking connections: the sheer strangeness of both figures when compared with those around them, the nervous dreams, almost semi-madness and the 'man's-energy' clarity of purpose, the obsessive hypochondriac sensitivity to pain, the visionary intensity of their seeing – but, in some ways it is imprecision itself that makes Carlyle's piece closest to Emily's depiction of Heathcliff: in terms of time they are, of course, more or less contemporary with each other.

Héger's requirement was that the girls should read these passages and 'sift and collect the elements of truth, and try to unite them into a perfect whole' (see above). It is almost possible to claim that the real material genesis, if the phrase has any meaning at all, of *Wuthering Heights* is to be located in this exercise. Heathcliff is a complete digest of these accounts of Cromwell with as many possible of the striking 'elements of truth' united into a 'perfect whole'.

If what I claim here is true then the sheer travesty of Charlotte's account of the creation of Heathcliff has to be accounted for:

> *Wuthering Heights* was hewn in a wild workshop, with simple tools, out of homely materials. The statuary found a granite block on a solitary moor: gazing thereon, he saw how from the crag might be elicited the head, savage, swart, sinister; a form moulded with at least one element of grandeur – power. He wrought with a rude chisel, and from no model but the vision of his meditations.[46]

Charlotte's evocation of the classic stereotype of the untutored romantic genius in fact achieves a number of specific strategic effects. In the first place it totally mythologizes the act of artistic creation: instead of locating the practice of writing, reading and learning in the material environment of an educational apparatus, it claims for it the status of a wholly ethereal and unaccountable gift, given to some and denied to others, with no court of appeal. It privileges the artist as someone 'special' and denies all others the possibility of being able actually to learn to read and write and create. If you haven't got it, then education will be no use to you anyway, which is precisely the opposite of what Emily's experience in Brussels proves.

The second effect of Charlotte's insistence on Emily's essential innocence – in fact downright ignorance – is to disguise the fact that Emily was a highly conscious artist and that *Wuthering Heights* is a highly worked out and crafted novel. It also serves to deny Emily's powerful intellect – 'unusual in a man, and rare indeed in a woman' – and to maintain the myth of her essential femininity.

The third important effect of Charlotte's note is to maintain the essential 'Englishness' of *Wuthering Heights* whereas what I have argued here is that the real origin of the novel is to be found in Emily's sojourn in Brussels. One of the boasts and myths of 'English' literature is that of its essential 'Englishness' – like roast beef and Yorkshire pudding. To risk a joke at this point: Yorkshire 'pudding' Emily was not; *Wuthering Heights* was very much a sprout of Brussels. More than that: the debt that Emily owed to her Brussels experience should alert us to the fact that so much of our so-called 'English' literature is shot through and dependent upon experiences and events elsewhere.

The fourth and perhaps the most significant effect of Charlotte's account of the creation of *Wuthering Heights* is that it disguises the fact that Heathcliff is modelled on two great revolutionary leaders, Mirabeau and Cromwell. To have recognized that Heathcliff owed his very existence to these two would have entailed the bringing into the full light of consciousness that spectre that at precisely that moment (1847–8) was haunting all Europe, the spectre not so much of 'communism' as that of revolution itself. In some ways it is precisely this blurring of Heathcliff's revolutionary provenance that is achieved by *Wuthering Heights* itself: it is one of its effects as an 'ideological operator', but had Charlotte been able to reveal the real origins of the book that particular act of ideological policing might have been less successful.

But Charlotte could never have made that revelation, and for a very good reason: she could not afford to face the truth of the Brussels experience for that truth would have been far too painful. This is the final reason for that construction of Emily as a 'wild, untutored, genius': it enabled Charlotte to disguise from herself the fact that the relationship between Emily Brontë and Constantin Héger had had a generative and productive intensity compared with which her own infatuation with Héger palled into adolescent mooning.

'Generative' and 'productive': Emily's relationship with Héger was certainly all of that. Due to an almost uncanny combination of circumstances what Brussels afforded Emily was the chance to resume contact with that real affective self that had had to be denied since that fateful Oakapple day so many years before. What the French exercises, first, and the readings of Cromwell, second, made possible was the re-establishment of contact with that self and that history which had been broken by the abrupt termination of that game of Cavaliers and

Roundheads. But now the 'civil war' can be negotiated not in terms of fugitive and hunters, not in terms of the exclusive disjunctions of either/or but in terms of a dispassionate assessment of the merits and limitations of both, not as polarities but as conditions one of the other. Instead of the paranoiac turmoil and the manic-depressive megalomania of the Gondal poems there is the celibate realization that the self can be residual to identity, that one can be one thing because one can also be another, that one can be the fugitive because one can be the hunter, Roundhead because a Cavalier, mother because father, man because woman – Emily Brontë because Ellis Bell.

There was one other text that Héger gave to the Brontës which we have not looked at yet. This was Casimir de la Vigne's celebrated poem on 'The Death of Joan of Arc':

> Qui t'inspira, jeune et faible bergère,
> D'abandonner la houllette legère,
> Et les tissus commencés par ta main?
> Qui t'inspira de quitter ton vieux père,
> De préférer aux baisers de ta mère,
> L'horreur des camps, le carnage et la mort?
>
> . . . . . .
>
> L'ange exterminateur bénit ton étendard;
> Il mit dans tes accents un son mâle et terrible,
> Et dit à la brebis paisible,
> Va déchirer le léopard
>
> . . . . . .
>
> Tu ne reverras plus tes riantes montagnes,
> Le temple, le hameau, les champs de Vaucouleurs,
> Et ta chaumière et tes compagnes,
> Et ton père expirant sous le poids de douleurs.[47]

This text, again, celebrates a great revolutionary, who was also a heretic and a mystic. In it de la Vigne asks what had prompted a simple country girl to abandon her humble home and grieving parents and become, instead, a great warrior. It is a poem that must have addressed itself directly at Emily for what Joan of Arc's example does, before anything else, is endorse and legitimize the momentous changes she feels taking place in herself.

For this is the real achievement of the Brussels experience: when Emily Brontë could spit out that stupid injunction to 'Honour thy father and mother' what emerged from the shell of the old self, like the butterfly of the 'Le Papillon' exercise, was a new being, Ellis Bell.

It is well known that Emily Brontë identified herself closely with her pseudonym and took to consistently referring to herself as Ellis. Indeed, at this point it is difficult to know how to gender 'E.B.': as in the incident at the signpost which set us off on this exploration there is an inconvenient slippage between the initials and what they are supposed to denote. In fact, what the resort to initials facilitates, and here we might recall the use of initials in the Gondal poems, is an epicene neutrality, like the Brontë pseudonyms, 'not positively masculine'[48] nor positively feminine either.

There is something else to note about 'Ellis Bell' too. Héger had said that Emily would have made a great navigator: it was an astonishingly perceptive piece of foresight for if we consider closely the combination of 'Ellis Bell' with Ellen/Nelly Dean, Ellis's narrator – and maybe throw in the most obvious rhyme of 'bell', 'knell' – then we get a peculiar acrostic.

Nelly
knell
E*lli*s
Ell*en*

which seems to be an anagrammatic play on the name 'Nelson'. What is astonishing about this is that it is not only the name of a great navigator but also the Name of the Father – to employ Lacanian parlance once again – for it was the name that E.B.'s father had given himself after Nelson, whom he greatly admired, had been made Duke of Brontë in 1799.[49] E.B., in other words, has made it after all: taken the name of the father or, more correctly, he/she has finally managed to transcend the gender allocations hitherto foisted upon him/her.

It was this transcendence that made the late great mystical poems possible and maybe *Wuthering Heights* too, though here I want to make a heretical statement of my own. I think that after Brussels E.B. had to write *Wuthering Heights*: she had 'Heathcliff' on her hands and she had to dump him somewhere but I don't think *Wuthering Heights* is a 'great' novel. I don't even think it is as good as the passages from Hugo, Bossuet, Guizot, Carlyle and de la Vigne that E.B. read in

Brussels. These are the 'unacceptable texts', passionate chronicles of revolution, that *Wuthering Heights,* for all its debt to them, effectively prevents us from reading. I also think that E.B. knew this and that this accounts for his/her total disinterest in the novel once it had been completed.

C. W. Hatfield ends his edition of the poems of 'Emily Brontë' by asking who was the author of the following poem: Emily Brontë or Charlotte:

> Often rebuked, yet always back returning
> To those first feelings that were born with me,
> And leaving busy chase of wealth and learning
> For idle dreams of things which cannot be:
>
> Today, I will not seek the shadowy region;
> Its unsustaining vastness waxes drear;
> And visions rising, legion after legion,
> Bring the unreal world too strangely near.
>
> I'll walk, but not in old heroic traces,
> And not in paths of high morality,
> And not among the half distinguished faces,
> The clouded forms of long-past history.
>
> I'll walk where my own nature would be leading:
> It vexes me to choose another guide:
> Where the gray flocks in ferny glens are feeding;
> Where the wild wind blows on the mountain side.
>
> What have those lonely mountains worth revealing?
> More glory and more grief than I can tell:
> The earth that wakes one human heart to feeling
> Can centre both the worlds of Heaven and Hell.[50]

It has to be by Ellis Bell.

5

Notes on a journey to *Vanity Fair*

Published in serial form in 1847 and as a volume in 1848, the definitive version of *Vanity Fair* was not achieved until the second, revised and popular edition of 1853, the edition on which all subsequent editions have been based. That 1853 edition may be seen as the result of a whole series of modifications, of deletions and compensatory interpolations, that chart, sometimes crudely, sometimes more subtly, shifts in consciousness and concern that may be regarded as stylistic and moral, professional and psychological, but all of which are, in the last resort, political.

Perhaps the most striking clue as to the nature of the changes that Thackeray's conception of his work underwent is to be found by considering briefly the various titles he used for it. When the manuscript first went to his publishers in 1846 it bore the title: *The Novel without a Hero: Pen and Pencil Sketches of English Society*.[1] The cover of the serial publication of 1847, however, bears a new title: *Vanity Fair: Pen and Pencil Sketches of English Society* as well as the illustration of the novelist as 'moralist . . . [in] long-eared livery'

(p. 116)[2] haranguing a similarly clad audience from the top of a barrel set against a background which includes an equestrian statue and a commemorative column (Plate 1).[3] Finally, there is the illustrated frontispiece of the 1848 volume which shows a dejected and introspective clown contemplating his face in a broken mirror against, this time, a background of cathedral towers, while the title now is simply *Vanity Fair: A Novel without a Hero* (Plate 2).[4]

Even with this minimal material a pattern may be discerned. With the shift from the first title to the second with its adoption of the Bunyanesque 'Vanity Fair' there is already the suggestion that Thackeray is deliberately moving away from the more rumbustious satirical mode of his earlier work towards the elaboration of a more sustained moral critique of his society grounded in the Puritan tradition. Moreover the equestrian statue and the commemorative column at least suggest a political and historical context for this critique. At the same time, however, the depiction of the moralist as wearing a fool's cap and as addressing other fools would seem to indicate some ambiguity, if not unease, in the adoption of this moralistic stance. By the time we get to the final title, *Vanity Fair: A Novel without a Hero*, all trace of the original satiric intention has disappeared or, at least, been subsumed within a universalistic *vanitas vanitatum*. Meanwhile the new illustration shows that the public harangue of the fool has collapsed into the melancholic and troubled introspection of the clown. Instead of the political and historical connotations evoked by the column and the statue of the serial cover we now have the meditative and reflective aura conjured up by the distant cathedral towers. Between 1846 and 1848, then, there has been a marked shift in emphasis from a satiric address to society, to a mood, instead, of introversion and self-analysis, from a concern with the external to a concern with the internal, from the social to the psychological.

This retreat from the social and satiric – this removal of cathexis from the real – is taken further in the revised version of 1853 where, albeit in the interest of cheapness (it would have been argued), all the illustrations of the serial version and the first edition were omitted. In the first place this was a serious aesthetic loss, for both contemporary and modern commentators have argued that *Vanity Fair* is one of the 'best illustrated books in the world',[5] 'an outstanding instance of the simultaneous pursuit of novel-writing and illustration'.[6] Secondly, the suppression of the illustrations means the loss of a good deal of

VANITY FAIR:

PEN AND PENCIL SKETCHES OF ENGLISH SOCIETY.

BY W. M. THACKERAY,

Author of " The Irish Sketch Book :" " Journey from Cornhill to Grand Cairo:" of " Jeames's Diary
and the "Snob Papers" in " Punch :" &c. &c.

LONDON:
PUBLISHED AT THE PUNCH OFFICE, 85, FLEET STREET.
J. MENZIES, EDINBURGH ; J. M'LEOD, GLASGOW ; J. M'GLASHAN, DUBLIN.
1847.

[Bradbury & Evans, Printers, Whitefriars.]

1   *Cover of the serial publication of Vanity Fair, 1847*

2   *Illustrated frontispiece to the 1848 volume of Vanity Fair*

information which materially affects any interpretation of the story: the best example of this is the plate showing Becky making her 'second appearance as Clytemnestra'[7] and which clearly implicates her in the death of Jos, a judgement the text carefully abstains from making. Finally, and most significantly, the suppression of the illustrations entails the loss of a mode of contemporary reference for, as Thackeray wryly notes in the first edition, the figures are clothed in the 'present fashion', the author having 'not the heart to disfigure [his] heroes and heroines' in the 'hideous' costumes of the beginning of the century.

While the illustrations disappeared between the first and second editions of the book, there had already been other significant and less than innocent deletions made between the serial version and the volume of 1848. Omitted, for example, is a long passage which originally appeared at the beginning of Chapter 6, the visit to Vauxhall. In the serial Thackeray playfully suggests how this chapter might have been written, parodying in the process the 'Newgate' and 'Silver Fork' (popular crime fictions and beau monde romances) novels of the period. The following is only a brief extract:

> Fancy this chapter having been headed:
> THE NIGHT ATTACK
> . . . it was dark, pitch dark; no moon. No, no. No moon. Not a star. There had been one at early evening, but he showed his face, shuddering, for a moment in the black heaven, and then retreated back.
>
> One, two three! It is the signal that Black Vizard had agreed on.
> 'Mofy! is that your snum?' said a voice from the area. 'I'll gully the dag and bimbole the clicky in a snuffkin.'
> 'Nuffle your clod, and beladle your glumbanions,' said Vizard, with a dreadful oath. 'This way men; if they screak, out with your snickers and slick! Look to the pewter room Blowser. You, Mark, to the old gaff's mopus box! and I,' added he, in a lower but more horrible voice, 'I will look to Amelia.'
>
> . . . . . .
>
> Or suppose we adopted the genteel rose-water style. The Marquis of Osborne has just despatched his petit-tigre with a billet-doux to the Lady Amelia. . . .

And Thackeray concludes:

Thus you see, ladies, how this story might have been written, if the author had but a mind; for, to tell the truth, he is just as familiar with Newgate as with the palaces of our revered aristocracy. But as I don't understand the language or the manners of the Rookery, nor the polyglot conversation which, according to the fashionable novelists, is spoken by the leaders of ton, we must if you please, preserve our middle course modestly, amidst those scenes and personages with which we are most familiar.[8]

Now, no doubt a case might be made for the omission of these passages on the grounds of 'literary merit': G. H. Lewes, for example, found them in very poor taste and severely censured Thackeray for relapsing 'into his old magazine manner'.[9] But another point should be made: in the first place the suppression is selective for elsewhere in *Vanity Fair* the 'palaces of our revered aristocracy' enjoy more than a passing attention. This means in effect that what *Vanity Fair* does reject are the colourful resources of popular slang. In the interests of a 'middle course' – in the interests, after all, of a 'literary style' – an alternative mode of discourse is 'judged "abortive" and "faulty", improper for the complex expression of ideas and sentiments'.[10] Elsewhere, in looking at *Wuthering Heights*, I have noted how the regional dialect of Joseph is effectively displaced by the bland literacy of Nelly Dean (see above, p. 75): here a similar operation is taking place with respect to an alternative contemporary mode of popular speech.[11] It should be unnecessary now to add that this suppression of popular language colludes at its level with the blunting of contemporary reference and satiric edge to be noted in the change of titles and the suppression of illustrations.

Over and against the curtailments and restraint exemplified by the change in titles and the deletions of slang and, in the second edition, the removal of the illustrations, must be set what Thackeray added to the novel as it evolved. The two most distinctive additions were that of the figure of Dobbin and that of a number of passages of what purport to be moral commentary – particularly the last six paragraphs of Chapter 8. These changes were first examined at length by Professor Gordon Ray in 1949 in an article entitled: '*Vanity Fair*: one version of a novelist's responsibility'[12] and his argument is that between 1845, when the first eight chapters of the novel were drafted, and 1846, when the revisions took place, Thackeray had developed a more serious and responsible

attitude to his work and both Dobbin and the moral commentary are
evidence of this new attitude, offering the reader both a moral yardstick
and guidance in interpretation. Ray's thesis, however, has been chal-
lenged by a number of later scholars, particularly Tillotson,[13]
Rawlins[14] and Sutherland.[15] While strongly subscribing to the view
that *Vanity Fair* is a moral work, Tillotson notes that the moral tone
and commentary is already to be found in the draft of 1845. The more
severe challenge to Ray's thesis, however, comes from Rawlins and
Sutherland in their close analysis of the fight between Cuff and Dobbin
and of the end of Chapter 8 respectively. Rawlins notes, for example,
that the outcome of the fight, when Cuff confesses that it had all been
his fault and then proceeds to coach Dobbin in Latin and Mathematics,
frustrates all our expectations:

> This is something other than a dramatic outcome against the odds;
> this is rather a reinterpretation of a dramatically perfect pattern,
> to the destruction of all clear dramatic commitments.[16]

In other words Cuff's good nature unsettles our judgement of the
episode and leaves us in a disconcerting double bind. Dobbin does not
emerge as the unequivocal champion and in this respect his status as
'hero' in a novel without a hero is already subject to mild suspicion. For
all his good nature Dobbin is afflicted with a lisp and is subject too, like
all the others, to the vice of vanity – as Thackeray makes clear in a letter
to one of his reviewers:

> – for instance if I had made Amelia a higher order of woman there
> would have been no vanity in Dobbin falling in love with her,
> whereas the impression at present is that he is a fool for his pains
> for he has married a silly little thing.[17]

The final paragraphs of Chapter 8 present an even more complex
instance of the construction of a double bind for they begin by the
author mocking those who get so involved in a story that they start to
hiss the villains or, where it is a play, refuse to play the parts of the bad
characters. It is a plea, then, for keeping distance and recognition that it
is 'only a story'. By the end of the outburst, however, Thackeray is
boldly proclaiming his right to abuse his characters if he thinks they
deserve it and is inviting his readers to do the same. It is as if – to resort
to an imagery Thackeray is all too conscious of – having stripped one
mask from his face he now reveals himself as already having donned

another. The effect is a kind of double irony like that of Swift where two diametrically opposed alternatives are both offered and denied. Sutherland, who analyses this passage in great detail, describes it as a kind of 'artistic impasse' and argues, against Ray, that far from evidencing a new assurance as to the responsibility of the novelist such an outburst is little more than narrative to make up the number:

> It is at least possible that the apostrophe's are less a cri de cœur than the early exercises in a narrative upholstery which was to become Thackeray's stock in trade. They may be there less to 'tell the reader what to think' than to furnish some much needed bulk.[18]

The truth, however, probably lies somewhere between Ray and Sutherland. In quoting from the manuscripts of this chapter Sutherland shows that Thackeray originally toyed with a cartographical metaphor that he subsequently left out. It would have come just before Thackeray mentions the Neapolitan story-teller:

> When Captain Beaufort and Captain Becher make charts at the Admiralty, they set down the rocks creeks bays quicksands in their proper places or the deuce wold be in it and the unwary mariner would find himself striking on a bar or floundering on a quicksand where he had been led to expect a clear channel and deep water so in our . . .[19]

That Thackeray suppresses such an image suggests that it was not mere padding or 'bulk' that he was looking for: it suggests rather that what he is doing is quite deliberately withdrawing all direction, all mapping, from his narrative. Ray is right to the extent that these passages were an added commentary; Sutherland is right that they are confusing: it is the confusion that is added. It is the same confusion that is effected by the omission of the plate showing Becky as the murderer of Jos – as contemporary readers noticed. Lady Eastlake, for example, counselled readers of the illustrated edition to 'cut out' the picture of Becky as Clytemnestra for it damagingly forecloses the question as to whether Becky was guilty or not:

> The whole use, too, of the work – that of generously measuring one another by this standard – is lost, the moment you convict Becky of a capital crime.[20] (her stress)

What Lady Eastlake recognized and welcomed was that *Vanity Fair* was designed to provoke discussion – 'was Becky guilty?' – to serve as, to use her telling expression, a social 'ether', to provide occasion for gossip and chit-chat. As such it offers an almost classic instance of that function which some marxist critics have alleged is of the essence of 'literature' as an institution: its promotion of an anodyne exchange of ideas, of the practice of a freedom of thought within a domain of value – of aesthetics and taste – uncontaminated by historical or political considerations.[21] Indeed, this might explain and resolve another difference between Thackeray's editors. Tillotson, for example, argues that the book has been very carefully constructed whereas Stewart acknowledges that there is considerable justice in regarding it as a 'hodge-podge':[22] it is both – a constructed hodge-podge. We would do well to recall the years of its composition and publication: 1845 to 1848 – years of acute crisis in England and abroad, when politics and history were very much in evidence and when any kind of distraction must have been more than welcome. As far as *Vanity Fair* was concerned, the relief of the early reviewers is all too evident:

> There are good people of quality as well as bad in his pages, – pretty much as we find them in the world; and the work is certainly not written with the view of proving the want of reorganisation in society, nor, indeed of proving anything else, which to us is a great relief. . . . Mr. Thackeray has kept his science and political economy (if he has any) for some other emergency, and given us a plain old-fashioned love-story, which any genuine novel reader of the old school may honestly, plentifully, and conscientiously cry over.[23]

The pattern of deletions and accretions, then, of an accumulation of lacks and excesses, that we have seen taking place in the production of the novel from its early drafts of 1845 to its revised edition of 1853 can be related, on the one hand, to an increasing curtailment of contemporary social reference and, on the other, to the elaboration of a specious and self-contradictory moral rhetoric: history – it is not too great a jump to suggest – is being suppressed in the interests of style, of the literary itself. And of course, while this movement might be seen to characterize the process of production of *Vanity Fair* it is also precisely this same dialectic that informs the structural axis of the novel: the first half centred on the absent Battle of Waterloo, the second on the caricature of the Wicked Nobleman, Lord Steyne.

Thackeray blithely acknowledges that his novel resides on the mere 'skirts of history' (p. 213) and is unabashed to admit that

> We do not claim to rank among the military novelists. Our place is with the non-combatants. (p. 346)[24]

In many ways, of course, Thackeray's depiction of Waterloo through its effects rather than by way of epic engagement is a masterly achievement. Nevertheless there is some evidence that the restraint of the artist answered to some fear in the man: Thackeray postponed writing the Waterloo number twice[25] and it is to be remarked how contorted the novel's time scheme becomes as Waterloo approaches:

> Our history is destined to this chapter to go backwards and forwards in a very irresolute manner seemingly, and having conducted our story to tomorrow presently, we shall immediately again have occasion to step back to yesterday, so that the whole tale get a hearing. (p. 293)

In an atrabilious remark, F. R. Leavis dismissed Thackeray as someone merely concerned to kill time:[26] in a sense Leavis was right. Sutherland has noted how Thackeray begins *Vanity Fair* with a scrupulous attention to his time scheme but later gives way to an almost total disdain for chronological credibility.[27] The marginalization of Waterloo and the indifference to chronology are correlative symptoms of a collapse of historical time and its substitution by a calendrical notation that lends itself to the most arbitrary permutations:

> those who know the present George Tufto would hardly recognise the daring Peninsular and Waterloo officer. He has thick curling brown hair and black eyebrows now, and his whiskers are of the deepest purple. He was light-haired and bald in 1815, and stouter in the person and limbs, which especially have shrunk very much of late. When he was about seventy years of age (he is now nearly eighty), his hair, which was very scarce and quite white, suddenly grew thick and brown and curly and his whiskers and eyebrows took their present colour. (p. 331)

General Tufto incarnates the temporal caesura of the text.

Of all the characters in *Vanity Fair* it is Lord Steyne who is most closely based on a real historical personage, the Marquis of Hertford, who died in 1842.[28] The proximity of his model threatened Thackeray both with anachronism – the time of the novel being much earlier – and with the reactivation of that mode of contemporary satire which we have seen him at such pains to suppress. If the historical disturbance of Waterloo is contained by reducing it to a lack, then that represented by Hertford – who had had a distinguished political career – is muffled by excess. Lord Steyne is introduced, from the very beginning, as a simulacrum, as a grotesque caricature of Becky:

> The great Lord Steyne was standing by the fire sipping coffee. The fire crackled and blazed pleasantly. There was a score of candles sparkling round the mantlepiece, in all sorts of quaint sconces, of gilt and bronze and porcelain. They lighted up Rebecca's figure to admiration, as she sat on a sofa covered with a pattern of gaudy flowers. She was in a pink dress, that looked as fresh as a rose; her dazzling white arms and shoulders were half covered with a thin hazy scarf through which they sparkled; her hair hung in curls round her neck; one of her little feet peeped out from the fresh crisp folds of silk: the prettiest little foot in the prettiest little sandal in the finest silk stocking in the world.
>
> The candles lighted up Lord Steyne's shining bald head, which was fringed with red hair. He had thick bushy eyebrows, with little twinkling bloodshot eyes, surrounded by a thousand wrinkles. His jaw was underhung, and when he laughed, two white buck-teeth protruded themselves and glistened savagely in the midst of the grin. He had been dining with royal personages, and wore his garter and ribbon. A short man was his Lordship, broad-chested and bow-legged, but proud of the fineness of his foot and ankle, and always caressing his garter knee. (p. 445)

To the extent that Becky is already a contrived (self-)composition, Steyne, whose description mimics that of Becky, is a kind of meta-composition, an artifice to the second power. Significantly it is a similar kind of arch-artifice that characterizes their first conversation which takes up Becky's expressed desire for a 'Sheep-dog':

> 'And so the shepherd is not enough,' said [Lord Steyne], 'to defend his lambkin?'
>
> 'The Shepherd is too fond of playing at cards and going to his clubs,' answered Becky, laughing.

'Gad, what a debauched Corydon!' said my Lord – 'what a mouth for a pipe!'

'I take your three to two,' here said Rawdon, at the card table.

'Hark at Meliboeus,' snarled the noble Marquis, 'he's pastorally occupied too: he's shearing a Southdown. What an innocent mutton, hey? Damme, what a snowy fleece!' (pp. 445–6)

It is a contrived exchange: a self-conscious abuse of a mock pastoral mode – a mocked mock-pastoral, a parody again to the second power. This excessive mode is to be found again later when we are given Tom Eave's account of Steyne's rooms in Gaunt House:

It conducts to the famous petits appartements of Lord Steyne – one, sir, fitted up all in ivory and white satin, another in ebony and black velvet; there is a little banqueting-room taken from Sallust's house at Pompeii, and painted by Cosway – a little private kitchen, in which every saucepan was silver and all the spits were gold. (p. 545)

This goes beyond connoting sensuality and begins to suggest fairy-story and pantomime. And this note of exotic unreality is only carried to a higher pitch of melodrama when Steyne's valet, Fiche, warns Becky to leave Rome:

'I tell Madame it is unwholesome now. There is always malaria for some people. The cursed marsh wind kills many at all seasons. Look here, Madame Crawley, you were always bon enfant, and I have an interest in you, parole d'honneur. Be warned. Go away from Rome, I tell you – or you will be ill and die.' Becky laughed, though in rage and fury. 'What! assassinate poor little me!' she said. 'How romantic! Does my lord carry bravos for couriers, and stilettos in the fourgons? Bah! I will stay, if but to plague him. I have those who will defend me whilst I am here.' (p. 752)

The theatricality is evident – even to Becky – but scarcely undercut by Thackeray: he seems to fail to notice that he has here relapsed into the 'polyglot' nonsense he had formerly satirized at the expense of the 'Silver Fork' romancers (see above, pp. 113–14). Meanwhile, our last glimpse of Steyne is of a 'worn-out wicked old man' with 'livid face and ghastly eyes' (p. 753) whirling past in a barouche, a figure of Hate in an Italian landscape: the Marquess of Hertford has become myth, history has become literature.

In a way the respective fates of Rawdon Crawley and Lord Steyne, the one sent to Coventry (Island), the other given a pantomime setting, are emblematic of two ways of treating history: consigning it to silence or elevating it to myth. Ironically Thackeray was a peculiarly privileged witness of what was happening in England and France in 1848: he was receiving almost daily reports from his mother of the street-fighting in Paris, while he himself went to the last great meeting of the Chartists on Kennington Common as reporter for the *Morning Chronicle*. For all that, he shows little analytical power, rather a sense of impotence and resignation:

> I can't find the end of the question between property and labour. We want something almost equal to a Divine Person to settle it. I mean if there is ever to be an elucidation of the mystery it is to be solved by a preacher of such novelty and authority, as will awaken and convince mankind – but O how and when? – the question of poverty is that of death disease winter or any other natural phenomenon.[29]

The appeal to the Divine Person and the resort to the natural analogue are no more than alternative ways of invoking silence and myth. The lack and the excess of *Vanity Fair* are symptomatic of a society that could no longer even pretend to know itself and that would seek by all means in its power for an alibi for its ignorance. There is a chapter in *Vanity Fair* which says it all, a chapter which at least one commentator finds 'insipid'.[30] It is that teasingly and significantly entitled: 'In which a charade is acted which may or may not puzzle the reader' (Chapter 51). In this charade one of the great tragedies of western culture, the *Agamemnon* of Aeschylus, is first reduced to an entertainment for a dissolute aristocracy and then reduced to the smutty ignominy of a pun: 'Mrs. Rawdon Crawley was quite killing in her part [of Clytemnestra]' (p. 596). The heroic has been whittled down to a cheap *double entendre*: a powerful analysis of politics and history has been reduced to the status of a slippery riddle, tragedy to farce.

If this were all that *Vanity Fair* had to offer then we would be forced to conclude with Thackeray that

> The best ink for *Vanity Fair* use would be one that faded utterly in a couple of days and left the paper clean and blank so that you might write on it to somebody else. (p. 231)

But ironically it is precisely in this 'insipid' chapter 'which may or may not puzzle the reader' that Thackeray prophetically anticipates, in the reduction of *Agamemnon* to a pun, the great – albeit apocryphal – analytical metaphor with which Marx opens his *Eighteenth Brumaire of Louis Bonaparte*:

> Hegel remarks somewhere that all great events and characters of world history occur, so to speak, twice. He forgot to add: the first time as tragedy, the second time as farce.[31]

Marx's text, written in early 1852, is a brilliant account – brilliant not only in its political insights but also in its stylistic ebullience – of the series of revolutions that took place in France between February 1848 and December 1851, from the collapse of the monarchy of Louis Philippe to the assumption of absolute power by Louis Napoleon. There is no space here to rehearse Marx's analysis in detail. Sufficient to note that what fascinated Marx was the spectacle of a history seemingly in reverse as a potentially socialist republic gave way to a bourgeois republic and this in turn to a dictatorship. Marx analyses in detail the contradictions of each stage of the struggle, the way in which all coalitions resolve themselves into their constituent elements and the way in which analysis itself finds itself confounded by the extraordinary phenomenon of Louis Bonaparte.[32] Thackeray, of course, lacks Marx's political insight but what is striking is the way in which they seem to share a number of metaphorical and stylistic obsessions. We have already referred to the celebrated 'tragedy/farce' characterization of history that informs both texts in their entirety. Similarly, for both there is the awareness that they are addressing a history without heroes: for Thackeray it is 'a novel without a hero'; for Marx the France of 1848–51 is a period 'poor in heroes and events'.[33] And just as Thackeray can be seen moving from an epic and historical time to a mere calendrical notation, so Marx remarks again and again on the mere calendrical significance of the events in France, where consequential time seems to have given way entirely to a mere sequential time.[34] The two writers share, too, a predilection for theatrical imagery, for a characterization of events and persons in terms of grotesque parodies and imitations of more heroic models. At the deepest level of all, perhaps, there is evidence that both novelist and political commentator are aware that in the face of a history of grotesque perversity, language itself finds itself at a loss. Marx observes, for example that the republican Constitution of 1848 was a tissue of contradictions:

> For each paragraph of the Constitution contains its own antithesis, its own upper and lower house, namely, freedom in the general phrase, abolition of freedom in the marginal note.[35]

Elsewhere he notes, surveying the period as a whole:

> In no period, therefore, do we find a more variegated mixture of elements, more high-flown phrases, yet more actual uncertainty and awkwardness.[36]

It is now, perhaps, that we can understand the real significance of the impasse and double bind of Thackeray's purported moral commentary (see above, p. 116): for all its ostensible suppression of history, *Vanity Fair* is historical through and through – it enacts the impasse of 1848 just as Chapter 51 enacts the collapse of tragedy into farce. And, indeed, it is in this enactment of a historical predicament that *Vanity Fair* gets closest to the *Eighteenth Brumaire* for, in the last analysis, Marx, no more than Thackeray, fully understood what was going on. As his account proceeds, Marx's imagery assumes an ever increasing degree of complexity. At times its dialectical richness reminds us of Swift:

> In the first French revolution the rule of the Constitutionalists was followed by the rule of the Jacobins. Each of these parties leaned on the progressive party. As soon as it had brought the revolution to the point where it was unable to follow it further, let alone advance ahead of it, it was pushed aside by the bolder ally standing behind it and sent to the guillotine. In this way the revolution moved in an ascending path. In the revolution of 1848 this relationship was reversed. The proletarian party appeared as the appendage of petty-bourgeois democracy. It was betrayed and abandoned by the latter on 16 April, on 15 May, and in the June days. The democratic party, for its part, leant on the shoulders of the bourgeois-republican party. As soon as the bourgeois republicans thought they had found their feet, they shook off this burdensome comrade and relied in turn on the party of Order. The party of Order hunched its shoulders, allowed the bourgeois republicans to tumble off, and threw itself onto the shoulders of

the armed forces. It believed it was still sitting on those shoulders when it noticed one fine morning that they had changed into bayonets. Every party kicked out at the party pressing it forward and leaned on the party in front, which was pressing backward. No wonder each party lost its balance in this ridiculous posture, and collapsed in the midst of curious capers, after having made the inevitable grimaces. In this way the revolution moved in a descending path.[37]

But as Marx seeks to characterize the enigmatic manœuvres of Louis Bonaparte who, while allied with no party subject to simple analysis, moved from a position of absolute powerlessness to that of absolute power, the logic of the argument becomes virtually impossible to follow:

He [Louis Bonaparte] has seemed to efface himself behind this ministry, resigning the power of government into the hands of the party of Order, and assuming the modest character mask worn by responsible newspaper editors in the time of Louis Philippe, the mask of the straw man. Now he threw away the mask, for it was no longer the light veil behind which he could hide his features, but an iron mask which prevented him from displaying any features of his own.[38]

John Coombes, in a brilliant analysis of the language of the *Eighteenth Brumaire*, draws the following conclusions:

The language of the *Eighteenth Brumaire*, collapsing as it does under the weight of its own increasingly baroque imagery, comes thus to mimic the artifice, crisis and failure of bourgeois society which it chronicles. . . . The text seems in its procedures ultimately to parody the parody of politics represented by Louis Bonaparte.[39]

The *Eighteenth Brumaire*, in other words, no more than *Vanity Fair*, offers us not so much a critical description of a historical moment as an enactment of that moment via its register of stylistic devices and convolutions which are themselves available for interpretation. It is not just that Agamemnon has been reduced to a pun, but a whole classical theatre of representation has given way to the elaboration of a conundrum that awaits decipherment. In a sense it is precisely that shift, from a concern with literature as reference and reflection to an awareness of its status as a practice *sui generis*, that the process of production of *Vanity Fair*, which we have examined in some detail, evidences. The suppression of the illustrations and the construction, instead, of a mannered self-congratulatory and self-abrasive style which allows of no appeal to a 'truth' beyond itself – 'Was Becky guilty or not?' – are part and parcel of a radical change in conception as to the nature of writing itself. Moeover it is possible to discover what enabled Thackeray to make that break. In Chapter 51 the collapse of Agamemnon into a riddle is facilitated by an Oriental setting: from August 1844 to February 1845 Thackeray himself travelled to the Middle East and his *Notes on a Journey from Cornhill to Grand Cairo*[40] are of crucial importance for an understanding of *Vanity Fair*.

We do not know exactly when Thackeray began writing *Vanity Fair* but Tillotson suggests that it might have been begun at the same time as he began the *Notes*.[41] It would not be surprising, then, to find a certain amount of cross-fertilization going on between the two texts. The most positive evidence that this is so relates to the origin of the figure of Dobbin. On the outward journey Thackeray made the acquaintance of a certain Lieutenant Bundy who had 'lean legs', had spent 'thirty seven years in the navy', was 'well educated' and 'contented' and whose 'doom is disappointment'.[42] The lieutenant clearly interested Thackeray:

> Is it breaking a confidence to tell Lieutenant Bundy's history? Let the motive excuse the deed. It is a good, kind, wholesome and noble character. Why should we keep all our admiration for those who win in this world, as we do, sycophants as we are? When we write a novel, our great stupid imaginations can go no further than to marry the hero to a fortune at the end, and to find out that he is a lord by right. O, blundering lick-spittle morality! And yet I would like to fancy some happy retributive Utopia in the peaceful cloudland where my meek lieutenant should find the yards manned of his ship as he went on board, all the guns firing an enormous salute (only without the least noise or vile smell of powder), and he be saluted on the deck as Admiral Sir James, or Sir Joseph – aye, or Lord Viscount Bundy, Knight of all the orders above the sun.[43]

There can be little doubt that here is the model for Dobbin with his clumsy feet, long service record, culture and long-suffering patience.

The second connection that might be established between the *Notes* and *Vanity Fair* is more complex but much more important for, in a sense, it accounts for the charade episode – that episode 'which may or may not puzzle the reader'. One of the great shocks of the *Notes* is Thackeray's disenchantment with Athens:

> When then I came to Athens, and saw that it was humbug, I hailed the fact with a sort of gloomy joy. I stood in the Royal Square and cursed the country which has made thousands of little boys miserable. They have blue stripes on the New Greek flag; I thought bitterly of my own. I wished that my schoolmaster had been in the place, that we might have fought there for the right; and that I might have immolated him as a sacrifice to the names of little boys flogged into premature Hades, or pining away and sickening under the destiny of that infernal Greek grammar.[44]

In his letters, in fact, the disenchantment becomes almost a kind of rage – Thackeray almost vomits up Athens:

> Athens is filthy beggarly racketty lousy buggy full of dogs donkeys and other vermin. . . .[45]

There is an animus here that goes beyond the mere disappointment of the tourist. Athens stirs up something very deep in Thackeray: the memory of being beaten at school haunted Thackeray all his life and it clearly had a traumatic significance for him. The outburst, then, is not simply against a dirty city, but against a whole system of education and discipline based on the classics, a protest against a whole grammar – with its declensions and conjugations and genders – that had literally lacerated him.

The next port of call was Smyrna, on the coast of Turkey, and the mood is quite different:

> How delightful is that notion of the pleasant Eastern people about knowledge, where the height of science is made to consist in the answering of riddles! and all the mathematicians and magicians bring their great beards to bear upon a conundrum![46]

Clearly, in the riddles and conundrums of the East Thackeray found an enormous relief from the severities and constraints of classical culture. His fascination with the Orient radiates from his letters as he savours each new word: cheboque, narghilch, sherbet, rebeck, papooshes,

Yackmack, etc.[47] The same kind of delight is to be found when Thackeray contrasts the 'sublimely beautiful, perfect loveliness' of the Parthenon with the architecture of Cairo:

> but these fantastic spirals, and cupolas and galleries, excite, amuse, tickle the imagination so to speak and perpetually fascinate the eye.[48]

There is, then, a world of difference between the classical tradition of the West and the Oriental tradition of the East. While the architecture of Athens and Rome imposes in terms of mass and volume, expressiveness ('sublimely beautiful') and teleology ('perfect loveliness'), that of Cairo works its effect in terms of surfaces, of decorative exuberance and referenceless fantasy. The penetrative zeal of the classical tradition (flogging) is set against the superficial fascination of the East (tickling). The tragic paraphernalia of the West – Hades, destiny, immolation – looks inert alongside the bazaars, veils and dissimulations of the Orient. A severe and oppressive grammar is gladly abandoned for the sovereign delight in the mere accumulation of exotic terms. *Agamemnon* – the starkest of classical tragedies with its scrupulous conjugation of roles and gender, of fate and destiny, of crime and punishment – yields to the sauciness of the riddle.

The Orient, then, marks for Thackeray a release from the constraints and taboos of his society and offers him instead all the indulgences of the flesh and spirit. But the adventure is not without risk – and here we come to the third and perhaps most disturbing connection between the *Notes* and *Vanity Fair*. To move off the map of one's society (we should recall here Thackeray's suppression of his cartographical metaphor at the end of Chapter 8 – see above, p. 116), to abandon its grammar, is, perhaps, to discover all the intoxication of perversity and desire but it is also to lose that security which a sanctioned and authorized codification of the relationship between desire and the body affords. When the ecstasy of desire subsides the unmapped and ungendered body will collapse into catatonic inertia and the pleasures it has courted will seem now alien barbs.[49]

That Thackeray thrilled to the sensual pleasures of the East is nowhere better evidenced than in his hilarious account of his visit to a Turkish bath:

> When you get into the Sudarium, or hot room, your first sensations only occur about half a minute after entrance, when

you feel that you are choking. I found myself in that state, seated on a marble slab; the bath man was gone; he had taken away the cotton turban and shoulder shawl: I saw I was in a narrow room of marble, with a vaulted roof, and a fountain of warm and cold water; the atmosphere was in a steam, the choking sensation went off, and I felt a sort of pleasure presently in a soft boiling simmer, which, no doubt, potatoes feel when they are steaming. You are left in this state for about ten minutes; it is warm certainly, but odd and pleasant, and disposes the mind to reverie. But let any delicate mind in Baker Street fancy my horror, when, on looking up out of this reverie, I saw a great brown wretch extended before me, only half dressed, standing on pattens, and exaggerated by them and the steam until he looked like an ogre, grinning in the most horrible way, and waving his arm, on which was a horse-hair glove. He spoke in his unknown nasal jargon, words which echoed through the arched room; his eyes astonishingly large and bright, his ears stuck out, and his head was all shaved, except a bristling top-knot, which gave it a demoniac fierceness. This description, I feel, is growing too frightful: ladies who read it will be going into hysterics, or saying, 'Well, upon my word, this is the most singular, the most extraordinary kind of language. Jane, my love, you will not read that odious book' – and so I will be brief. This grinning man belabours the patient violently with the horse brush. When he has completed the horse-hair part, and you lie expiring under a squirting fountain of warm water, and fancying all is done, he reappears with a large brass basin, containing a quantity of lather, in the midst of which is something like old Miss MacWhirter's flaxen wig that she is so proud of, and that we have all laughed at. Just as you are going to remonstrate, the thing like the wig is dashed into your face and eyes, covered over with soap, and for five minutes you are drowned in lather; you can't see, the suds are frothing over your eyeballs; you can't hear, the soap is whizzing into your ears; you can't gasp for breath, Miss Mac-Whirter's wig is down your throat with half a pailful of suds in an instant – you are all soap. Wicked children in former days have jeered you, exclaiming, 'How are you off for soap?' You little knew what saponacity was till you entered a Turkish bath. When the whole operation is concluded, you are led – with what heartfelt joy I need not say – softly back to the cooling-room, having been robed in shawls and turbans as before. You are laid gently on the reposing bed; some body brings a narghile, which taste as tobacco must taste in Mahomet's Paradise; a cool sweet dreamy languor takes possession of a purified frame; and half an hour of such delicious laziness is spent over the pipe as is unknown in Europe, where vulgar prejudice has most shamefully maligned indolence, calls it foul names, such as the father of all evil, and the like; in fact, does not know how to educate idleness as these honest Turks do, and the fruit which, when properly cultivated, it bears.[50]

It is difficult not to sense Thackeray's rather scary delight at the whole experience of being stripped, pummelled and man-handled in a sweltering atmosphere of sweat and steam. It comes as all the more of a shock, then, when, after so much celebration of the Orient and the obvious pleasure of the Turkish bath, towards the end of the *Notes*, Thackeray seems to round on and savage all his earlier enthusiasm:

> The life of the East is a life of brutes. The much maligned Orient, I am confident, has not been maligned near enough; for the good reason that none of us can feel the amount of horrible sensuality practiced there.[51]

At one level, of course, it would be easy to interpret this outburst as a moment of contrition after 'a night before', a shameful recoil from sensual indulgence. But it is possible, also, that it is the index of a much deeper disturbance. In a letter to his wife Thackeray reveals that the helpless abandon of the Turkish bath touched off a deep-rooted fear:

> Then I could describe to you a Turkish bath I took – how I was sweated and shampooed and kneaded by a great grinning Turk, as bad as you used to be at Château Boppart.[52]

The passive voice is itself significant but the reference to Château Boppart is even more ominous. Château Boppart was a clinic for the mentally ill. Mrs Thackeray's baths were part of a course of treatment to cure her of acute psychotic withdrawal.

Let us try to summarize briefly the significance of the Eastern trip and the *Notes*. In the first place, if the two major additions to the early chapters of *Vanity Fair* were, as has been established, Dobbin and the equivocating moral commentary, then it is possible to trace the origins of both to the *Notes*, to the figure of Lieutenant Bundy (Dobbin, be it recalled, is first introduced immersed in an Oriental text – *The Arabian Nights* (p. 79)), and to the riddling wisdom of the East. Dobbin and the commentary, then, are in dialectical tension for as the commentary ceaselessly works to effect perplexity, Dobbin remains as a kind of residual sheet-anchor of common decencies and values. Secondly, the journey to the Orient marked a break with the constraints and taboos of the West but while, on the one hand, that break meant the freedom to indulge in an excess of pleasure, on the other it courted the risk of the lack of all control: over and against the serpentine arabesques of desire must be set the inertia and catatonic arrest of the body without organs.[53] That schizophrenic polarity of excess and lack, of desire and inertia, of delirium and death is to be found figured in *Vanity Fair* in the bewitching bohemianism of Becky Sharp and in the turgid Regency buck, Jos Sedley.

As we anticipated, prompted by the striking change between the title page of 1847 and the frontispiece of 1848, analysis of *Vanity Fair* finds itself having to move inwards, into the psychology of Thackeray himself – though whether in doing so we abandon the historical and social altogether remains to be seen. Thackeray was born in India in 1811 and sent to school in England in 1816. The schools he attended were harsh and he suffered even more from the separation from his mother – 'Pray God, I may dream of my mother'[54] was his cry each night as he went to bed. His mother returned to England in 1820 and they were reunited, but by now

> Thackeray [had come] to see life permanently in terms of a dichotomy between the warmth and trust of a happy home circle and the brutality and indifference of the outside world.[55]

Throughout his life Thackeray was to maintain an extremely close relationship with his mother. Beyond her circle of warmth and influence he found the world harsh and alien: at Charterhouse he had his nose broken in a boxing match and when he went to Cambridge he soon lost interest in his studies and became involved instead with a gambling set. In 1832 he came into his fortune, but by 1833 had wasted most of it away. By 1835 he had failed, too, to achieve success as an artist. All the evidence, then, is of a young man of some talent and intelligence whose dependence on his mother makes it difficult for him to develop that 'masculine' robustness that would enable him to cope with the world at large.

In 1835 he met the 19-year-old Isabella Shawe and in 1836, despite resistance from her mother, Thackeray married her – ominously giving her a 'mourning ring' in place of a wedding ring. Isabella was a mere child and though the two were happy together to begin with she found the burden of marriage too great and after the birth of her first two children she became subject to increasingly intense fits of depression. In 1840 she tried several times to commit suicide and in 1841 was committed to a mental home. Isabella's breakdown affected Thackeray deeply and the next three years were of great emotional and financial strain – indeed, not resolved until the successful publication of *Vanity Fair*. In other words, the years leading up to *Vanity Fair* were years of acute crisis and if Isabella was the obvious victim of the strain it is not too difficult to see that Thackeray skirted the edge of the abyss too – our analysis of the *Notes* has shown that. Caught between a doting mother and a child-bride, for months separated from his daughters and without a house, in desperate financial straits and yet ambitious to make his way in the world, Thackeray, too, came close to breakdown. Came close, that is, to his Waterloo.

We noted earlier (see above, p. 118) that Thackeray postponed the Waterloo episode twice and we suggested then that it might mark some fear in the writer himself. In June 1848, Thackeray sent a small note to a Miss Smith:

> Ah, dear Miss Smith! I shall be outatown on Sunday 18th: and I never dine out on that day because it is the Hannawussary of the death of my dear friend Captain George Osborne of the -th regiment.[56]

The note itself is set in a framework of crude sketches of the scene of death (Plate 3). It is a curious design but it lends itself to quite a sustained interpretation. On the right Thackeray's signature sets in motion a clockwise reading – first a movement of descent to the foot of the page. At the bottom of the page is the inert body of George Osborne; around him are scattered miscellaneous cannon balls, an upturned cannon, scattered limbs and marching heads, the torso of the Duke of Wellington and a three-quarter length sketch of Captain Dobbin. What we have, then, is the juxtaposition of an inert body and its scattered pieces and adjuncts, a 'corps morcelé'.[57] It is a moment of acute schizophrenia: the *Vanity Fair* equivalent of the Turkish bath incident in the *Notes* when the body sensed itself helpless in the clutch of a desire to which it felt indifferent. Here the cannon-balls, cannon, swords and bayonets figure that barbed threat of no longer codified desires and which are free to indulge in perverse excesses: the cannon – note: A canning – a caning? – is pointed at Osborne's backside and Dobbin's sword, too, seems to be penetrating its victim from behind. What is desperately needed is a new relation – a new narrative – of desire, the body in pieces and its objects. We can see the new relation evolve as we move clockwise round the sketches: the pile of legs, the torso, the heads, the three-quarter length body, the full figure and, finally, the full figure of the mounted 'Bony runninaway like any-think'. The design as a whole, then, traces a descent into schizophrenic crisis, a splitting between the body and desire, and the gradual construction of a new relation which in its togetherness might achieve escape.

The drawing celebrates the anniversary of George Osborne's death and to this extent it can see a completed pattern which might not have been so clear at the moment of death: Napoleon's triumph in the drawing anticipates an outcome that at Quatre Bras – notice that even this name suggests a fragmented body – would hardly have been in prospect. For at Waterloo what Thackeray kills in that one chilling and climactic sentence is his old self: the wastrel and rake married to a child-bride, the gambler and profligate, the spoilt son and heir. The death of George Osborne is the death of Thackeray's former ideal of himself, the ideal of the Regency dandy. His model, of course, was Beau Brummell.

In May 1844 Thackeray reviewed for the *Morning Chronicle* Jesse's *Life of George Brummell Esq.* He begins by himself summarizing Brummell's life:

> It may be consoling to the middle classes to think that the great Brummell, the conqueror of all the aristocratic dandies of his day, nay, the model of dandyhood for all time, was one of them, of the lower order. There is comfort to consider that his grandfather was a footman – a Treasury lackey, who had a son who rose to be a treasury clerk, and to enjoy the confidence of great people, and who amassed sixty thousand pounds, a third part of which sum came to George Brummell at his majority.[58]

Thackeray records Brummell's great rivalry with and triumph over George IV:

13 Young St. Kensington.
June 6. 1845.

Bony running away like anything

Ah, dear Miss Smith! I shall be out of town on Sunday the 18th: and I never dine out on that day because it is the Hannaversary of the death of — my dear friend Captain George Osborne of the —th Regiment.

Capting Dobbing

Soders

A Cannon

Pate de voile!

Capting Hosbin
ded a bullick through his Art.

Yours
always
W
M
T.

3   *Thackeray's letter of 6 June 1848*

Young Brummell, the footman's descendant, engaged and over-came this gigantic power. All the profligate splendours of Carlton House could not compete with the Beau's small tenement in Chesterfield-street. . . . Brummell overcame him by simplicity, elegance, and neat impudence of mind. There seems to have been a calmness about him which flustered and intolerably annoyed the unwieldy antagonist with whom he contended for the first place in a certain society. That question of 'Who's your fat friend?' must have quivered like a poisoned arrow in the flesh of the Prince: how superior it is to all the latter's clumsy attempts at bullying and bravado.[59]

Later:

Having expended his patrimony, not merely in country washing, but in gambling and other species of debauchery, and having run into debt as far as his tradesmen would possibly allow him, and having failed (although he told lies for the purpose) to get money from his friends, Mr. Brummell quitted the country, and, cheating his creditors, established himself at Calais.[60]

Brummell incurred more debts at Calais and then became Consul at Caen. Eventually, however, he was thrown into prison for debt and died insane in the hospital of the Bon Sauveur at Caen. Thackeray then concludes his review by quoting extensive extracts from Jesse's book. The first is a description of Brummell's person:

His face was rather long, and complexion fair; his whiskers inclined to sandy, and his hair light brown. His features were neither plain nor handsome; but his head was well-shaped, the forehead being unusually high; showing, according to phreno-logical development, more of the mental than the animal passions – the bump of self-esteem was very prominent. His countenance indicated that he possessed considerable intelligence and his mouth betrayed a strong disposition to indulge in sarcastic humour; this was predominant in every feature, the nose ex-cepted, the natural regularity of which, though it had been broken by a fall from his charger, preserved his countenance from degenerating into comicality. His eyebrows were equally express-ive with his mouth, and while the latter was giving utterance to something very good humoured or polite, the former, and the eyes themselves, which were grey and full of oddity, could assume an expression that made the sincerity of his words very doubtful.[61]

Brummell's career and person as here recounted in the review must surely remind us of two other careers: those of Becky Sharp and Thackeray himself. Indeed, it would be a teasing exercise to disentangle the Becky strands from the Thackeray strands in the above passages: of Becky there is the society triumph in the face of all the odds, the debts, the flitting, the wit, the out-facing even of monarchs – there is, too, her colouring, her eyes, her 'simplicity, elegance and neat impudence of mind'; of Thackeray there is the squandered patrimony, the gambling, the high forehead and, of course, the broken nose. At Waterloo this composite buck splits into the inert body of Osborne and the scattered pieces of his illusions; in the *Notes* it splits into the helpless body in the Turkish bath and the 'fantastic spirals, and cupolas and galleries [that] excite, amuse, tickle the imagination so to speak and perpetually fascinate the eye'; in *Vanity Fair* it splits into Becky Sharp and the bloated, Humpty-Dumpty-like bulk of Jos Sedley – the 'fat friend', the Other, the foil, to Brummell's triumph.

The relationship of desire to the body is one of inscription: desire is 'written' on the body, it maps its erogenous zones, allocates points of intensity, articulates lines of force, traces relations between function and structure that ignore anatomical determinations. In a crisis – a breakdown – it is possible for the body to shed such a mapping, cast off its cartography as if it were a transfer that had not taken, and in such an event the body becomes organless and inert. This is what happens to Jos – or, rather, it is what Jos figures: barely able to move, inarticulate, helplessly reduced to the condition of a mere digestive organism, a bloated polyp. Vainly he tries to don ever more flamboyant and exotic waistcoats in an endeavour to shape and contour his grossness. At Waterloo his blubbering cry is 'Coupez-moi, coupez-moi': unwittingly his bad French expresses his prime need – to be 'cut', incised, scripted.

Over and against Jos is Becky Sharp, an instrument of incision *par excellence*, the most finely honed of writing machines. Becky is the heterogeneity of a desire that has lost its surface of inscription, lost all secure reference, and which is alluring and threatening in its sovereign autonomy. She is to Jos what the 'fantastic spirals, and cupolas and galleries' of the Orient are to the grey domes and inert masses of Rome and Athens. Becky's serpentine writhings and machinations are as devoid of origin, reference and end as are the arabesques of Cairo. Significantly she is not seen as beginning life so much as beginning it all over again (p. 53); motherless, she must become her own mother. Becky, that is, re-presents herself: she epitomizes that original repetition which must legitimate all or any desire. But here, as we have seen, the schizophrenic moment has separated desire from the body, Becky from Jos – so that the latter is like a Schlemiel who has lost his shadows[62] – and has eschewed all orthodox register: the dictionary is hurled from the carriage window; B. Sharp designates no note on any scale. Becky enters the text in a postscript and it is in postscripts that she is discussed by Mrs Bute Crawley and Miss Pinkerton: she is, in a sense, a perpetual supplement, ever elsewhere, most at home in a foreign language and environment. She delights in the sheer excess of language – in its 'false notes' (p. 144), in its riddles and repartee, in the vertiginous abandon afforded by its referenceless autonomy. Her letters to Miss Crawley are a tissue of fabrications and bear as much reference to the reality they purport to register as do the handful of battlefield souvenirs that she includes with them. And this is the point: what Becky 'represents' – if we can use that word without confusion – is the breakdown of representation itself, i.e. of that notion of representation conceived of as a specular reflection of the represented by the representative. 'Chili', it is discovered, no longer means 'cool' (p. 61); a pineapple turns out to be not an apple off a pine-tree (p. 75). Indeed, much of the brio of *Vanity Fair* itself derives from a delight in the gratuity of signification:

> After dinner Mrs. Crawley had an assembly, which was attended by the Duchess (Dowager) of Stilton, Duc de la Gruyere, Marchioness Alessandro Strachinor, Comte de Brie, Baron Schapzuger, Chevalier Tosti, Countess of Slingstone, and Lady F. Macadam, Major-General and Lady G. Macbeth and (2) Miss Macbeths; Viscount Paddington, Sir Horace Fogey, Hon. Sands Bedwin, Bobbachy Bahawder, and an etc. which the reader may fill in at his pleasure through a dozen lines of small type. (p. 589)

At another level, of course, this breakdown of representation means that it is wholly appropriate that Becky's household should survive on 'nothing a year': credit, like language and like desire, must thrive in an inflationary economy where it is never called to account.

Desire, language, credit: the crisis of representation, then, is not simply Thackeray's local schizophrenic impasse, but one that is invested through and through with ideological, political and economic determinations. The melancholic clown gazing wistfully into a broken mirror testifies not to a personal but to a whole social crisis of consciousness – that loosely but conveniently denominated '1848'.

Perhaps the major theme of the *Eighteenth Brumaire* is the collapse of representation. As Marx records the events in France from February 1848 to December 1851 he is evidently fascinated by the spectacle of a historical pageant coming apart at the seams. He watches in amazement as Legitimists and Orleanists, while subjectively motivated by monarchist aspirations, collude in practice to further republican ends; or as the coalition of Order courts, in effect, anarchy and dictatorship; or as the peasantry, seduced by the illusions of enfranchisement, vote to absolute power the principal agent of their oppression. At the centre of it all was the critical confusion of the bourgeoisie:

> Not only was the parliamentary party of Order split into its two great fractions, and each of these fractions divided within itself, but the party of Order within the parliament had also fallen out with the party of Order outside parliament. The spokesmen and writers of the bourgeoisie, its platform and its press, to put it briefly the ideologists of the bourgeoisie, had become alienated from the bourgeoisie itself. *Representatives and represented faced each other in mutual incomprehension.*[63] (my emphasis)

Frightened by the spectacle of the Parisian 'mob' the French bourgeoisie broke with its revolutionary heritage and rounded savagely on its ideological representatives:

> The bourgeoisie demonstrated its anger with its literary representatives, its own press, even more unambiguously than its break with its parliamentary representatives. Not only France but the whole of Europe was astonished by the sentences of ruinous fines and shameless terms of imprisonment inflicted, on verdicts brought in by bourgeois juries, for every attack by bourgeois journalists on Bonaparte's usurpationist desires, and for every attempt by the press to defend the political rights of the bourgeoisie against the executive power.[64]

This split between representative and represented, between ideological stance and material support, is even more acutely epitomized in the relationship between Louis Bonaparte and his notorious Society of 10 December:

> The Society of 10 December belonged to him, it was his work, his very own idea. Whatever else he laid hold of was put into his hands by the force of circumstances, whatever else he did either circumstances did for him or he copied from the deeds of others; but he himself became an original author when he combined official turns of phrase about order, religion, family and property, spoken publicly before the citizens, with the secret society of disorder, prostitution and theft, behind him. The history of the Society of 10 December is his own history.[65]

Finally, nowhere is a rampant schizophrenia more manifest than when we place alongside each other Marx's descriptions of the constituent elements of the Society of 10 December and of its leader:

> The society dated from 1849. Under the pretext of founding a charitable organisation, the Paris lumpenproletariat had been organised into secret sections, each section led by Bonapartist agents and the whole headed by a Bonapartist general. Alongside decayed roués of doubtful origin and uncertain means of subsistence, alongside ruined and adventurous scions of the bourgeoisie, there were vagabonds, slaves, swindlers, confidence tricksters, lazzaroni, pickpockets, sleight-of-hand experts, gamblers, maquereaux, brothel keepers, porters, pen-pushers, organ-grinders, rag-and-bone merchants, knife-grinders, tinkers and beggars: in short, the whole indeterminate fragmented mass, tossed backwards and forwards, which the French call la bohème; with these elements, so akin to himself, Bonaparte founded the Society of 10 December.[66]

> 10 December 1848 was the day of the peasant insurrection. The symbol that expressed their entry into the revolutionary movement, clumsy but cunning, rascally but naïve, oafish but sublime, a stupid anachronism, a momentous, historic piece of buffoonery, an undecipherable hieroglyph for the understanding of the civilised – this symbol bore unmistakably the physiognomy of the class which represents barbarism within civilisation.[67]

Part of the anomaly, of course, is that the symbol of the peasant insurrection should be the adopted leader of the Parisian lumpen-proletariat but, for the moment, let us content ourselves by noting the impossible conjunction of la bohème – with all its energetic hetero-geneity manifest in the writing itself – with the 'oafish . . . stupid anachronism, a momentous, historic piece of buffoonery' that is Louis Bonaparte. Over and against the originless and fragmented body of the Parisian underworld is set the clumsy inertia of an 'undecipherable hieroglyph' – the unscripted body without organs. It is Cairo and Athens again, the Turkish bath at Smyrna, Becky Sharp – how well she epitomizes la bohème as described here by Marx – and the oafish, anachronistic buffoon, Jos Sedley.

The number of parallels that might be drawn between Marx's writings on France and Thackeray's text is, indeed, striking but, clearly, it would be naïve to suggest 'influence' or any other kind of positivistic or structural connection. Much of the similarity is to be explained by considering the extent to which both writers are addressing a common crisis – that we have characterized as the breakdown of representation. For Marx, as we have seen, that breakdown derived primarily from the bourgeoisie's abandonment of its revolutionary tradition and its rounding on its ideological representatives. What emerged from this was the establishment of an autocratic state under Louis Bonaparte and the institution of a state machinery no longer allied to any particular class. In England a similar shift in patterns of power and representation might be traced.

The years 1846 to 1852 – roughly coincident, be it noted, with the time of production of *Vanity Fair* – saw what is generally regarded as the last administration in England to be formed on a designedly Whig basis.[68] It marked the end, in other words, of that hegemony exercised by the landed interest that stretched back to the Glorious Revolution of 1688. Perhaps the single most telling evidence of this shift in power was the collapse of political patronage and the institution of a profess-ional Civil Service, i.e. as in France, the emergence of an autonomous state machinery. At the time, however, the waning power of the landed interest was most clearly marked by the repeal of the Corn Laws in 1846. This act, more than any other, heralded the wholesale capitula-tion to the gospel of *laissez-faire* which held that economic prosperity and expansion depended on the free flow of labour, the free flow of capital, and the freedom of contract between the two.[69]

The flows of labour and capital, then, are no longer inscribed in or governed by an economy based on the land – literally they have become deterritorialized[70] and as such can be seen as enjoying an autonomy we have earlier ascribed to desire, language, and credit. At the same time, however, it became evident that if *laissez-faire* was not to result in a mad free-for-all – and the speculative booms and crises of the 1840s gave more than a hint of this – then alternative modes of control and legislation had to be found. It is no coincidence, therefore, that the same administration that was responsible for the repeal of the Corn Laws also introduced the Ten Hours Bill of 1847. This Bill, in regulating the number of hours a man might work, marked the first intrusion by the state into the private domain of the family – and, indeed, was most hotly contested for this very reason. In other words, whereas power had formerly been mediated via land it was now to be mediated via the family: the affiliative nexus of aristocratic 'blood' gives way to the taboos of the nuclear household.[71] The pattern of representation and identification hitherto underwritten by landed wealth find a new and virulent purchase in the home. It is this re-inscription in the family of a system of representation that has collapsed elsewhere that marks the final melancholy achievement of *Vanity Fair*.

The whole process of production of *Vanity Fair*, as we have seen, entailed a series of breaks with representation (the loss of illustrations) and reference (the suppression of slang, the curtailment of contemporary allusion) and this crisis of representation can also be seen to characterize the stylistic (the use of non-referential language) and thematic achievement (particularly the break between the body and desire) of the novel. If, however, in the Jos/Becky Sharp theme we see the dread and the hope yielded by the collapse of representation and reflection it is nevertheless possible to see the re-institution and re-inscription of representation and reflection in the domestic romance of Dobbin, Amelia and little Georgy. Here the exuberances and excesses of desire are contained and controlled within a new axiomatic of identities and relationships grounded on the lack supplied by the dead George Osborne: the free flows of schizophrenic abandonment succumb to the neurotic syndrome centred on castration – to, that is, the double bind of the Oedipal complex. In a wry moment Terry Eagleton has suggested that the mid-nineteenth century had difficulty in resolving its Oedipal complex:[72] rather, its problem was to consti- tute it – to constitute, that is, a mechanism of social reproduction and legitimacy in lieu of that formerly afforded by land and 'connection'. If Becky is able to whittle down *Agamemnon* to a riddle, Dobbin, with his big feet and li(s)p – chiasmatically the two yield a 'li(m)p'! – returns as Oedipus.

The whole of Dobbin's long infatuation with Amelia as well as hers with first George and then Georgy is mediated by way of images, fetishes and tokens, by a whole apparatus of representations that lends itself to voyeurism, perversion and parasitism. The system is most intense and incestuous in Amelia's determination that little Georgy should look 'like' his father:

> The elder George returned in him somehow, only improved, and as if come back from heaven. In a hundred little tones, looks and movements, the child was so like his father, that the widow's heart thrilled as she held him to it; and he would often ask the cause of her tears. It was because of his likeness to his father, she did not scruple to tell him. She talked constantly to him about his dead father, and spoke of her love for George to the innocent and wondering child; much more than she ever had done to George himself. (p. 457)

George and Georgy: pictures, images, repetitions one of another – Amelia sleeps with pictures of both of them on the wall and another of Georgy under the pillow (p. 652), images and secrecy. Poor Dobbin is graciously allowed to 'look and long, no more' (p. 693) and must find but scant relief drooling over a figure from a book of fashions which he fancies has some resemblance to Amelia (p. 510) while Amelia closely guards a pair of his gloves in a secret drawer (p. 782). The whole set of relationships is secretive, voyeuristic, parasitic – neurotically familial. In this minimal but disseminated labyrinth of mirrors desire is ever excited and ever denied, its objects always displaced, lost at the very moment they are found, ever elsewhere, circling on an empty place. It is this above all that guarantees that the system will reproduce itself: at the end it is not Amelia that Dobbin loves most, but his daughter, and there is a certain irony in noting that Dobbin's predicament as he embarks upon his *History of the Punjab* – caught between a child-bride and a beloved daughter – is very similar to that of Thackeray when he embarked upon *Vanity Fair*.

Thackeray's closing note is properly sombre:

> Ah! Vanitas Vanitatum! which of us is happy in this world? Which of us has his desire? or, having it, is satisfied? – Come children, let us shut up the box and the puppets, for our play is played out.

Yet, for Thackeray, *Vanity Fair* was a great triumph and, as he would have put it, 'it made him'. Perhaps we should here recall the impish conclusion of the drawing of George Osborne's death – 'Bony runnin-away like anythink'. Bony looks a little like Thackeray and the pose is rampant. Escape, then, is possible – but how does one cope with exile?

6

Dickens: the commodification of the novelist

In May 1846, when he began *Dombey and Son*, Dickens's career as a writer was at something of a crisis point. Sales of *Martin Chuzzlewit* and his *American Notes* had been disappointing, he had rowed and broken with his publishers, Chapman and Hall, and his flirtation with newspaper publication, with the *Daily News*, had resulted in little less than a shambles. If he was to retain – even regain – his position as England's pre-eminent and most popular novelist, and satisfy his new publishers, Bradbury and Evans, into the bargain, it was imperative that his next book be an unqualified success.

It is a notorious fact, then, that *Dombey and Son* was, as we would say today, 'hyped':

> The publishers conducted an extensive advertising campaign. By 29 August they had printed 160,000 demy 8vo bills; within three weeks another 60,000 rolled off the presses. On 5 September, 5000 double royal posting bills were prepared, and in October two more printings doubled the total; in December a third printing sported green ink. In Exeter, Edinburgh, Glasgow, Coventry,

Bath, and London, bill stickers posted the broadside announce-
ments of Mr. Dickens's new work, while salesmen eagerly distributed 300 cards announcing the terms for advertising, and 3,000
red and black show cards with specially designed and engraved
lettering.[1]

Moreover we know that Dickens set about the planning and overall
organization of *Dombey and Son* with a ruthlessness and determination unprecedented with his previous works. Everything was designed
for maximum effect. The very title, itself to be kept a closely guarded
secret prior to publication, is arch with contrivance: *Dealings with the
Firm of Dombey and Son, Wholesale, Retail, and for Export.* Most
obviously the title prepares the ground for the great *coup* of the novel,
the death of little Paul and Miss Tox's stunned outburst 'that Dombey
and Son should be a Daughter after all!' (p. 298). But, possibly more to
the point, the title manifests a significant ambiguity: the 'Dealings . . .
Wholesale, Retail and for Export' are not so much the narrative theme
of the novel as the marketing machinery that was to make *Dombey and
Son* a best-seller on both sides of the Atlantic.

For a success it was. On 11 October 1846,[2] Dickens could write to
Forster: 'The Dombey success is BRILLIANT!' There had been a first
run of 25,000 copies which was supplemented by two further runs of
5000 and 2000 more copies and subsequent numbers never fell short of
30,000. Thackeray's outburst after reading the number depicting the
death of Paul is well known but it still conveys as well as anything the
sheer sensation that *Dombey* created:

> There's no writing against such power as this – One has no
> chance! Read that chapter describing young Paul's death: it is
> unsurpassable – it is stupendous.[3]

And the financial reward for Dickens was in due proportion, his profit
from the book amounting to just over nine thousand pounds. So that
R. L. Patten can write:

> These sums 'were so much in excess of what had been expected
> from the new publishing arrangements,' Forster reports, 'that
> from this date all embarrassments connected with money were
> brought to a close.'[4]

In short, it was not so much a matter of Dickens having 'made' *Dombey
and Son* as *Dombey and Son* having 'made' Dickens.

Now this is a thesis – 'that it is not so much authors who create their works as works which create their authors' – that has already been propounded with respect to *Dombey and Son* by Gabriel Pearson. Pearson writes:

> *Dombey* becomes Dickens's first 'real' novel, in the sense claimed for it by its critics, partly because that is the project it sets itself.[5]

> *Dombey and Son*, I would argue, is precisely a work designed to create its author.[6]

Moreover, Pearson goes on to suggest that

> In creating *Dombey*, he [Dickens] partly created himself as Dombey, the linear, purposive, selfish architect of a unique destiny. . . . It requires Dombey-like powers to engineer so purposive a construct, the autonomy of the object corresponding to the autonomous self that designed it.[7]

At the same time, however, this massive act of self-management and self-promotion – of self-control, even – must have entailed a certain cost. For Pearson, at one level, this is to be found figured in the death of little Paul:

> In little Paul . . . he [Dickens] acknowledges a cost – the death of that innocent, childish spontaneity which was the well head of his own common humanity.[8]

while, at a more general level, the cost is what Pearson characterizes as 'the communal identity of Boz':[9]

> With *Dombey*, Dickens ceased definitively to be Boz, the old, popular 'Inimitable', with Boz's peculiar showman's gusto, his ringside intimacy, his mountebank's creative mendacity.[10]

For Pearson, then, with *Dombey* a 'division of labour entered into the marrow of the writing process',[11] a division 'between the professional craftsman and his more capacious and public identity as mime, manipulator and performer'.[12]

As far as it goes I am substantially in agreement with Pearson's argument. Where I would differ, however, is essentially on two points. In both cases it may be no more than a matter of emphasis but it seems to me that that change in emphasis is all-important. The first is concerned with the *seriousness* of the division in Dickens that takes place with the production and self-production of *Dombey and Son*: in my opinion that division is much more radical and traumatic than Pearson gives us to believe. The second is concerned with just *what* was lost with the abandonment of 'Boz': again, for me, it is something much more important than what is suggested by the rather dismissive allusions to Boz's 'showman's gusto, his ringside intimacy, his mountebank's creative mendacity'.

That Dickens was suffering from almost intolerable mental distress at the time of writing the first few numbers of *Dombey* is testified to over and over again in his letters to Forster from Switzerland. The distress seems – and seemed to Dickens – to stem very much from the absence of streets and crowds:

> The absence of any accessible streets continues to worry me, now that I have so much to do, in a most singular manner. It is quite a little mental phenomenon. I should not walk in them in the daytime, if they were here, I dare say: but at night I want them beyond description. I don't seem to be able to get rid of my spectres unless I can lose them in crowds. (20 September 1846)

and the principal symptom of this distress is a very bad *head*:

> There are no streets and crowds of people here to divert the attention. My head suffers. And that is unusual, as you know, with me. (25 September 1846)

The references to a 'bad head', to 'headaches', to 'a damaged head' occur again and again. On 23 October he mentions again

> still occasional giddiness and headaches, attributable, I have not the least doubt, to the absence of streets.

It is this juxtapositioning of a 'damaged head' and crowded streets as, in some ways, its antidote that I would like to consider more closely. It is a juxtapositioning of 'mental distress' and a nomadic, fretful wandering, of mental anguish and a frenzied mobility, of intense psychological stress and the dispersal of self in the anonymity and volatility of the crowd.

We are going to have problems with terminology throughout what follows and I feel already burdened with distinctions – such as 'head/streets' and its correlatives such as 'inside/outside', 'internal/external' – that are at once facile and ungainly. Part of the problem is that these distinctions are so 'pat', so untroublesome. It is the patness of such distinctions – between 'professional craftsman' and 'public identity', or between 'purposive, selfish architect' and 'innocent, childish spontaneity' – that makes me dissatisfied with Pearson's essay. In a way such 'distinctions' run so easily in harness, form part of a readily recognized paradigm, are discursively at ease with each other. Clearly there are philosophical and epistemological questions at stake here but perhaps we can be satisfied for the moment in noting the ideological cosiness of these distinctions between 'public' and 'private', between 'head' and 'streets', between 'inside' and 'outside': they clearly inform and underwrite, as it were, historically specific notions of property, identity and status. The problem is in thinking *outside* the distinction between 'inside/outside', or of conceiving of an 'identity' that is neither private nor public, neither in the head nor in the streets, and yet is both, or the one because the other – intensely personal because intensely public, highly individual because dispersed, autonomous because residual.

Part of my concern here is the extent to which *Dombey and Son* so readily lends itself to a reading in terms of 'inside' and 'outside', between the 'personal' and the 'public', between the 'domestic' and the 'wider commercial world'. Raymond Williams, for example, points out that much of the tension of the novel hinges on what we are to understand by a 'House'[13] – the trading House or the house as a 'home'. We learn from Butt and Tillotson, moreover, that this struggle between the 'public' and the 'domestic' can be traced in the very plans that Dickens drew up before committing himself to his final project. In the cover design Dickens planned with Hablot K. Browne all the interest seems to be focused on the *public* career of Dombey while, in a long letter written to Forster at about the same time the emphasis is almost exclusively on the domestic drama of Dombey's relationship with first young Paul and then with Florence, and his, Dombey's, 'struggle with himself'. What the Forster letter shows, conclude Butt and Tillotson, is that

> The novel is thus to be a new departure for Dickens – a novel founded upon a relationship, and upon a character's inner conflict.[14]

As the novel progresses, of course, it is the personal drama that increasingly predominates; so much so, in fact, that the firm of

Dombey and Son becomes less and less a viable business venture than a psychological allegory wherein the 'good' and 'bad' Carkers, Morfin and Walter become figures of 'good' and 'bad' conscience, probity and promise, respectively. Everything has reverted to the 'Head' – be that understood, narratively, as Dombey's paranoia or, structurally, the psychological register we have just described. Perhaps we can understand now just how implicated in this scheme is the suffering of young Paul, narrated as it is – and Dickens was proud of this – *from inside*: he is less that that has been sacrificed than the very principle of this new determination to see things *from within*. It is not a question of a division between a 'purposive selfishness' and 'childish spontaneity': the death of 'childish spontaneity' in *Dombey and Son* is the most contrived moment in all of Dickens and was, as we have seen, a tremendous boost to sales.

Before we go any further I think it might be as well to issue a caution as to the level at which I hope to conduct the following argument. The kind of shift I have just described – from public to private, from the commercial to the domestic – is very much a *thematic* shift which it requires very little ingenuity to discover. What concerns me more is that this more overt shift has more serious implications at the level of the writing itself which are far less easy to describe but the effects of which are far more serious and far-reaching.

In a way I think that the deeper crisis that I wish to draw attention to is, oddly but, perhaps, not surprisingly, to be found indicated in what is probably the most unlikely and unconvincing relationship in the novel, that between an 'interpolation' and a 'permanency', between Toots and Susan Nipper. Toots, we know, did not figure in the original plans of the novel and was a late addition to what Dickens termed his 'stock' whereas, from the beginning, Susan Nipper was regarded as being of great importance. Dickens writes in a letter to Forster:

> I rely very much on Susan Nipper grown up, and acting partly as Florence's maid, and partly as a kind of companion to her, for a strong character throughout the book. I also rely on Toodles, and on Polly, who, like everybody else, will be found to have gone over to his daughter and become attached to her. (26 July 1846)

Toots, we learn, is the 'head boy' at Blimber's Academy and his title is tragically ironic for poor Toots's head – a large one – has been 'blown' by the Blimbers' hothouse regime. If there is a 'damaged head' in

Dombey and Son it is that of Toots and I would want to argue that it is with Toots that Dickens could in some ways relieve himself by comic sublimation of some of the distress he felt in his swollen head in Geneva. Moreover Toots's endless correspondence with himself, not to mention the self-reference of his name: To – oT, might well bear some allusion to Dickens's own self-scrutiny and introspection at the time of writing *Dombey*. Toots is as close – but for one exception to which I shall refer in a moment – to a mental block as it is possible to imagine.

Susan Nipper is Toots's diametrical opposite, a principle of in-exhaustible energy and initiative, of resource and incisiveness. In place of Toots's tongue-tied 'How d'ye do? . . . I'm very well, thank you; how are you?' (p. 321)[15] we have the Nipper's comma-only improvisations of proverbial saws and street-wise directness. She has, that is, a language of her own ungoverned by any alien restraint, asyntactical and agrammatical, and it is she alone who is prepared to take on Dombey face to face, to square up, that is, to the frigidity that so holds everyone else in thrall. The 'unnatural' conjunction of Toots and Nipper is the 'yoking forcibly together' of the polar forces of the novel, of a head become numb by the pressures within it and an energy and volubility – an articulateness – that are potentially anarchic.

What encourages me to insist on the peculiar importance of this relationship between Toots and Nipper is that it is redoubled in the novel by another unlikely relationship (the word relationship is hardly satisfactory as I hope to make clear later): the farcical marriage of Bunsby and Mrs MacStinger. I did say earlier that Toots was as close – but for one exception – to a mental block as could be imagined: the exception, of course, is the sagacious Bunsby who has 'took as many bars and bolts about the outside of his head when he was young as you'd want a order for on Chatham-yard to build a pleasure yacht with' (p. 411). Bunsby, like Toots, suffers from a severely damaged head and while Toots is merely tongue-tied Bunsby simply swallows his words, like a head eating itself – a *Bun*-sby. It is this extraordinary creature that Mrs MacStinger manages to net as a suitable spouse and 'father' for her children. And Mrs MacStinger, in her way, is as formidable as Susan Nipper, a daunting antagonist and endowed with seemingly inexhaustible energy – as her house cleaning testifies.

But what Nipper and MacStinger figure, not only in the parts they play in the story, but in their very names, are an energy that marks – nips and stings – and reproduces itself, that threatens and exceeds everywhere and on all sides the damaged cerebralism which is the theme and condition of existence of the novel as a whole. The recurring headaches and the longing for streets and crowds which promise relief that we find in the letters to Forster are symptoms of a far more serious crisis than has generally been recognized – a schizophrenic division between the head that thinks – and thinks until it can no longer think – and a quantum of energy that is mobile, popular and anarchic.

II

We have seen earlier how much mental distress Dickens suffered at the time of the composition of *Dombey*. Part of that distress, however, was not related to *Dombey* or, at least, only indirectly so. It was caused by the great trouble Dickens was finding in producing his 'Christmas' book for 1846, *The Battle of Life*. Forster relates this episode at length for he seemed to find it a peculiarly exemplary illustration of the way in which Dickens worked. Forster writes:

> I might grudge the space thus given to one of the least important of his books but that the illustration goes farther than the little tale it refers to, and is a picture of him in his moods of writing, with their weakness as well as strength upon him, of a perfect truth and applicability to every period of his life.[16]

I think we should try to understand what makes this little book so peculiarly exemplary for Forster. The title itself is sufficiently ominous: *The Battle of Life* clearly suggests some kind of acute crisis of consciousness.

The story is trivial enough: it concerns the love of two sisters, Marion and Grace, for the same man, Alfred Heathfield. Marion, the younger sister, who at the beginning of the story is about to be married to Heathfield, senses that her older sister loves Alfred at least as well as she does and that Alfred, albeit as yet unconsciously, reciprocates that love. Marion therefore decides to sacrifice her own happiness to that of her sister and runs away. After a proper interval Alfred does, in fact, marry Grace and it is only when this marriage is satisfactorily concluded that Marion returns to explain her motives for running away and become reconciled to her family.

Steven Marcus[17] suggests that much of the 'disproportionate agony' suffered by Dickens while writing this novel was due to an increasing sense of frustration, emotional and sexual, in Dickens's private life at this time and that with the names 'Marion' and 'Grace' Dickens is beginning to play what Marcus calls his 'alphabet game' – that is the use of names with first letters offering a clue as to the 'original' on whom the character is modelled. The best example is David Copperfield whose reversed initials yield the first letters of Charles Dickens. For Marcus 'there can be little doubt' that the names 'Marion' and 'Grace' 'elaborate some fantasy about Dickens's relation to his wife's two sisters, Mary and Georgina (Hogarth)'.[18] What Marcus is arguing, in effect, is that in *The Battle of Life* Dickens 'is trying to have it all ways; he possesses all the sisters now'.[19] That is, by allowing Heathfield to marry Grace while retaining the devotion of Marion (even in her long absence) while Dickens himself is married to Catherine, Dickens can fantastically possess all the sisters at once – even the tragically dead Mary whose death, in the story, is translated into a willing self-sacrifice.

I am not fully convinced that Marcus has properly located where the distress comes from; or, maybe he has located an aspect of it – the fantastical possession of all the sisters – but misinterpreted what this 'possession' really meant.

While Dickens was writing *The Battle of Life* and, for that matter, the early parts of *Dombey*, in Geneva in October 1846, a brief revolution took place there of which Dickens himself was an extremely interested observer. Shortly afterwards, writing to Forster about his difficulties with *The Battle of Life*, we find him describing his distress as follows:

> I dreamed all last week that the *Battle of Life* was a series of chambers impossible to be got to rights or to be got out of, through which I wandered drearily all night. On Saturday night I don't think I slept an hour. I was perpetually roaming through the story, and endeavouring to dove-tail the revolution here into the plot. The mental distress, quite horrible. (20 October 1846)

What is clear from this is that the crisis, whatever it is, cannot be contained, as Marcus attempts to do, within a familial context, that of Dickens and the three Hogarth sisters. The 'mental distress' embraces, is plugged into, a much wider social and political context, one here that concerns directly the movements of crowds and revolutionary disturbance. In the manically exuberant letter of 11 October – in which he

refers to the *Dombey* success and in which he moots for the first time
the idea of giving public readings – Dickens gives a spirited account of
the revolution and declares that his 'sympathy is all with the radicals'.
Compared with this euphoric 'high' is it not possible that the return to
the familial context, even when it affords fantastical gratifications –
indeed, *because* it can only afford fantastical gratifications – is itself a
source of distress? In other words, the permutation of the Hogarth
sisters is less a fantastical consolation than that very 'series of chambers
impossible to be got to rights or to be got out of' he refers to in his
letter, his prison not his escape.

For all his recognition of the distress *The Battle of Life* caused
Dickens, Marcus does not seem to take the book too seriously, seeing it
as 'no more than a day dream'.[20] 'And', he adds,

> for all the value it offers as a work of literature one might as well
> read *The Battle of Life* backwards.[21]

If, in fact, we take Marcus's advice we find ourselves in for a shock
for we find ourselves moving backwards from the intra-familial gratifications of the alphabet game to a primal scene that knows no persons
nor inter-personal relations but only supra-personal aggregates and
sub-personal composites, the primal scene of a battle and its attendant
carnage:

> Once upon a time, it matters little when, and in stalwart England,
> it matters little where, a fierce battle was fought. It was fought
> upon a long summer day when the waving grass was green. Many
> a wild flower formed by the Almighty Hand to be a perfumed
> goblet of dew, felt its enamelled cup fill high with blood that day,
> and shrinking dropped. Many an insect deriving its delicate colour
> from harmless leaves and herbs, was stained anew that day by
> dying men, and marked its frightened way with an unnatural
> track. The painted butterfly took blood into the air upon the edges
> of its wings. The stream ran red. The trodden ground became a
> quagmire, whence, from sullen pools collected in the prints of
> human feet and horses' hoofs, the one prevailing hue still lowered
> and glimmered at the sun. (pp. 135–6)[22]

Dickens then goes on to relate how the fields were subsequently
worked through the centuries and traces of the battle became less and
less visible:

But there were deep green patches in the growing corn at first, that people looked at awfully. Year after year they reappeared; and it was known that underneath those fertile spots, heaps of men and horses lay buried, indiscriminately, enriching the ground. The husbandmen who ploughed those places, shrunk from the great worms abounding there; and the sheaves they yielded, were, for many a long year, called the Battle Sheaves, and set apart; and no one ever knew a Battle sheaf to be among the last load at a Harvest Home. (pp. 137–8)

And this is a *Christmas* story! One cannot imagine it adding much relish to the mince pies and Christmas pudding.

Seriously, though, is there not something strange about a piece of writing like this at the beginning of a *Christmas* book? Something is being ploughed up here – that's exactly what the passages are saying – but it is something larval, writhing, contagious, composite – NOT fantastical gratifications with a series of sisters, not even a perverse necrophilia for the dead Mary. Here there are no molar identities, familial or otherwise, just the schizoid fear of the dissolution of identity into molecular and aggregative compoundings of the alive and the dead, the organic and inorganic, the human and the inhuman. Here is the *battle of life* not in the silly little alphabet game but in the nightmare fear that one is many and multiple, aggregative and dispersed, connected but scattered. It is the same fear that we have seen haunting *Dombey* between the head that thinks – and thinks of fantastical consolations that only become a prison – and a state of being that is molecular, fluid, migratory; a state that is both a nightmare and a terrible hope.

III

There is yet another text associated with this extremely critical period of Dickens's life. This is the 'Autobiographical Fragment' given to Forster in 1849, much of the material of which was subsequently incorporated into *David Copperfield* and then into Forster's *Life*. The version I shall use will be that supplied by Forster as I will be drawing on some other material concerning Dickens's childhood that figures in the *Life*.

The 'Autobiographical Fragment' is a notoriously difficult document to interpret for there seems to me to hover around it a peculiarly insinuating air of deceit. It will be one of the objects of what follows to trace the source whence that uneasy feeling comes. For the moment we might just mention some of our original reasons for suspicion. In the first place it seems to me to be just too opportune, coming, as it does, at just this moment in Dickens's career when he is so much concerned to constitute himself as a major author. Nor do I believe in its celebrated 'secrecy', all that 'hush, hush' with which Dickens so contrived to surround it – that it contained material too painful to mention to his wife, for example: not only was Dickens well aware, as was Forster, that in supplying the material to the latter he was making sure that it would be included in the biography that had already been planned[23] but the incorporation of almost all the same material in a barely disguised form in *David Copperfield* makes a nonsense of his avowed fear of revelation. Indeed such is the frequency with which the experiences recounted in the 'Fragment' are returned to again and again in the various works – in essays as well as novels – that the whole 'Warrens' Blacking' episode is as much flaunted as it is repressed.

Secondly we need to remind ourselves – as does Steven Marcus to whose reading of this document we will turn in a moment – that the 'Fragment' 'was written by the greatest *comic* genius who ever lived'.[24] It was written, that is, by a consummate master of the art of pulling his audience's leg and one, moreover, who is concerned most of all at this particular moment of his career with promoting and decently packaging himself. It's not very likely that he is going to give too much away.

Thirdly, the whole thing, to me, is just too well done, too professional if you like. Forster writes of the 'Fragment' that it

> present[s] to us a picture of tragical suffering, and of tender as well as humorous fancy, unsurpassed in even the wonders of his published writings.[25]

I think that's the point: Dickens is in the business of surpassing himself (and everybody else) yet again. So much of the 'Fragment' reads like a skit on what is to become that popular middle-class pastime of proving one's working-class roots ('Crusts? we had to make do with croissants!'). Again and again the whole thing teeters on the edge of a mawkish self-pitying self-indulgence. One can sense the damp-eyed self-beholding of the following:

> I know my father to be as kind hearted and generous a man as ever lived in the world. Everything I can remember of his conduct to

his wife, or children, or friends, in sickness or affliction, is beyond all praise. By me, as a sick child, he has watched night and day, unweariedly and patiently, many nights and days. He never undertook any business, charge or trust that he did not zealously, conscientiously, punctually, honourably discharge. His industry has always been untiring. He was proud of me, in his way, and had a great admiration of the comic singing. But, in the ease of his temper, and the straitness of his means, he appeared to have utterly lost at this time the idea of educating me at all, and to have utterly put from him the notion that I had any claim on him in that regard, whatever. So I degenerated into cleaning his boots of a morning, and my own; and making myself useful in the work of the little house; and looking after my younger brothers and sisters (we were now six in all); and going on such poor errands as arose out of our poor way of living.[26]

or, again:

It is wonderful to me how I could have been so easily cast away at such an age. It is wonderful to me that, even after my descent into the poor little drudge I had been since we came to London, no one had compassion enough on me – a child of singular abilities: quick, eager, delicate, and soon hurt, bodily or mentally – to suggest that something might have been spared, as certainly it might have been, to place me at any common school. Our friends, I take it, were tired out. No one made any sign. My father and mother were quite satisfied. They could hardly have been more so, if I had been twenty years of age, distinguished at a grammar-school, and going to Cambridge.[27]

and, again, a little later:

No words can express the secret agony of my soul as I sunk into this companionship; compared these everyday associates with those of my happier childhood; and felt my early hopes of growing up to be a learned and distinguished man crushed in my breast. The deep remembrance of the sense I had of being utterly neglected and hopeless; of the shame I felt in my position; of the misery it was to my young heart to believe that, day by day, what I had learned, and thought, and delighted in, and raised my fancy and emulation up by, was passing away from me, never to be brought back any more; cannot be written. My whole nature was so penetrated with the grief and humiliation of such considerations, that even now, famous and caressed and happy, I often forget in my dreams that I have a dear wife and children; even that I am a man; and wander desolately back to that time of my life.[28]

and, finally:

From that hour until this at which I write, no word of that part of my childhood which I have now gladly brought to a close, has passed my lips to any human being. I have no idea how long it lasted; whether for a year, or much more, or less. From that hour, until this, my father and mother have been stricken dumb upon it. I have never heard the least allusion to it, however far off and remote, from either of them. I have never, until I now impart it to this paper, in any burst of confidence with anyone, my own wife not excepted, raised the curtain I then dropped, thank God.[29]

I must say that I find the almost universal credence given to this tale of woe quite extraordinary. What on earth does all the suffering amount to? That at nearly 12 years of age the young Dickens has been 'reduced' to cleaning his father's – and his own!!! – boots of a morning? that he has been asked to help look after his brothers and sisters and run errands? and that for *just 'four months, five at the most'*[30] he has been given a job in a small factory producing boot-blacking at a salary of six or seven shillings a week – not a bad salary for a child at this period? What Dickens seems to be complaining most about – and it really is the height of unreasonableness – is that his poor harassed and pressed parents didn't realize that it was not just their nearly teenage son that they had to do with but the great popular novelist Charly Dickens. It's a bit like that Jarry joke of the skull of the child Voltaire.

No, it won't do. There is something going on in all this and it is painful but it is like Mrs Gradgrind's pain, somewhere in the room but not here. Where, then, is the charge coming from?

The most ingenious and persuasive attempt to trace the source of this charge, at least as far as I am aware of, is that of Steven Marcus in his appendix, 'Who is Fagin?', to his *Dickens: from Pickwick to Dombey*. Marcus begins by considering the excessively casual way in which Dickens mentions where he had got the name 'Fagin' from. In the 'Fragment' Dickens recounts his first day at Warrens':

> My work was to cover the pots of paste-blacking: first with a piece of oil-paper, and then with a piece of blue paper; to tie them round with string; and then to clip the paper close and neat all round, until it looked as smart as a pot of ointment from an apothecary's shop. When a certain number of grosses had attained this pitch of perfection, I was to paste on each a printed label; and then go on again with more pots. Two or three other boys were kept at similar duty downstairs on similar wages. One of them came up, in a ragged apron and a paper cap, on the first Monday morning, to show me the trick of using the string and tying the knot. His name was Bob Fagin; and I took the liberty of using his name, long afterwards, in *Oliver Twist*.[31]

Marcus comments:

> So casual and off-hand a revelation of what must by nature be a highly charged fact is itself evidence of the high charge.[32]

I think we can probably go along with Marcus in this observation but it is worth pausing just a moment to note the risk in this strategy: that that which is casually mentioned is that which is highly charged, the least significant is an index of the most significant. Given this tactic why should we take Dickens at his word elsewhere in the 'Fragment' when he claims that when he witnessed his sister receiving a prize at the Royal Academy of Music 'there was no envy in this'.[33] Could not the disavowal be the index of a seething rage? We will have occasion to recall this later.

Let's leave that for a moment and trace Marcus's argument a little further. What Marcus establishes by means of something like a simple structural analysis is that while Bob Fagin was extremely kind to the young Dickens whereas Fagin himself is a terrible threat to the young Oliver, the feelings excited by both figures share something of the same 'attraction of repulsion' – a phrase of some considerable importance in Dickens, as we shall see. Bob's kindness to Dickens is attractive but that kindness threatens Dickens with a certain loss of status, a putting of him on a level which is rather lower socially than that which he felt to be his due. Fagin, of course, is a threat to little Oliver but, nevertheless, he is the first person to have ever shown the child any kindness, and even manages to make him laugh.

Marcus argues the parallels rather more fully than I have suggested here but I think I have said enough to convey the gist of his argument.

Still, even Marcus does not think these parallels are sufficient to explain the charge around the figure of Bob Fagin or the even greater intensity of fascination and horror associated with Fagin in the novel. At this point Marcus begins a different tack by considering that brief episode which seems to have brought Dickens's sojourn in the blacking factory to an end. When Warrens' moved to new premises such was the skill of Bob Fagin and Dickens in tying up the blacking pots that they were set to work in the shop-window and their briskness and dexterity often attracted quite a little crowd of onlookers. On one occasion, Dickens writes:

> I saw my father coming in at the door . . . and I wondered how he could bear it.[34]

Shortly afterwards Dickens is taken away from Warrens' and he thinks 'it may have had some backward reference . . . to my employment in the window'.[35]

What attracts Marcus about this brief incident is the association of exposure and being spied upon and being 'caught in the act' by his father. Returning to *Oliver Twist* Marcus then compares this episode with two rather odd moments in the novel when Oliver is in a kind of 'hypnogogic state', somewhere between sleeping and waking. The first is when, but half awake, he sees Fagin gloating over his hoarded treasures and is caught by the latter and threatened with a knife (pp. 106–8).[36] The second is when, albeit asleep in the relative security of the Maylies' house, Oliver senses the malign, watching presence of Monks and Fagin (pp. 309–11). The pattern of seeing and being seen, of exposure and threat, suggests to Marcus that the shop-window scene in the 'Fragment' is a 'screen memory' for an earlier, more infantile, scene of seeing/being-seen/seen-seeing involving the very young child and his parents. It is here that the horrific murder of Nancy by Sykes – Sykes haunted by the memory of Nancy's eyes and then by the eyes of the crowd – furnishes Marcus with the last bit of his little exercise in psychoanalysis: for what the murder 'represents' is the buried infantile memory of the child seeing his parents making love for, as Marcus remarks:

> In the mind of a very small child, we know, sexual intercourse is first apprehended as a form of violence, specifically of murder, inflicted by the male on the female.[37]

As further corroboration of Dickens's morbid fascination with this 'primal scene' Marcus goes on to cite the fact that when, towards the end of his life, Dickens engaged in public readings of episodes from his work it was the scene of Sykes's murder of Nancy that became an obsession with him, so much so that the nervous energy expended on it was largely responsible for his death.

Now we know where the charge that informs the 'Autobiographical Fragment' comes from. The off-hand connection established by Dickens between Bob Fagin and Fagin, the highly ambiguous feelings aroused by these two figures, and the patterns of fascination and violence, of exposure and threat, all stem from what Marcus takes to be 'the master theme of Dickens's novels',[38] 'his relation to his father'. It is a complex compounded of a sense of betrayal and unrequited love, of exposure and the threat of castration, of identity and alienation, of rivalry and terror. In a word: the Oedipus complex.

Now this is all very well but after quite properly saying that there is no such thing as a 'key'[39] for a great artist it seems to me that Marcus has got very close to supplying us with one – 'his relation to his father . . . the master theme of Dickens's novels'. Such a reduction to the familial and oedipal of the massive complexity and heterogeneity of Dickens's work is surely impoverishing, to say the least – though we have seen Marcus operating a similar reduction in his analysis of the anguish surrounding *The Battle of Life*. But what concerns me now is that even with regard to the 'Autobiographical Fragment' which is at the heart of Marcus's thesis it is wilfully perverse for at least two related and complementary reasons. The first is that what the 'Fragment' seems to show almost in spite of itself is the extraordinary casualness of the relations between Dickens and his parents. I know it is the burden of the 'Fragment' that poor little Dickens was hard done by but that is from an ideological vantage point – that of the notion of the exceptional and exclusive intimacy and intensity of familial relationships – that Dickens was very largely responsible for constructing, indeed, it is the argument of this chapter, is in the process of constructing. Through Dickens's whining self-pity it is quite clear that his parents hardly had time to give him a second thought and probably wouldn't have done so if they had had the time. The second, related and complementary, reason why Marcus's thesis is perverse is that his oedipal/familial reduction refuses to see just how *crowded* is the extra-familial and intra-familial environment in which the young

Dickens lives and thrives. The 'Autobiographical Fragment' itself is crammed with incidents and events and persons and things that impinge far more directly and immediately on Dickens than his family does. If we expand our catchment area to include, for example, the other incidents of Dickens's young life recounted by Forster or garnered by Christopher Hibbert in his *The Making of Charles Dickens*,[40] what must astound us is the sheer crowdedness of his existence in the context of which familial determinations shrink into insignificance. There was James Lamert, for example, the son of a Dr Lamert who had married Dickens's mother's sister whose first husband had died in Rio de Janeiro. It was James Lamert, a Sandhurst cadet, who first wakened Dickens's passion for the theatre and it was a cousin of this same James who found Dickens the job in the blacking factory.[41] Or there was the extraordinary influence of Mary Weller, Dickens's nurse, whose weird and macabre stories haunted him all his life. In London Dickens visited his mother's elder brother and his godfather, a rigger, and mast, oar and block maker at Limehouse who was reported to have an Indian connection.[42] And the 'Fragment' itself is studded with visits to pawnbrokers, second-hand bookshops, restaurants and public houses.

Perhaps the way in which the 'Autobiographical Fragment' consistently spills out of the familial framework is in no way better indicated than in recalling that Dickens's 'home' at the period which the 'Fragment' is describing was none other than the Marshalsea Prison where his father was held for debt. What inhabit the prison are not families but collectivities, conglomerates, non-familial and a-familial groupings. Even the familial is unfamilial: witness Captain Porter upstairs, from whom Dickens borrows a knife and fork:

> I knew (God knows how) that the two girls with the shock heads were Captain Porter's natural children, and that the dirty lady was not carried to Captain P.[43]

and one of Dickens's happiest memories of the prison is having witnessed all the prisoners lining up to sign a petition asking for permission to be allowed to drink to His Majesty's forthcoming birthday:

> Their different peculiarities of dress, of face, of gait, of manner, were written indelibly upon my memory. I would rather have seen it than the best play ever played; and I thought about it afterwards, over the pots of paste-blacking.[44]

The fascination and the connections are again not with discrete individuals or with the familial group but with heterogeneous series, unpredictable aggregations, crowds and migrant collectivities.[45]

But Dickens's experience of London as it is recorded in the 'Fragment' is not just of collectivities and multiplicities of persons that exceed the family – important enough as it is to recognize that. It is also an experience of objects and miscellanies, of textures and surfaces, of smells and detritus. The 'Fragment' is pungent with the smell of saveloys and bread-pudding, cabbage leaves and hat-making cement, of coffee and blacking. The most unlikely combinations and conjugations attract his attention – 'the Fat Pig, the Wild Indian, and the Little Lady'.[46] It is the sheer swarming of the streets that seduces him, that constitutes that 'profound attraction of repulsion'[47] that Marcus appropriates to describe his relationship with *persons* and, it follows from his analysis, to his *father*. It is that grotesque reduction to the familial, to daddy, mummy and poor little me, the oedipal fix, that needs to be called into question.[48]

At almost every moment Dickens's childhood seems to have been invested and entranced by those fractures and disjunctions, those conglomerates and multiplicities that spill over and wash round and stream through the oedipal scene.

Take the two extra-familial agents we have mentioned earlier, James Lamert and Mary Weller. James, as we noted, introduced Dickens to the theatre and its wonders 'of which not the least terrific', Dickens recalls,

> were, that the witches in *Macbeth* bore an awful resemblance to the thanes and other proper inhabitants of Scotland; and that the good King Duncan couldn't rest in his grave, but was constantly coming out of it and calling himself somebody else.[49]

Fractures, that is, of identity, status and vital state, disturbingly schizoid. And what are we to make of Mary Weller's story of 'Chips', a shipwright, who sold his soul to the Devil, part payment for which was a rat that could speak and which Chips couldn't kill and which swore to stick to him like pitch:

> Soon the rat was joined by other rats that filled Chips's pockets and got into his pocket and into the sleeves of his coat. And they could all speak to one another, and he understood what they said. And they got into his lodging, and into his bed, and into his teapot, and

into his beer, and into his boots. And he was going to be married to a corn-chandler's daughter; and when he gave her a workbox he had himself made for her, a rat jumped out of it; and when he put his arm round her waist a rat clung about him, so the marriage was broken off.[50]

And that's not the end of the story. But again it is the swarm, the furtive, migrant multiplicity, that gnaws at identity and prevents conjugal couplings. This nightmare looks forward, of course, to the delirium tremens of the dying clown in *Pickwick*. But this apprehension of swarming intensities, of migrating and shifting and haphazard identities, need not always entail paranoiac phobias as here, for elsewhere the assembling and parading of large anonymous aggregates can create elation and a sense of impregnable sovereignty – the excitement, for example, recaptured early in *Pickwick*, of

> the gay bright regiments always going and coming, the continual paradings and firings, the successions of sham-sieges and sham-defences[51]

that were to be witnessed at Chatham.

The child at play blithely transcends the familial context, travelling widely in time and space, implicated in history and politics, permutating identities and places, objects and persons, each and all a delicious heap of indifferent partial-objects at his capricious disposal:

> It was in the boys' playing-ground near Clover Lane in which the school stood that, according to youthful memories, he had been, in the hay-making time, delivered from the dungeons of Seringapatam, an immense pile ('of haycock'), by his countrymen, the victorious British ('boy next door and his two cousins') and had been recognised with ecstacy by his affianced one ('Miss Green'), who had come all the way from England ('second house in the terrace'), to ransom and marry him. It was in this playing-field, too, as he himself has recorded, he first heard in confidence from one whose father was greatly connected, 'being under Government,' of the existence of terrible banditti called *the radicals*, whose principles were that the prince regent wore stays; that nobody had a right to a salary; and that the army and navy ought to be put down.[52]

I think it is time that we gave ourselves some help and called a halt to this ungainly expression 'the young Dickens'. There was no 'young Dickens' – at least no 'young Dickens' such as the forlorn creature concocted for us by the 'Autobiographical Fragment'. There were only sham-sieges and sham-defences, regiments coming and going, continual paradings and firings, congregations and migrations of rats, duplications and reduplications of roles, Tom Jones and Roderick Random, Captain Somebody of the Royal British Navy, the victorious British and terrible banditti. The 'young Dickens' was himself a crowd opening upon and invested by other crowds, a composite whose identity was constituted by a radical dispersal.[53]

It is this coextension of the composite that is the 'individual' with the multiplicities that are its environment and the eclectic, haphazard, appropriations and disappropriations between the one and the other that needs to be understood, not the forlorn neurotic drama of the oedipal triangle. What the threnodic descant of the 'Autobiographical Fragment' seeks to drown out is a marvellous clatter of collisions and engagements and feints and purchases between an endlessly mobile and flexible consciousness and an environment that is itself alarmingly alive and volatile. There is no inside/outside here but a ceaseless exchange of doffings and castings between the aggregate subject and the circumambient context. It is the marvellous mode of the pilgrim crab which at one and the same time makes an environment of itself and makes a self of its environment. It is the primal mode of display, where one becomes discrete by simulation, original by copying.

I think we are now in a better position to understand where the hysterical charge of the 'Autobiographical Fragment' comes from though it will give us a completely different reading from that of Marcus.

What the 'Autobiographical Fragment' offers us first and foremost is, in every sense of the term, a *relation*. That is, it is a narrative – a relation – which constructs a relation: Dickens's relation with his parents.[54] Thus, what Dickens achieves in the relation that is the 'Fragment' is the production of a fitting childhood for the man who is to be Dickens the author. It is a brilliantly fictive achievement, the construction – indeed appropriation – of the myth of the boyhood trials of the unrecognized genius. It is the retrospective construction of an eminently marketable identity – the extent to which this relation has been 'bought' is evidence enough for that. But what that relation has also achieved is the massive reduction of all those multifarious and heterogeneous determinants – those crowds, those collectives, those dispersals – that, indeed, made him what he was, to a narrowly delimited familial drama, to a triangle of love and hate and rivalry, which so easily lends itself to an oedipal reading. The whole aggregate of social, economic and political determinations that made Dickens what he was has been reduced to the family scene, and the outrage and protest against an unjust society that informs so much of Dickens's early work can now be understood as deriving from the 'master theme' of his novels, 'his relation to his father'. It is the classic oedipal ploy:

> It is in one and the same movement that the repressive social production is replaced by the repressing family, and that the latter offers a displaced image of desiring production that represents the repressed as incestuous familial drives.[55]

I think it is worth recalling that this is precisely the pattern of *The Battle of Life*: the collapse of the outrage and horror of battle and its attendant carnage and its substitution by quasi-incestuous fantastical gratification and guilt. Trapped in Oedipus the pain is there – recall now Mrs Gradgrind – but in the wrong place.

It is only by refusing to be seduced by the oedipal trap, the allure of the relation, that we are able to see that the 'Autobiographical Fragment' recounts also what the reduction is at the expense of. For what the 'Fragment' narrates is the collapse of a marvellous capacity for *display*, for 'showing off', for mimicry – that pilgrim-crab delight of doffing and donning a whole repertoire of identities and roles the prime thrill of which is *being seen* but not *labelled*. We should perhaps recall here that the young Dickens, that is the Dickens of the 'Boz' period, was a notorious *flâneur*. The traumatic experience of the blacking factory had less to do with the fear of a loss of caste than the bitter forging of a specific, no longer mobile identity. The whole narrative posture of the 'Fragment' – that of Dickens seeing himself seeing himself – is the forlorn and unconvincing surrogate for the loss of the glory of being the object of a universal gaze. It is this wistfulness derived from a terrible self-deception that gives the 'Fragment' its lack of conviction, its sense of effecting some kind of 'sleight of hand'.[56] It is here, I think, that we must locate that source of unease that the 'Fragment' evokes and to which I referred earlier.

What is remarkable is that the 'Autobiographical Fragment' tells us exactly what is going on without any need for interpretation or analysis at all. The glory of display has given way to labelling blacking pots. The facility for mimicry and the nomadic capacity for establishing heterogeneous and eclectic connections – all that that Pearson's pithy but inadequate characterization of as 'Boz's peculiar showman's gusto, his ringside intimacy, his mountebank's creative mendacity' refers to – has become reduced to a small, carefully marshalled and distributed, supply of ink.[57]

What the 'Autobiographical Fragment' narrates then is the painful transition from the nomadic buz of Boz to the labelled identity of Dickens. The experience of the blacking factory is a shrewd allegorization of the reduction of a brilliant talent for display to the marketable status of a commodity. The blacking pots, bound and labelled to look like the aseptic products of an apothecary's shop, are no more and no less than an image of Dickens's own reduction of himself to authorship and his work to a commodity.

Now, once that decision has been made, once one has become labelled, what haunts one is the fear of a return of that heterogeneity that one has reneged upon, the unfixing of identity and the flux of difference. Dickens talks of that fear:

> My whole nature was so penetrated with the grief and humiliation . . . that even now, famous and caressed and happy, I often forget in my dreams that I have a dear wife and children; even that I am a man; and wander desolately back to that time of my life.[58]

But is Dickens, and are we, sure as to exactly what this fear really is? Is it not, precisely as he says, the fear of forgetting that he has a 'dear wife and children; even that [he is] a man'? The fear, that is, of falling back into that undifferentiated state that escapes designations of 'husband, man, child' because it exceeds them on all sides?[59]

I think we can now return to the fear provoked in the young Dickens by Bob Fagin and in young Oliver by Fagin. When Dickens is ill in the blacking factory Bob Fagin takes care of him:

> Bob Fagin was very good to me on the occasion of a bad attack of my old disorder. I suffered such excruciating pain that time, that they made me a temporary bed of straw in my old recess in the counting house, and I rolled about on the floor, and Bob filled empty blacking bottles with hot water, and applied relays of them to my side half the day.[60]

We have to imagine and *feel* the scene: the small passive body with the relays of warm bottles distributed around it – like so many leeches – or rats? – or phalluses? The body without organs feeling a myriad intensities crossing and recrossing it, annihilating boundaries, scorning determinations, relay after relay – the return of regiments and rats, sieges and defences. The return, in other words, of all that threatens labels and identities.

This, too, is the appalling threat of Fagin. Consider the game that Fagin plays with the boys. He distributes around himself a motley collection of objects – a snuff box, a watch, a guard chain, a mock diamond pin, a spectacle case and a handkerchief and little Oliver laughs as the members of the gang bump against him and knock into him and rifle his pockets. It is like the mass rape of a proliferation of small vaginas scattered about a helpless body. It is, again, the nightmare that the body is not a molar whole but a series of discrete orifices, open on many sides, a molecular, volatile conglomerate.

This is the 'master theme' of Dickens's work, the motor of his manic-depressive genius. The titanic and never resolved struggle between, on the one hand, a profound awareness of the diabolical and transcendent allure of manifold intensities, while on the other, the determination to hold fast to a hardly constructed heroic identity, between a potentially schizoid longing for flight and a paranoiac clinging to a fragile ego, between Boz and Dickens.

If my reading of the 'Autobiographical Fragment' is correct then what we have in the 'Fragment' is a paradigmatic illustration of the simultaneous reduction of literature to the status of a commodity and the emergence of a familial complex that will shortly be labelled as oedipal. For Deleuze and Guattari the two go hand in hand:

The Oedipal form of literature is its commodity form.[61]

In our case we can see that Dickens at one and the same time 'relates' himself to his parents – crushing the heterogeneity and splendour of Boz into a familial triangle – and reconstitutes the author as commodity.

We cannot leave discussion of the 'Autobiographical Fragment', however, without addressing, albeit briefly, the last two pieces of 'evidence' that Steven Marcus appeals to to support his reading. The first concerns the watching/being-watched couples which Marcus so swiftly identifies with the parents making love. Firstly it surely has to be remarked that in the crowded petty-bourgeois household in which so many Victorian children were brought up and to which the Dickens's household was no exception the chances of a child seeing his or her parents making love must have been more than considerable. Indeed it would have been more remarkable if Dickens had never seen his parents making love.

But another point needs to be made. For all the fulsome outpouring of the 'Autobiographical Fragment' Dickens remains curiously silent on the very incident that is supposed to have triggered it off. This is Forster's reporting to Dickens that he had been seen in the blacking factory by Charles Dilke and had been given a half-crown by the latter for which he, Dickens, had returned a 'very low bow'.[62] It is the same incident that closes the 'Fragment' – though it is not made very clear. Dickens records that his father had rowed with Lamert and he supposes that 'it may have had some backward reference, in part, for anything I know, to my employment in the window.'[63] I don't want to pursue this farther than the evidence allows but I do feel that Dickens's reticence and obliqueness here is very intriguing. In fact it seems at times that Dickens concocted the whole 'Autobiographical Fragment' for no other purpose than to divert attention from that incident with Dilke, the memory of which clearly unsettled him when Forster first broached it. If we are to locate an embarrassment at being discovered by a watching couple then it seems to me that the scene in the window at the blacking factory, given that it is so avoided, might have had much more traumatic associations – of exposure and violation – than has hitherto been supposed.

The final piece of corroborative evidence used by Marcus for his interpretation is Dickens's late obsession with Sykes's murder of Nancy. About this I would like to make the following two points. The first is that Dickens did not perform a public reading of 'Sykes and Nancy' until his very *last* programme was arranged in 1869 and it was performed only 28 times in all – compared with 164 times for 'Pickwick' and 127 times for the 'Carol'. It is true that once it had been introduced into his repertoire it exercised a particular fascination for him. But – and this is the second point I want to make – was the obsession with 'Sykes and Nancy' due to a fixation on some primal scene of his parents' making love? For what I want to suggest is that the obsession with Sykes and Nancy is an obsession with that dreadful hybrid that hovers between the aggregative consciousness of the group

and the neurotic identifications of the family – the *couple*. The
obsession with the 'couple', therefore, is less due to the failure to
exorcise a troubled memory than to the bewilderment at finding
oneself in a fatal impasse. The 'couple' is not something we are trying
to escape from but something we arrive at; the 'couple' comes not at the
beginning but at the end. The 'couple' is essentially the result of a
dreadful and fateful hesitation between the anarchic appeal of the
group and the cosy proprieties of the legitimate family, between
rhizomic flight and structured restraint. It is a struggle, I suppose, that
most of us have known and Dickens's peculiar preoccupation with it
differs only in its public intensity. On his way to the platform, the last
time he performed 'Sykes and Nancy', Dickens whispered to a friend: 'I
shall tear myself to pieces.'[64] That promise, or threat, or maybe just an
observation, perhaps more than anything reveals the principal motor
of the 'Sykes/Nancy' performance: the desperate, forlorn, impossible
attempt to dash the couple and all coupling – be that understood
however one wishes – into a myriad scattered fragments.

IV

I think it is time now that we looked a little more closely at what exactly
was lost in the abandonment of Boz's 'showman's gusto, his ringside
intimacy, his mountebank's creative mendacity'. To do this, and to
gauge more accurately the shift from 'Boz' to 'Dombey', it might be
helpful to look at a number of those passages in the *Sketches* that can be
most conveniently compared with similar passages in *Dombey*. I have
in mind, for example, the essays on 'Brokers and Marine-Store Shops'
and on 'The Pawnbroker's Shop' that might be illuminatingly brought
alongside the descriptions of The Little Midshipman and Brogley's
brokerage in the novel.

In the essay on 'Brokers and Marine-Store Shops' Dickens begins by
saying that by 'Brokers' he does not have in mind prestigious warehouses with 'long perspectives of French-polished dining tables', etc.,
nor, for that matter, the 'posher' second-hand shops catering to the
pretensions of an aspirant petite-bourgeoisie with such execrable
hybrids as 'sofa-bedsteads'. No, what he has in mind are other, far
inferior establishments:

> Our readers must often have observed in some by-street, in a poor
> neighbourhood, a small dirty shop, exposing for sale the most

extraordinary and confused jumble of old, worn-out, wretched articles, that can well be imagined. (p. 178)[65]

and he goes on to list some random examples, concluding:

Although the same heterogeneous mixture will be found in all these places, it is curious to observe how truly and accurately some of the minor articles which are exposed for sale – articles of wearing apparel, for instance – mark the character of the neighbourhood. Take Drury Lane and Covent Garden for example. (p. 179)

– which he then does, showing how these poor pawnshops reveal the theatrical activities of this particular neighbourhood. Next he turns to some

marine-store dealer's, in that reservoir of dirt, drunkenness and drabs; thieves, oysters, baked potatoes, and pickled salmon – Ratcliff Highway (p. 180)

which is a naval area. After listing some of the typical contents of these 'marine-brokers' he makes the following concluding point:

A sailor generally pawns or sells all he has before he has been long ashore, and if he does not, some favoured companion saves him the trouble. In either case, it is an even chance that he afterwards unconsciously repurchases the same things at a higher price than he gave for them at first. (p. 180)

Finally, Dickens turns to the last example of these poor brokers' shops:

Again: pay a visit with a similar object, to a part of London, as unlike both of these as they are to each other. Cross over to the Surrey side, and look at such shops of this description as are to be found near the King's Bench prison, and in 'the Rules'. How different, and how strikingly illustrative of the decay of some unfortunate residents in this part of the metropolis! Imprisonment and neglect have done their work. There is contamination in the profligate denizens of a debtor's prison; old friends have fallen off; the recollection of former prosperity has passed away; and with it all thoughts of the past, all care for the future. First watches and rings, then cloaks, coats, and all the more expensive articles of dress, have found their way to the pawnbroker's. That miserable resource has failed at last, and the sale of some trifling article at one of these shops has been the only mode left of raising a shilling or two, to meet the urgent demands of the moment. Dressing-cases and writing desks, too old to pawn but too good to keep; guns, fishing-rods, musical instruments, all in the same condition; have first been sold, and the sacrifice has been but slightly felt. But hunger must be allayed, and what has already become a habit is easily resorted to when an emergency arises. Light articles of clothing, first of the ruined man, then of his wife, at last of their children, even of the youngest, have been parted with, piecemeal. There they are, thrown carelessly together until a purchaser presents himself, old, patched and repaired, it is true; but the make and the materials tell of better days; and the older they are, the greater the misery and destitution of those whom they once adorned. (pp. 180–1)

In turning to the second essay, 'The Pawnbroker's Shop', I will try to make my quotations briefer, though it is difficult to do so and still make all the points that I wish to make. There is, again, a long description of the heterogeneity of the objects to be found in these places which concludes with a kind of 'zoom' effect or of multi-perspective collage of 'foreground' and 'background' which I think is worth recording:

An extensive collection of planes, chisels, saws, and other carpenters' tools, which have been pledged and never redeemed, form the foreground of the picture; while the large frames full of ticketed bundles, which are dimly seen through the dirty casement up-stairs – the squalid neighbourhood – the adjoining houses, straggling, shrunken, and rotten, with one or two filthy, unwholesome-looking heads, thrust out of every window, and old red pans and stunted plants exposed on the tottering parapets, to the manifest hazard of the heads of the passers-by – the noisy men loitering under the archway at the corner of the court, or about the gin-shop next door – and their wives patiently standing on the curbstone, with large baskets of cheap vegetables slung round them for sale, are its immediate auxiliaries. (pp. 189–90)

Within the shop Dickens (Boz) depicts three small 'scenes'. The first is of a woman hurrying to do a deal:

'Now, Mr. Henry, do make haste, there's a good soul, for my two grandchildren's locked up at home, and I'm afeer'd of the fire.' (p. 190)

The second concerns a half-drunken, wife-beating lout trying to redeem his tools for a job the money for which he has already spent and the railing he is subject to from a number of the women in the group:

> 'What do you strike the boy for, you brute?' exclaims a slipshod woman, with two flat irons in a little basket. 'Do you think he's your wife, you willin?' 'Go and hang yourself!' replies the gentleman addressed, with a drunken look of savage stupidity, aiming at the same time a blow at the woman which fortunately misses its object. 'Go and hang yourself; and wait till I come and cut you down.' – 'Cut you down,' rejoins the woman, 'I wish I had the cutting of you up, you wagabond! (loud). Oh! you precious wagabon! (rather louder.) Where's your wife, you willin? (louder still; women of this class are always sympathetic, and work themselves into a tremendous passion on the shortest notice.) Your poor dear wife as you uses worser nor a dog – strike a woman – you a man! (very shrill;) I wish I had you – I'd murder you, I would, if I died for it!' (p. 192)

The third looks at three other groups of women: a young girl with her mother trying to make a deal for the first time; the second a case-hardened prostitute and the third an old woman – 'the lowest of the low; dirty, unbonneted, flaunting, and slovenly' – who looks on. And Dickens (Boz) concludes:

> Who shall say how soon these women may change places? The last has but two more stages – the hospital and the grave. How many females situated as her two companions are, and as she may have been once, have terminated the same wretched course, in the same wretched manner! One is already tracing her foosteps with frightful rapidity. How soon may the other follow her example! How many have done the same! (p. 195)

Let us now look at the two passages from *Dombey and Son.* The first is the description of the stock of The Little Midshipman – that being a kind of marine-broker's store:

The stock in trade of this old gentleman comprised chronometers, barometers, telescopes, compasses, charts, maps, sextants, quadrants, and specimens of every kind of instrument used in the working of a ship's course or the keeping of a ship's reckoning, or the prosecuting of a ship's discoveries. Objects in brass and glass were in his drawers and on his shelves, which none but the initiated could have found the top of, or guessed the use of, or having once examined, could ever have got back again into their mahogany nests without assistance. Everything was jammed into the tightest cases, fitted into the narrowest corners, fenced up against the most impertinent cushions, and screwed into the acutest angles, to prevent its philosophical composure from being disturbed by the rolling of the sea. (p. 88)

The second is the description of Brogley's shop:

There lived in those days, round the corner – in Bishopsgate Street Without – one Brogley, sworn broker and appraiser, who kept a shop where every description of second-hand furniture was exhibited in the most uncomfortable aspect, and under circumstances and in combinations the most completely foreign to its purpose. Dozens of chairs hooked onto washing stands, which with difficulty poised themselves on the shoulders of sideboards, which in their turn stood upon the wrong side of dining-tables, gymnastic with their legs upward on the tops of other dining-tables, were among its most reasonable arrangements. A banquet array of dishcovers, wine-glasses, and decanters was generally to be seen, spread forth upon the bosom of a four-post bedstead, for the entertainment of such genial company as half-a-dozen pokers, and a hall lamp. A set of window curtains with no windows belonging to them, would be seen gracefully draping a barricade of chests of drawers, loaded with little jars from chemists' shops; while a homeless hearthrug severed from its natural companion the fireside, braved the shrewd east wind in its adversity, and trembled in melancholy accord with the shrill complainings of a cabinet piano, wasting away, a string a day, and faintly resounding to the noises of the street in its jangling and distracted brain. Of motionless clocks that never stirred a finger, and seemed as incapable of being successfully wound up, as the pecuniary affairs of their former owners, there was always great choice in Mr.

Brogley's shop; and various looking glasses, accidentally placed at compound interest of reflection and refraction, presented to the eye an eternal perspective of bankruptcy and ruin. (pp. 176–7)

Now, of course context is important and both The Little Midshipman and Brogley's shop have to be considered within the structure of *Dombey and Son* as a whole. And it can be argued that, in the description of Brogley's shop, for example, where objects have lost all trace of their use value and have assumed instead purely arbitrary exchange relationships of self-referentiality – relationships of 'compound interest of reflection and refraction' – Dickens is making a very serious point. This commodification and quantification of social and economic relationships – indeed of all relationships – is one of the principal themes of *Dombey and Son*. Nevertheless what bothers me is that some of the archness of this passage – gymnastic tables and decanters entertaining pokers – seems to me much more like a 'showman's gusto' and a 'mountebank's creative mendacity' than can be found in the passages quoted from the *Sketches*. There is some risk that the creative brio might detract from the essentially serious point that is being made. Put another way, the fetishization and commodification has entered into the very language itself. Moreover, in the description of Sol's stock, a similar process of commodification and fetishization can already be seen to be taking place. There again the objects have lost all use value and assumed no more than a mere curio value for would-be collectors. There is a strong sense that the whole collection of instruments has become insulated and cocooned, muffled and displaced by their packaging, cases and wrappings. This is all the more serious when we realize how often the 'Sol' and 'Little Midshipman' theme is regarded as representing 'good' values opposed to 'bad' 'Dombey' values – all that fatuous opposing of 'dry' values by 'wet' values, 'linear' time by 'cyclic' time, etc. It's only when one stops to think for a moment just how characteristic of capitalism is cyclic time – indeed it *is* capitalist time: the 'cycle of investment, commodity production, profit, reinvestment' – that we realize just how inane is this Dombey/Gills opposition.

If we now return to the passages from the *Sketches* what must surely strike us at once is their essential seriousness, their uncanny attention to detail, their controlled purposefulness. The *Sketches* convey strongly the sense of a real economy – albeit a local one – with real variety and real, specific, histories. The locales are categorized according to professional and occupational interests and the objects depicted are marked with use and history. Moreover the people in these scenes are not just victims of their condition but are capable of reacting against it – as is the case with the women who turn on the drunken labourer in the pawnshop. Dickens lacks – indeed never aspires to – the statistical precision or investigative procedures of Henry Mayhew's later work for the *Morning Chronicle* but there seems to me to be implicitly present in these *Sketches* something like the notion of a 'sub-culture' – though not formulated as such by either Dickens or Mayhew – which Eileen Yeo has claimed to have been the major discovery of the latter.[66]

But it is not simply a matter of subject matter. It is also a question of style, of a mode of writing which in turn raises questions bearing on tone, focus, authority and on structures of time, location and identity. It might help if we looked at one more passage from the *Sketches*, from the essay on 'Seven Dials' which, as we know from the 'Autobiographical Fragment', was a part of London that had a peculiar fascination for Dickens:

> The peculiar character of these streets, and the close resemblance each one bears to its neighbour, by no means tends to decrease the bewilderment in which the unexperienced wayfarer through 'the Dials' finds himself involved. He traverses streets of dirty, straggling houses, with now and then an unexpected court, composed of buildings as ill-proportioned and deformed as the half-naked children that wallow in the kennels. If the external appearance of the houses, or a glance at their inhabitants, presents but few attractions, a closer acquaintance with either is little likely to alter one's first impression. Every room has its separate tenant, and every tenant is, by the same mysterious dispensation which causes a country curate to 'increase and multiply' most marvellously, generally the head of a numerous family.
>
> The man in the shop, perhaps, is in the baked 'jemmy' line, or the fire-wood and hearth-stone line, or any other line which requires a floating capital of eighteen pence or thereabouts: and he and his family live in the shop, and the small back parlour behind it. Then there is an Irish labourer and *his* family in the back kitchen, and a jobbing man – carpet beater and so forth – with *his* family in the front one. In the front one-pair, there's another man

with another wife and family, and in the back one-pair, there's 'a young 'oman as takes in tambour-work, and dresses quite genteel,' who talks a good deal about 'my friend' and can't 'a-bear anything low.' The second floor front, and the rest of the lodgers, are just a second edition of the people below, except a shabby-genteel man in the back attic, who has his half-pint of coffee every morning from the coffee-shop next door but one, which boasts a little front den called a coffee-room, with a fire-place, over which is an inscription, politely requesting that, 'to prevent mistakes,' customers will 'please pay on delivery.' The shabby-genteel man is an object of some mystery, but as he leads a life of seclusion, and never was known to buy anything beyond an occasional pen, exept half-pints of coffee, penny loaves, and ha'porths of ink, his fellow-lodgers very naturally suppose him to be an author; and rumours are current in the Dials, that he writes poems for Mr. Warren. (pp. 71–2)

What I think is the most characteristic *stylistic* feature of the *Sketches* is a curious impersonality or transparency of tone: there is very much a sense that the scenes and episodes reveal or display themselves. The most frequent voice is what linguists might be prepared to describe as the 'aorist' – that is a kind of neuter 'fourth person': one, we, 'the unexperienced wayfarer'. True, it falters now and again for it is a most difficult voice to maintain in English. Now and again the moralist stands apart – as at the end of 'The Pawnbroker', asking 'Who shall say how soon these women will change places?' or, as in the 'Seven Dials' piece when we get that rather gratuitous allusion to 'the same mysterious dispensation which causes a country curate to "increase and multiply"'. But, on the whole, it is this curiously anonymous voice that prevails, letting the scenes and the episodes seemingly 'tell' themselves. Coupled with this anonymity is that multi-perspectival collage effect I have mentioned earlier: where each scene seems to be seen simultaneously from different angles and different points of view by a kind of ubiquitous eye scanning rather than simply looking. I think it is also a part of this peculiarly 'degree zero' style – its absence of person and what Jakobson has termed 'shifters', i.e. indices of person, time and space – that time is given a particularly arbitrary status – as when, again at the end of 'The Pawnbroker's' piece, we are invited to contemplate the three women, young, older and old, changing place, a sense of an 'induration' of time rather than 'enduration' or endurance, so that different times become strangely simultaneous, imbricated one in another.

I said earlier that we were going to have problems with terminology and nowhere does this become more apparent than in attempting to characterize the style of these *Sketches*. Even specialist commentators on Dickens's early work seem to be groping ineffectually for a suitable set of critical terms – 'amiable humour', 'pictorial style', 'vivification of character'[67] to describe the peculiarly transparent flexibility of the style of these pieces.

This being the case I think it might be of help to us here – first to help us characterize the *Sketches* more satisfactorily but, more importantly, to enable us to understand more clearly that break between 'Boz' and 'Dickens' with which this essay began – to consider for a moment Deleuze and Guattari's distinction between 'rhizomic' structures and 'tree' structures.[68] And, unorthodox though it may be, perhaps the easiest way to do this is adapt a technique from computer word-processing and 'open up a window' on my Appendix I (pp. 236–7) where I discuss this very distinction.

For Deleuze and Guattari rhizomic structures are hardly structures at all: they resist totalizations. Instead they are essentially conglomerates and aggregates of molecular heterogeneous multiplicities whose relationships with each other are poly- and multivalent, arbitrary and volatile, provisional and unstable. What the rhizome dispenses with and outflanks are molar, that is totalized, identities and unities. The rhizome is nomadic and multiple rather than sedentary and fixed. It is the tribe versus the state, 'Go' as opposed to 'chess', the pack as opposed to the individual, the negotiation of borders rather than the focusing of centres. For Deleuze and Guattari what meet are not molar individuals but heterogeneous clusters and each cluster will be a composite of molecular inconsistencies, pieces of this and pieces of that, vegetable and animal, mineral and organic, alive and dead. So that between clusters all sorts of permutations and combinations may take place or may not take place, connections and disconnections, feints and parries, assaults and repulses, and so on. For Deleuze and Guattari we are all such clusters: we are not molar individuals with separate identities but congeries of partial objects and molecular intensities all of which are capable of multiple imbrications with other similar, albeit different,

congeries, groups, composites. The 'individual' is an arbitrary construct on a field of intensities, like a biscuit shape on a field of pastry.
The field extends far beyond the individual and meets up with other
fields – what Deleuze and Guattari call 'plateaux' or 'planes' – of
consistency with which it overlaps, merges with, slips under. In this
sense the shimmering field that is 'me' flows far beyond me and makes
all sorts of breaks and connections with the many other fields that
surround it – with the office, the kitchen, the street – all these not so
much designations of places as of affective spaces. We are plugged in,
then, to the world around us by all manner of cables and currents. Here
there are no 'mediations', just a complexity of connections and disconnections. This is how love works – through multiple connections and
disconnections – and also how power works: political repression works
not through 'ideology' or 'mediations' but through pot-holes in the
street, through queues, through dirty and unpunctual trains, through
baton charges and tapped telephones. We are all 'tapped': clipped onto
and drained.

Less needs to be said about 'tree' structures for it is with a whole
arborescent culture that we are too sadly familiar. So many disciplines,
from biology to linguistics, are structured on trees:

> It is curious how the tree has dominated Western reality, and all of
> Western thought, from botany to biology and anatomy, and also
> gnosticism, theology, ontology, all of philosophy . . .

The 'tree' is that hierarchical organization of separate and individual
entities which is best illustrated by the genealogical 'tree': it arranges
and distributes molar figures in fixed locations that are the co-ordinates
of power and domination. The tree allocates designations of gender,
descent and vital state and is allied to and underwrites the despotic
power of the state. It is all this that the notion of the rhizome threatens:
the rhizome is anti-genealogical and anarchic, essentially subversive
and revolutionary.

With these distinctions in mind I think we are now in a better position to
understand the peculiar fascination and radical thrust of the *Sketches*.

Take the description of the house in the passage from 'Seven Dials':
it is not presented as a coherent totality but as an aggregate of locales – a
bit like a register in a computer and which, like a register, can be quickly
loaded and unloaded with endlessly permutated 'bits'. It is, that is,

rhizomic. The occupants are not presented as characters but as a series of instances of a shared and collective condition. What is further to be remarked is that this structure which refuses to be totalized has its own discrete though eccentric modes of categorization: what is the 'baked "jemmy" line'? what is a front one-pair or a back one-pair? These are not so much topographical locations as affective spaces – a bit like the notion of the 'best room' or the 'study': it's amazing how a study, for example, can migrate around a house! Here, as elsewhere in the *Sketches*, we are confronted with distinctions and categorizations that refuse to stay in place, that are essentially volatile, elusive, nomadic.

There is one further point to be made about this passage that is connected with this notion of a molecular, non-totalized space, this absence of privileged individuals or of an all-embracing point of view, and that is the presence within the narrative of the narrator himself. For who else could the 'shabby-genteel man' be, who 'writes poems for Mr. Warren', but Dickens/Boz himself? In other words there is a sense that the narrator is in the same plane as the narration itself, a display within a display, his idiosyncracies – 'half-pints of coffee, penny loaves, and ha'porths of ink' – part and particle of the mêlée which he describes but by which he is embraced and seen.[69]

V

What I am arguing is that what was lost by the shift from Boz to Dickens, if I may put it that way, was far more than a 'mountebank's creative mendacity' or even what can be more generously glossed as a 'communal identity'. It was much more the loss of a mode of seeing and writing which in its 'shifterless' or rhizomic flexibility could thread the complexities of an urban environment in a way that the later more strictly 'authorial' style could not. What gives this 'aoristic' style its impact is its preconceptionless ability to register an environment and be registered within that environment. What we have is not so much a 'communal identity' which invokes all sorts of jolly cosiness as a 'collective' or 'aggregate' consciousness which is nomadic rather than privileged, dispersed rather than stable. To a certain extent the *Sketches* show the potential of this style only in embryo and probably Dickens, as much as Gabriel Pearson, is right in sensing their short-comings. The point I wish to make is that their shortcomings are not that they do not yet show the narrative or structural skills of the 'mature' works – which is a kind of teleological fallacy and, besides, it is precisely what is gained by 'narrative' and 'structure' that I wish to question here – but that they do not yet fully achieve what they might have achieved if they had themselves been developed. Some clue as to what might have been achieved is perhaps to be found in the description of Jacob's Island towards the end of *Oliver Twist* and which reminds us, in many ways, of the kind of writing we have met in the *Sketches*:

To reach this place, the visitor has to penetrate through a maze of close, narrow, and muddy streets, thronged by the roughest and poorest of waterside people, and devoted to the traffic they may be supposed to occasion. The cheapest and least delicate provisions are heaped in the shops; the coarsest and commonest articles of wearing apparel dangle at the saleman's door, and stream from the house-parapet and windows. Jostling with unemployed labourers of the lowest class, ballast-heavers, coal-whippers, brazen women, ragged children, and the raff and refuse of the river, he makes his way with difficulty along, and assailed by offensive sights and smells from the narrow alleys which branch off on the right and left, and deafened by the clash of ponderous wagons that bear great piles of merchandise from the stacks of warehouses that rise from every corner. Arriving, at length, in streets remoter and less-frequented than those through which he has passed, he walks beneath tottering house-fronts projecting over the pavement, dismantled walls that seem to totter as he passes, chimneys half crushed, half hesitating to fall, windows guarded by rusty iron bars that time and dirt have almost eaten away, every imaginable sign of desolation and neglect. In such a neighbourhood, beyond Dockhead in the Borough of Southwark, stands Jacob's Island, surrounded by a muddy ditch, six or eight feet deep and fifteen or twenty wide when the tide is in, once called Mill Pond, but known in the days of this story as Folly Ditch. It is a creek or inlet from the Thames, and can always be filled at high water by opening the sluices at the Lead Mills from which it took its old name. At such times, a stranger, looking from one of the wooden bridges thrown across it at Mill Lane, will see the inhabitants of the houses on either side lowering from their back doors and windows, buckets, pails, domestic utensils of all kinds, in which to haul the water up; and when his eye is turned from these operations to the houses themselves, his utmost astonishment will be excited by the scene before him. Crazy wooden galleries common to the backs of half a dozen houses, with holes from which to look upon the slime beneath; windows, broken and patched, with poles thrust out, on which to dry the linen that is never there; rooms so small, so filthy, so confined, that the air would seem too tainted even for the dirt and squalor which they shelter; wooden chambers thrusting themselves out above the mud, and threatening to fall into it – as some have done; dirt-besmeared walls, decaying foundations; every repulsive lineament of poverty, every loathsome indication of filth, rot, and garbage; – all these ornament the banks of Folly Ditch.

Here is the same 'aorist' voice of the *Sketches* – 'the visitor', 'a stranger' – and the quick shifting of points of view together with the sense that the scenes themselves 'excite' the attention. But it is also a very *strong* piece of writing: there is the density of detail in the first paragraph that conveys the sense of a specific and complex local economy: there is also the concise historical contextualization – from Mill Pond to Folly Ditch – how much is conveyed by that! There is the sheer horror in the casual mention that the ditch can be filled at high water by opening the sluices at the Lead Mills. And so it goes on: the water drawn for drinking from a veritable pool of excrement and the final bitter irony of the notion of the fact that all this squalor 'ornament(s) the banks of Folly Ditch'.

I have suggested earlier that some of the *Sketches* might be regarded in some ways as anticipating the more strictly sociological studies of Mayhew. This is not to suggest that Dickens 'should' have been a social scientist rather than a novelist. The comparison was rather to suggest that in the *Sketches* Dickens/Boz was developing a style of writing which has a power and potentiality to *move* us, to implicate us, catch us up, as it were. With a power of mobilization, that is, that is potentially explosive. It seems to me now, for example, that the above extract from *Oliver Twist* is much better – not just as 'literature' but as 'social science' even, than Mayhew's own – 'famous' according to E. P. Thompson[70] – account of Jacob's Island:

We then journeyed on to London-street, down which the tidal ditch continues its course. In No. 1 of this street the cholera first appeared seventeen years ago, and spread up it with fearful virulence; but this year it appeared at the opposite end, and ran down it with equal severity. As we passed along the reeking banks of the sewer the sun shone on the narrow slip of water. In the bright light it appeared the colour of strong green tea, and positively looked as solid as black marble in the shadow – indeed it was more like watery mud than muddy water; and yet we were assured this was the only water the wretched inhabitants had to drink. As we gazed in horror at it, we saw the drains and sewers emptying their filthy contents into it; we saw a whole tier of doorless privies in the open road, common to men and women, built over it; we heard bucket after bucket of filth splash into it, and the limbs of the vagrant boys bathing in it seemed by pure force of contrast, white as Parian marble.[71]

What weakens this, it seems to me, is precisely that reportage stance of the observing eye which is so missing from the *Sketches*: 'We then journeyed . . . we passed . . . it appeared . . . we gazed . . . we saw . . . we heard' – that is the mediation of the scene by a subjective, authorial, point of view. And the intrusive comparison of the 'vagrant boys' with 'Parian marble' at the end is simply grotesque. What I am arguing, in short, is that the mode of writing of the *Sketches*, of Boz, has a power and radical energy that is due above all to its stylistic flexibility, its mobility of point of view, its 'shifterless' shifts, its aggregative disjunctions, its discrete and dispersed collective register, the rhizomic imbrication of the recorder in the plane of the recorded.

VI

What I want to suggest now is two things. The first is that it is possible to see the whole trajectory of Dickens's career from the *Sketches* onwards as a series of attempts to break with this radically decentred and aggregatively collective, rhizomic, style and espouse instead a more authoritative and collected narrative control. The second thing I want to suggest is that this change, to the extent that it took place, did not necessarily make him a better *writer*. Now I know that this kind of comparing the 'early' and the 'late', or the 'young' and the 'mature' Dickens tends to be rather invidious if not downright silly and I would not do it if I did not think that there was something at stake that was of some importance at least politically and morally if not aesthetically. This having been said there seems to me to be no need to hide the fact that what I am indeed arguing is that 'Boz' was a far better – more original, more varied, more humanly wise, more vitally exciting – writer than was 'Dickens'.

Pickwick, of course, is Dickens's most rhizomic work, a scatter-brained romp around the greater part of southern and eastern England and up and down and along and across the literary register. I don't want to detract from its reputation as a great comic masterpiece but what must strike any reader coming to it for the first time – given the associations that 'Pickwick' evokes – is the extraordinary vein of seriousness that runs through it. The first intercalated story of the dying clown with delirium tremens comes as a great shock and this is only the first of a number of stories dealing with madness and insanity, that is with a threat to the sovereignty of reason and identity. But these stories are not so much aberrations as the obverse side to the manic improvisation and comic inventiveness of the work as a whole. *Pickwick* is a compendium of collective registers and multiplicities and its humour, as well as its seriousness, derives most of all from a delight in incongruities, impossible coincidences, incredible connections and improbable alliances. This rhizomic delight in the collective and the heterogeneous, in multiplicities, rather than in individuals and pro-prieties, is manifest at every level from the stenographic anagram-maticism of Jingle and the street-wise saws of Sam Weller, through the endless proliferation of group activities – parties, picnics, elections, games, the 'Club' itself – to the masterly description of conditions in the Fleet prison:

> It was getting dark; that is to say, a few gas jets were kindled in this place which was never light, by way of compliment to the evening, which had set in outside. As it was rather warm, some of the tenants of the numerous little rooms which opened into the gallery on either hand, had set their doors ajar. Mr. Pickwick peeped into them as he passed along, with great curiosity and interest. Here four or five great hulking fellows, just visible through a cloud of tobacco smoke, were engaged in noisy and riotous conversation over half-emptied pots of beer, or playing at all-fours with a very greasy pack of cards. In the adjoining room, some solitary tenant might be seen, poring, by the light of a feeble tallow candle, over a bundle of soiled and tattered papers, yellow with dust and dropping to pieces from age: writing for the

hundredth time, some lengthened statement of his grievances, for the perusal of some great man whose eyes it would never reach, or whose heart it would never touch. In a third, a man, with his wife and whole crowd of children, might be seen making a scanty bed on the ground, or upon a few chairs, for the younger ones to pass the night in. And in a fourth, and a fifth, and a sixth, and a seventh, all came over again in greater force than before.

In the galleries themselves, and more especially on the staircases, there lingered a great number of people, who came there, some because their rooms were empty and lonesome, others because their rooms were full and hot: the greater part because they were restless and uncomfortable, and not possessed of the secret of exactly knowing what to do with themselves. There were many classes of people here, from the labouring man in his fustian jacket, to the broken down spendthrift in his shawl and dressing-gown, most appropriately out at elbows; but there was the same air about them all – a listless jail-bird careless swagger, a vagabondish who's afraid sort of bearing, which is wholly indescribable in words, but which any man can understand in one moment if he wish, by setting foot in the nearest debtor's prison, and looking at the very first group of people he sees there, with the same interest as Mr. Pickwick did. (pp. 665–6)[72]

This is very much the mode of the *Sketches*: a marvellous registering of a collective predicament, a sense of the seriality of connections, the specificities of micro-histories contingent upon one another, a nomadic tracking along galleries and up and down staircases, conveying so well – albeit that it is 'indescribable in words' – the 'listless jail-bird careless swagger, [the] vagabondish who's afraid sort of bearing'. The whole scene is so packed and crammed: just how many of the later novels, for example, are jammed into this passage?

There are other passages in the book that illustrate this strangely immediate mode of description (the description, for example, of the Temple (pp. 504–5) and of Lant Street (pp. 520–1)) but, sadly I think, *Pickwick* is the last (as well as the first) novel in which this mode is predominant.

The first move away from this collective mode is to be found in the novel that immediately followed upon *Pickwick*. We have already seen, while discussing the 'Autobiographical Fragment' the dangerous cast given to Fagin's fascination for Oliver, the threat he poses of a radical dispersal of identity. In a sense the whole of *Oliver Twist* is Oliver's struggle to establish and maintain a 'proper' way of speaking in the face of the popular slang and clan ideolect used by Fagin's gang and associates. The threat to Oliver is not just that he might become a criminal but that he might become a member of a *group* and in some ways the burden of *Oliver Twist* is to suggest that Fagin, the Dodger, Charlie Bates and the rest are not simply bound into a group by their shared criminality but that because they are a group they are to be criminalized. Albeit delivered with the utmost cynicism Fagin's notion of a 'general number one' admirably encapsulates the essence of group consciousness:

> 'In a little community like ours, my dear,' said Fagin, who felt it necessary to qualify this position, 'we have a general number one; that is, you can't consider yourself as number one, without considering me too as the same, and all the other young people.'
> (p. 387)

The name bestowed on young Oliver, 'Twist', actually enshrines the very project of the novel, to 'twist' into a single thread of identity the aggregate consciousness of the group – that 'group', after all, with its 'Charlie' and 'Dawkins' – its Charles Dickens that is – which is the author's own heterogeneity. And of course, as has been noted many times before, all the energy of *Oliver Twist* is invested in the group compared with which the world of the Maylies and Brownlows is incredibly vapid.

Again, in *Nicholas Nickleby* the great strengths of the book are not to be found in the rather fey and very much blessed stories of Nicholas and his sister with their very unlikely benefactors, the Cheerybles, but in the 'group' episodes. First there is the memorable account of the condition of the pupils at Dotheboys Hall. It is, after all, for this episode that the book is best known and it is some surprise to find how brief it is in the context of the tale as a whole. Here is Nicholas's first glimpse of the poor wretches:

> But the pupils – the young noblemen! How the last faint traces of hope, the remotest glimmering of any good to be derived from his efforts in this den, faded from the mind of Nicholas as he looked in dismay around! Pale and haggard faces, lank and bony figures, children with the countenances of old men, deformities with irons

upon their limbs, boys of stunted growth, and others whose long
meagre legs would hardly bear their stooping bodies, all crowded
on the view together; there were the bleared eye, the hare-lip, the
crooked foot, and every ugliness or distortion that told of unnatural aversion conceived by parents for their offspring, or of young
lives which, from the earliest dawn of infancy, had been one long
endurance of cruelty and neglect. There were little faces which
should have been handsome, darkened with the scowl of sullen,
dogged, suffering; there was childhood with the light of its eye
quenched, its beauty gone, and its helplessness alone remaining.
There were vicious-faced boys, brooding with leaden eyes, like
malefactors in a jail; and there were young creatures on whom the
sins of their frail parents had descended, weeping even for the
mercenary nurses they had known, and lonesome even in their
loneliness. With every kindly sympathy and affection blasted in
its birth, with every young and healthy feeling flogged and
starved down, with every revengeful passion that can fester in
swollen hearts eating its evil way to their core in silence, what an
incipient Hell was breeding here! (pp. 82–3)[73]

The sense of a general condition here is conveyed not by isolating any
particular individual victim but by piling the various symptoms in a
heap, as it were, so that each distress is not the peculiar property of any
one but of the whole, a collective condition not a contingent plight. And
because it is a collective condition redress, when it comes, must be
collective too. When the boys finally turn on the Squeers family they
do so as a group, their solidarity the product of their common
condition. I think this is the real achievement of the passage I have
quoted: that despite the apparent allocation of responsibility to parental neglect – that is to a familial context – what is brought across is that
this is a 'general', and therefore social and mass, condition and for that
reason, indeed, an 'incipient Hell'. It is perhaps the radical energy
generated by this sense of a mass condition that explains the tear-
jerking role of Smike in the novel. What Smike makes possible is the
concentration of the outrage provoked by the account of the exploitation in institutions like Dotheboys Hall on one token individual and
his solitary fate. When, at the end of the novel, by an incredible
amount of not very convincing string-pulling and manipulation,
Smike turns out to be Ralph Nickleby's long-lost son it means that that

radical flow that momentarily escaped familial accountability in the Dotheboys episode is once again firmly inscribed within a father/son relationship, thus no longer a general social condition. The anarchic energy of the rhizome has given way to the genealogical tree.

If the tragic strength of the novel comes from the Dotheboys Hall episode, then its comic strength undoubtedly comes from another trans-individual and trans-familial group or collective: the Crummles travelling troupe of non-stable identities. There is no space here, alas, to quote at length the scene when Nicholas first meets the troupe and marvels at their bizarre ability to assume any number of seemingly incompatible roles (pp. 275–6) but some idea of the sheer exhilaration of this facility can be gained from the following briefer account of a subsequent meeting:

> Here all the people were so much changed, that he scarcely knew them. False hair, false calves, false muscles – they had become different beings. Mr. Lenville was a warrior of blooming propor-tions; Mr. Crummles, his large face shaded by a profusion of black hair, a Highland outlaw of most majestic bearing; one of the old gentlemen a gaoler, and the other a venerable patriarch; the comic countryman, a fighting man of great valour, relieved by a touch of humour; each of the Master Crummles a prince in his own right; and the low-spirited lover, a desponding captive. (p. 284)

The Crummles troupe, that is, is totally anarchic, subversive of all proprieties. They are an essentially molecular, 'crumbly', conglomer-ate. It is part and parcel of their subversive energy that they pay scant respect to copyright – a sore point with Dickens at this period:

> 'Invention! what the devil's that got to do with it!' cried the manager [who has just asked Nicholas to write a new play for the following Monday].
> 'Everything, my dear sir.' [replies Nicholas]
> 'Nothing, my dear sir,' retorted the manager, with evident impatience. 'Do you understand French?'
> 'Perfectly well.'
> 'Very good,' said the manager, opening the table drawer and giving a roll of paper to Nicholas. 'There! Just turn that into English, and put your name on the title-page.' (p. 278)

– and that any 'positively final performance' should take place at least three times (p. 360). Subversive, then, of identity, property and any real regard for time, it is to be lamented that Crummle's troupe can be accommodated, in the end, only abroad – in America.

What seems to be happening, then, in *Oliver Twist* and *Nicholas Nickleby*, is that Dickens is increasingly endeavouring to write the kind of narrative of bourgeois and petty-bourgeois familial romance and in doing so he is, in many ways, losing touch with the more creative and original aspects of his earlier work, with a group sensibility, with a collective register, with an anarchic flair, which is not just a stylistic loss but a political one as well, the loss of a powerfully mobilizing rhetoric – such as the description of Jacob's Island referred to earlier, or the description of Dotheboys Hall found in *Nicholas Nickleby*.

I think it is, in fact, in *Nicholas Nickleby* that the real failure of nerve comes. After the Dotheboys Hall episode the narrative turns for a time to dwell on the fate of Kate Nickleby in London where she gains employment in Madame Mantalini's dressmaking and millinery establishment. Now, it was a notorious fact that these establishments were well known for their abuse of sweated and 'dishonourable' (that is, un-unionized) labour and that so poor were the rates of pay that any poor woman seeking to keep body and soul together, not to mention those of any dependants, was almost bound sooner or later to turn to prostitution. Dickens knew all this: his description of Mantalini's establishment, its showroom, entrance, type of clientèle, hierarchy of employees, even rates of pay (seven shillings a week) are spot on and there is no doubt that he could have provided as powerful an exposé of this trade as he did of Dotheboys Hall.

In the novel, as we have it, however, Dickens cops out. Kate is promoted from the sweatshop to the showroom almost immediately, the Mantalinis are allowed to get away with being simply a farcical husband-and-wife comedy act, and the real threat of prostitution is turned into the totally unconvincing stagy pursuit of Kate by Sir Mulberry Hawke and his 'gull' (the fact that such a term springs to mind is indicative as to how stagy it is) Lord Frederick Verisopht.

The Old Curiosity Shop now seems to me to be, perhaps, the key text for understanding Dickens's early work and the kinds of shift – from 'Boz' to 'Dickens', from the 'collective', 'rhizomic' mode to the 'familial romance', 'tree-structure' mode – that I have been trying to explore.

In looking at *Nicholas Nickleby* I have suggested that the radical potential of the 'Boz' mode, as exemplified in the Dotheboys Hall episode, was, if it had been deployed in exposing the plight of the seamstresses in the Mantalini episodes, in danger of drawing Dickens into a far more radical critique of his society than he could perhaps sustain without alienating his public. The suggestion was, in short, that Dickens lost his nerve.

What I think is happening in *The Old Curiosity Shop* is that the old rhizomic energy still flows but now becoming increasingly subject to censure and frustration and, at the same time, increasingly deployed to purely comic as opposed to comic and critical ends.

Quilp is, perhaps, the finest achievement of the Boz mode and his compressed, concentrated energy and rage indicative of the restraints now placed upon it. It is typical of Quilp that he should be a 'ship-breaker' – an anarchical little modification to the status of a 'ship-broker' – and that he is directly plugged into a whole gamut of economic activity:

> Mr. Quilp could scarcely be said to be of any particular trade or calling, though his pursuits were diversified and his occupations numerous. He collected the rents of whole colonies of filthy streets and alleys by the water side, advancing money to the seamen and petty officers of merchant vessels, had a share in the ventures of divers mates of East Indiamen; smoked his smuggled cigars under the very nose of the Custom House, and made appointments on 'Change with men in glazed hats and round jackets pretty well every day. On the Surrey side of the river was a small rat-infested dreary yard called 'Quilp's Wharf', in which were a little wooden counting-house burrowing all awry in the dust as if it had fallen from the clouds and ploughed into the ground; a few fragments of rusty anchors; several large iron rings; some piles of rotten wood; two or three heaps of old sheet copper, crumpled, cracked and battered. On Quilp's Wharf, Daniel Quilp was a ship-breaker, yet to judge from these appearances he must have been a ship breaker on a very small scale, or have broken his ships up very small indeed. (pp. 72–3)[74]

or, again, in a passage which seems to me to show, as did the Jacob's Island episode in *Oliver Twist*, some of the potential of the Boz mode:

> It was flood tide when Daniel Quilp sat himself down in the wherry to cross to the opposite shore. A fleet of barges were

coming lazily on, some sideways, some head first, some stern first; all in a wrong-headed, dogged, obstinate way, bumping up against the larger craft, running under the bows of steamboats, getting into every kind of nook and corner where they had no business, and being crunched on all sides like so many walnut-shells; while each with its pair of long sweeps struggling and splashing in the water looked like some lumbering fish in pain. In some of the vessels at anchor all hands were busily engaged in coiling ropes, spreading out sails to dry, taking in or discharging their cargoes; in others no life was visible but two or three tarry boys, and perhaps a barking dog running to and fro upon the deck or scrambling up to look over the side and bark the louder for the view. Coming slowly on through the forest of masts was a great steam ship, beating the water in short impatient strokes with her heavy paddles as though she wanted room to breathe, and advancing in her huge bulk like a sea monster among the minnows of the Thames. On either hand were long black tiers of colliers; between them the vessels slowly working out of harbour with sails glistening in the sun, and creaking noise on board, re-echoed from a hundred quarters. The water and all upon it was in active motion, dancing and buoyant and bubbling up; while the old grey Tower and piles of building on the shore, with many a church-spire shooting up between, looked coldly on, and seemed to disdain their chafing, restless neighbour. (pp. 86–7)

I know that Quilp is constructed as the villain of the piece but his diabolical and mercurial energy is very much the genius of the dark commercial city and dockland areas that Dickens is here describing, and it is fitting that in his death at the end he should merge with it like a long wrack of kelp. But Quill-p too is the very energy of the writing, the manic motor keeping the story going.

If Quilp is Boz concentrated, then Mrs Jarley's wax-works is Boz immobilized. The wax-works shows the reduction of the mobile and nomadic energy of the Crummles troupe to the status of passive automata. The mercurial shifts of personae, the doffing and donning of roles which constitute so much of the relish of the earlier works are still hilariously funny, but they have become mere artifice perpetrated for purely commercial ends:

And these audiences were of a very superior description, including a great many young ladies' boarding schools, whose favour Mrs. Jarley had been at great pains to conciliate, by altering the face and costume of Mr. Grimaldi as clown to represent Mr. Lindley Murray as he appeared when engaged in the composition of his English Grammar, and turning a murderess of great renown into Mrs. Hannah More – both of which likenesses were admitted by Miss Monflathers, who was at the head of the head Boarding and Day Establishment in the town, and who condescended to take a Private View with eight chosen ladies, to be quite startling from their extreme correctness. Mr. Pitt in nightcap and bedgown, and without his boots, represented the poet Cowper with perfect exactness; and Mary Queen of Scots in a dark wig, white shirt-collar, and male attire, was such a complete image of Lord Byron that the young ladies quite screamed when they saw it. (p. 288)

Now what is surprising is that Quilp and Mrs Jarley's wax-works, which, apart, seem like a polarization of the constituent attributes of the rhizomic mode, come together again to threaten Nell in her dreams:

Notwithstanding these protections, she could get none but broken sleep by fits and starts all night, for fear of Quilp, who throughout her uneasy dreams was somehow connected with the wax-work, or was wax-work himself, or was Mrs. Jarley and was wax-work too, or was himself, Mrs. Jarley and a barrel organ all in one, and yet not exactly any of them either. (pp. 278–9)

Quilp indeed was a perpetual nightmare to the child, who was constantly haunted by a vision of his ugly face and stunted figure. She slept, for their better security, in the room where the wax-work figures were, and she never retired to this place at night but she tortured herself – she could not help it – with imagining a resemblance, in some one or other of their death-like faces, to the dwarf, and this fancy would sometimes so gain upon her that she almost believed he had removed the figure and stood within the clothes. Then there were so many of them with their great glassy eyes – and, as they stood one behind the other all about her bed, they looked so like living creatures, and yet so unlike in their grim stillness and silence, that she had a kind of terror of them for their own sakes, and would lie watching their dusky figures until she was obliged to rise and light a candle, or go and sit at the open window and feel the companionship in the bright stars. (pp. 288–9)

Nell's dread is of the terrifying conjunction of demonic energy and dehumanized automata. It is the fear, that is, of those forces and material conditions of existence that Dickens as 'Boz' – in his 'Quilp' mode or his 'wax-works' mode – was peculiarly, if not uniquely, equipped to depict and expose. It is the dread, that is, of the industrial landscape and its spectral slaves, such as are described later in the book:

It needed a strong confidence in this assurance to induce them to enter, and what they saw inside did not diminish their apprehension and alarm. In a large and lofty building, supported by pillars of iron, with great black apertures in the upper walls, open to the external air; echoing to the roof with the beating of hammers and roar of furnaces, mingled with the hissing of red-hot metal plunged in water, and a hundred strange unearthly noises never heard elsewhere; in this gloomy place, moving like demons among the flame and smoke, dimly and fitfully seen, flushed and tormented by the burning fires, and wielding great weapons, a faulty blow from any one of which must have crushed some workman's skull, a number of men laboured like giants. Others reposing upon heaps of coals or ashes with their faces turned to the black vault above, slept or rested from their toil. Others again, opening the white-hot furnace-doors, cast fuel on the flames, which came rushing forth to meet it, and licked it up like oil. Others drew forth, with clashing noise upon the ground, great sheets of glowing steel, emitting an insupportable heat, and a dull deep light like that which reddens in the eyes of savage beasts. (p. 417)

It is too long to quote here but one should also read the long description of the industrial landscape on the Birmingham–Wolverhampton road that Dickens describes later (pp. 423–4) and the account he gives also of the plight of the working men and women and their families, their poverty, abjection and mutinous rage. It is, by far, Dickens's most outspoken indictment of the conditions of industrial squalor and exploitation.

Here is the real threat to Nell – that of severe industrial unrest and revolutionary outrage. This is what the nightmare of Quilp and the wax-works really represents. It is a threat that can be related to social, political and economic conditions but this, in many ways, is precisely what Dickens refuses to do. What he does, instead, is really quite an astonishing stroke of audacity. He transfers the massive charge generated by the social conjuncture and earths it in the seemingly less dangerous context of the family. The jump-lead – it has to be a heavy-duty one for so much energy – is the 'rape' of Nell.

Part of the prurient fascination of *The Old Curiosity Shop* is surely how long it can be before little Nell suffers some kind of sexual assault and the major threat seems to be that offered by Quilp. And yet when the 'rape' does come, it does not come from Quilp at all, but from her momentarily deranged grandfather:

> At last, sleep gradually stole upon her – a broken, fitful sleep, troubled by dreams of falling from high towers, and waking with a start and in great terror. A deeper slumber followed this – and them – What! That figure in the room.
>
> A figure was there. Yes, she had drawn up the blind to admit the light when it should dawn, and there, between the foot of the bed and the dark casement, it crouched and slunk along, groping its way with noiseless hands, and stealing round the bed. She had no voice to cry for help, no power to move, but lay still watching it.
>
> On it came – on, silently and stealthily, to the bed's head. The breath so near her pillow, that she shrank back into it, lest those wandering hands should light upon her face. Back again it stole to the window – then turned its head towards her.
>
> The dark form was a mere blot upon the lighter darkness of the room, but she saw the turning of the head, and felt and knew how the eyes looked and the ears listened. There it remained, motionless as she. At length, still keeping the face towards her, it busied its hands in something, and she heard the chink of money.
>
> Then, on it came again, silently and stealthy as before, and, replacing the garments it had taken from the bedside, dropped upon its hands and knees, and crawled away. How slowly it seemed to move, now that she could hear but not see it, creeping along the floor! It reached the door at last, and stood upon its feet. The steps creaked beneath its noiseless tread, and it was gone. (pp. 301)

In other words, instead of being violated by Quilp – by, that is, the social forces which in a sense he represents – Nell is violated within the bosom of her own family. What is remarkable about *The Old Curiosity Shop* is that, in the end, Nell is not killed by Quilp, for all his leering lechery, but by the vices and obsessions of her grandfather in relation to whom she plays all the familial roles of child and mother, daughter and sister. What Dickens manages to do in *The Old Curiosity Shop* is to transfer the energy and the threat of a specific historical moment – that of the raw dawn of industrial society – to the more confined and controllable space of the family which becomes at one and the same time a place of safety and of perversion. It was not just a question of creating the family as a safe little retreat from the powerful forces in society at large but of giving that retreat a charge that would give it sufficient cohesion – the kind of charge that could only be provided by a taboo and its threatened violation – such, in fact, as rape.

Here I want to make a tricky point but one which a reading of *The Old Curiosity Shop* forces upon me. What Dickens seems to be doing in the novel is to promote at one and the same time an ideological myth of the sanctity of the home (see the 'hymn to home' on pp. 363–7) *and* the demonology which, later, in the formulation of the Oedipus complex both underwrites and threatens it. Take the four principal families of the text, for example: Nell and her grandfather, the Garland family, Kit's marriage to Barbara, and Dick Swiveller's late betrothal to the 'Marchioness'. Between them they contain an old man obsessed by 'games of chance', a compulsive gambler, that is, prepared to risk his fate on the turn of a card; a hereditary club foot (the Garlands) which is the mark of an 'Abel' not a nomadic 'Cain'; the production and reproduction of children who are 'exact facsimiles and copies' of their parents and their parents' parents' offspring; and, finally, a Sophronia *Sphynx*, the name chosen for the Marchioness 'as being both euphonious and genteel, and furthermore indicative of mystery' (p. 667). Divination, club foot, confusion of generations, a Sphynx and a mystery: Oedipus, no less. It is very disconcerting: how on earth had Dickens managed to have read Freud at such a date?

But that, surely, is to put the wrong question. Instead of pondering the enigma as to how Dickens could have read Freud we should be considering, rather, to what extent Freud was familiar with Dickens or, at least, with the whole heritage of bourgeois literature in the nineteenth century. In other words, did Freud 'discover' Oedipus in the unconscious or in his reading and interpretations of the classics of bourgeois culture. The possibility suggests itself, then, that Oedipus was not the product of the unconscious nor the discovery of psychoanalysis, but the complexly wrought agent of a social formation that needed the refuge and the taboos of the nuclear family. It is this that makes the Oedipal reading of literature possible for it was this literature itself that first produced Oedipus:

> It is correct to measure established literature against an Oedipal psychoanalysis, for this literature deploys a form of superego proper to it, even more noxious than the non-written superego. Oedipus is in fact literary before being psychoanalytic. There will always be a Breton against Artaud, a Goethe against Lenz, a Schiller against Hölderlin.[75]

or – can we not now add here? – a 'Dickens' against 'Boz'?

What we see happening in *The Old Curiosity Shop*, therefore, is the gradual elimination of that nomadic and collectivist style we have labelled 'Boz'. It becomes concentrated in Quilp, frozen in the wax-work statues, with bits of it adhering now only to small migrant groups – the 'Punch and Judy' and little forlorn troupes like 'Grinders' lot'. The career of Dick Swiveller is symptomatic of what is happening. In many ways he still shares some of the zany unpredictability of the 'Boz' mode – see, for example, pp. 348–9:

> It was upon this lady (Sally Brass), then, that Mr. Swiveller burst in full freshness as something new and hitherto undreamed of, lighting up the office with scraps of song and merriment, conjuring with ink-stands and boxes of wafers, catching three oranges in one hand, balancing stools upon his chin and penknives on his nose, and constantly performing a hundred other feats of equal ingenuity.

But Swiveller is, as his name suggests, a 'swiveller' and he moves across from the Boz side of the text – it is perhaps worthy of note that his fight with Quilp (p. 154) is less a matter of engagement than of 'dislodgement', of self-separation, that is, rather than evidence of affinity – to the Dickens side of the text where he remains funny but no longer very serious. And perhaps another point can now be made. In many ways it seems to me that it is to this 'swiveller' mode of gratuitous nonsense that Pearson's 'showman's gusto', 'ringside intimacy' and 'mountebank's creative mendacity' might with some justness be applied; but it is not, now, 'Boz'. In fact what we find happening is that the 'showman', the 'ringmaster' and the 'mountebank' do not designate an *earlier* stage of Dickens's career which he grew out of into some kind of 'maturity' but most aptly characterizes features of his work that emerge simultaneously with his determination to attain a more rigorously professional stature. Much earlier we remarked how the description of Brogley's shop in *Dombey* seemed much more 'gusto-ish' than the corresponding *Sketches* passages. Is it not possible to see, now, that many of the 'characters' of *Dombey* – Captain Cuttle, Major Bagstock, Cousin Feenix, for example – are very much the product of a showman's gratuitous fun. The 'mountebank's creative mendacity', that is, does not so much come before as accompany the construction of the 'purposive architect of a unique destiny'. When you give it a moment's thought, though, this should hardly come as a surprise.

Still, the Boz side does not go down without a fight. Much of the rage of Quilp seems to stem from an awareness that a new stiffness is entering into the writing, a principle of authority and control and delegation profoundly at odds with his own mercurial and anamorphic energies. It is this, I think, that explains the frenzied havoc Quilp wreaks on the huge ship's figure-head he drags into the corner of his summer-house:

> All this time, Sampson was rubbing his hands, and staring with ludicrous surprise and dismay at a great, goggle-eyed, blunt nosed figure-head of some old ship, which was reared up against the wall in a corner near the stove, looking like a goblin or a hideous idol whom the dwarf worshipped. A mass of timber on its head, carved into the dim and distant semblance of a cocked hat, together with the representation of a star on the left breast and epaulettes on the shoulders, denoted that it was intended for the effigy of some famous admiral; but without those helps, any observer might have supposed it the authentic portrait of a distinguished merman, or great sea-monster. Being originally much too large for the apartment which it was now employed to decorate, it had been sawn off short at the waist. Even in this state it reached from floor to ceiling; and thrusting itself forward with that excessively wide-awake aspect, and air of somewhat obtrusive politeness, by which figure-heads are usually characterised,

seemed to reduce everything else to mere pigmy proportions. (p. 564)

The frenzy with which Quilp assails this massively inert body without organs stems from the consciousness of an energy of desire that has lost its place of register: the gougings and scarifications inflicted on the figure-head are the paranoiac compensations and anguish of a loss of inscription. At another level, of course, what the figure represents is a massively erect phallus and what that phallus connotes for Quilp is the protrusion into the text of a new and despotic signifier which threatens to encode, once and for all, his own dispersed and heterogeneous sexuality within the crushing axiomatic of the patriarchal law of a despotic superego. No wonder he takes an axe to it.

The massive, albeit tongue-in-cheek, genealogical table with which it opens signals at once that *Martin Chuzzlewit* marks the triumph of the familial structure over the looser and more heterogeneous patternings of the earlier novels, of the 'tree' over the 'rhizome'. It is the focus on the family and the relationships within it that give the novel its structural coherence. *Chuzzlewit*, in fact, is very much determined by the capricious whims of an almost dynastic patriarch. In proportion to this increasing reliance on the family as a structural principle and centre of concern there is correspondingly less interest in more collective phenomena such as groups and non-familial conglomerates. If a strong group might have been found in the novel, that is an area where we might have found further examples of that peculiarly nomadic and investigative style of the *Sketches* and the Jacob's Island passage, it surely would have been in those chapters that describe Todgers's – significantly referred to as

that noun of multitude signifying many. (p. 191)[76]

But, in this sense, Todgers's is disappointing. It is interesting, in fact, to compare the description of Todgers's with the description of the house depicted in the 'Seven Dials' essay referred to above. Compared with that earlier description the account of Todgers's is in many ways far too 'finished', the décor and furnishings too heavy, its atmosphere too rigid. The occupants, too, have become 'characters' – Jinkins, Moddle and the rest – with a rigorous hierarchy depending on age and length of residence. In many ways Todgers's is too much of a 'set-piece' and for all its internal coherence or even that of its setting it remains curiously detached from the world outside. (In fact, not quite, for it has that curious hidden cellar:

> But the grand mystery of Todgers's was the cellerage, approachable only by a little back door and a rusty grating: which cellerage within the memory of man had had no connexion with the house, but had always been the freehold property of somebody else, and was reported to be full of wealth: though in what shape – whether in silver, brass, or gold, or butts of wine, or casks of gunpowder – was a matter of profound uncertainty and supreme indifference to Todgers's, and all its inhabitants. (pp. 187–8)

The 'cellerage' seems to exist, therefore, in a strange adjacency to the house like some kind of atrophied rhizomic root.)

It is possibly worth noting, too, that the one figure associated with Todgers's who retains some of the mobility and vitality that we associated with the collectives and groups of the earlier works, young Bailey, quickly abandons Todgers's and is to be found next associated with the only other possible group identity, the phenomenal Anglo-Bengalee Disinterested Loan and Life Assurance Company masterminded by the mercurial Montague Tigg, or Tigg Montague, as you wish. The Anglo-Bengalee is, in fact, a wonderfully comic achievement though there is a sense that Dickens conjured it up off the top of his head, as it were – indeed that is probably why it is such an achievement. What is remarkable about it is that its whole mode of operation, duplicitous and fraudulent though it may be, is fully explained and, moreover, we can see that it probably *works*. I think this is another point that is worth making with regard to the groups in Dickens – whether we refer to Fagin's gang, Crummle's troupe, or Tigg's Anglo-Bengalee, or even Quilp's brokerage: they actually *work*, we see how the money is made, how an economy operates. Whereas it is a notorious fact that so many of Dickens's 'respectable' well-off middle-class characters – the Brownlows, Maylies, Cheerybles, the Garlands, later Jarndyce – seem to be guaranteed secure incomes from no source whatsoever. In other words, in increasingly losing interest in groups Dickens increasingly loses touch with economic reality.

It may be that it was the lack of 'group' possibilities offered by the Chuzzlewit theme – the Anglo-Bengalee operation seeming very much like a brilliant but late improvisation – that accounts for Dickens making his two most notorious additions to the novel as it had been planned: the introduction of Mrs Gamp and the sudden trip to America. Mrs Gamp, of course, with her phantom familiar, Mrs Harris, is a 'group' in herself and her perpetual alcoholic twilight and an incomprehensible ideolect all her own makes her the most memorable character in the book.

The animus that informs the American episodes of *Chuzzlewit* has always taken a bit of explaining and certainly made Dickens unpopular in that country. In many ways the American episodes are very uneven: there is a wonderful gallery of memorable types with their unforgettable names – Mr Jefferson Brick, Mr Lafayette Kettle, Colonel Driver, the ominous Mrs Hominy – and the equally memorable onslaught on the muck-raking of the American press and such giant land-swindles as the Eden Land Corporation. The journey up-river, too, on the Esau Sludge, to Eden where young Martin finally begins to come to terms with himself, does not lack in epic potential – sufficient for it to have been suggested that Conrad modelled *Heart of Darkness* on it. On the whole, however – I was about to say – the narrative itself is pretty thin and undeveloped. But I don't think that is what is the problem: what is distinctive about the American episodes is not the failure of narrative but the collapse of that sense of the viability of collective groups which until now has been Dickens's principal strength. The America of *Martin Chuzzlewit* is haunted by spectral, illegitimate and bastard collectivities, ranging from Mrs Pawkins' boarding house:

> Dyspeptic individuals bolted their food in wedges; feeding, not themselves, but broods of nightmares, who were continually standing at livery with them. (p. 334)

through to the nightmare of Eden. I would suggest that the bitterness of the American episodes are as much due to Dickens sensing a collapse of something important in himself – of all those facilities, indeed faculties we have associated with Boz – as to the 'objective (and) correlative' disappointment with America. Speaking of 'Boz' for the last time – as we now must for the next novel is to be *Dombey* – it might be worthwhile recalling the origin of this pseudonym: it was a corruption of a nickname given to one of Dickens's brothers – Moses. Moses was the great leader of a nomadic and exiled multitude, a great marshal in the wilderness, the great defier of the state. Almost the last memorable character we meet in the American section of *Chuzzlewit* is that most egregious apologist of the United States the Honourable

Elijah Pogram, Member of Congress, 'one of the master minds of our country' (p. 604). Elijah, too, had been a great prophet notorious for crying in the wilderness and there is irony enough in that; but it is hard not to recognize the closeness of 'Pogram' to 'pogrom' – to, that is, a word that connotes the organized annihilation of masses. With Elijah/Pogram the genius of Boz turns on itself and self-destructs.

VII

In the light of the foregoing it is, perhaps, easier now to understand more fully the nature of the achievement of *Dombey and Son* and, though it might seem paradoxical, the *weaknesses* of that achievement, as well as to gauge more accurately what was lost with Dickens's construction of himself as the 'purposive architect of a unique destiny'.

The change, the achievement, and what was lost can be illustrated, not surprisingly, by considering the impact of the railway – which is the dominant metaphor of the novel and its production – on Staggs's Gardens. Early in the novel we are shown the Garden still just managing to keep the railway at a distance:

> But as yet, the neighbourhood was shy to own the Railroad. One or two bold speculators had projected streets; and one had built a little, but had stopped among the mud and ashes to consider farther of it. A bran-new Tavern, redolent of fresh mortar and size, and fronting nothing at all, had taken for its sign The Railway Arms; but that might be rash enterprise – and then it hoped to sell drink to the workmen. So, the Excavators' House of Call had sprung up from a beer-shop; and the old-established Ham and Beef Shop had become the Railway Eating House, with a roast leg of pork daily, through interested motives of a similar immediate and popular description. Lodging-house keepers were favourable in like manner; and for the like reasons were not to be trusted. The general belief was very slow. There were frowzy fields, and cow-houses, and dunghills, and dustheaps, and ditches, and gardens, and summer houses, and carpet-beating grounds, at the very door of the Railway. Little tumuli of oyster shells in the oyster season, and of lobster shells in the lobster season, and of broken crockery and faded cabbage leaves in all seasons, encroached upon its high places. Posts, and rails, and old cautions to trespassers, and backs of mean houses, and patches of wretched vegetation, stared

it out of countenance. Nothing was the better for it, or thought of being so. If the miserable waste ground lying near it could have laughed, it would have laughed it to scorn, like so many of the miserable neighbours.

Staggs's Gardens was uncommonly incredulous. It was a little row of houses, with little squalid patches of ground before them, fenced off with old doors, barred staves, scraps of tarpaulin, and dead bushes; with bottomless tin kettles and exhausted iron fenders, thrust into the gaps. Here, the Staggs's Gardeners trained scarlet beans, kept fowls and rabbits, erected rotten summer-houses (one was an old boat), dried clothes, and smoked pipes. Some were of opinion that Staggs's Gardens derived its name from a deceased capitalist, one Mr. Staggs, who had built it for his delectation. Others, who had a natural taste for the country, held that it dated from those rural times when the antlered herd, under the familiar denomination of Staggses, had resorted to its shady precincts. Be this as it may, Staggs's Gardens was regarded by its population as a sacred grove not to be withered by Railroads; and so confident were they generally of its long outliving any such ridiculous inventions, that the master chimney-sweeper at the corner, who was understood to take the lead in the local politics of the Gardens, had publicly declared that on the occasion of the Railroad opening, if ever it did open, two of his boys should ascend the flues of his dwelling, with instructions to hail the failure with derisive cheers from the chimney-pots. (pp. 121–2)

No, I am not going to argue that this is 'Boz'-like. There are a number of Boz-like features: the aggregative accumulation of details and the suggestions of a number of micro-economies and, indeed, of what we have earlier referred to as a sense of a 'sub-culture'. But it is Boz become a little mannered and arch, patronizing even, and it is significant that there are a number of very awkward grammatical shifts and jolts in the passage – 'but that might be rash enterprise – and then it hoped to sell drink to the workmen'; 'through interested motives of a similar immediate and popular description' – and the bewildering paralogism of the final sentence: 'the master chimney-sweeper at the corner . . . had publicly declared that on the occasion of the Railroad opening, if ever it did open, two of his boys should ascend the flues of his dwelling, with instructions to hail the failure with derisive cheers from the chimney-pots'. The word 'failure' here just does not seem to me to be right.

Let us turn now to the same scene after the triumph of the railway:

> There was no such place as Staggs's Gardens. It had vanished from the earth. Where the old rotten summer-houses once had stood, palaces now raised their heads, and granite columns of gigantic girth opened a vista to the railway world beyond. The miserable waste ground, where the refuse-matter had been heaped of yore, was swallowed up and gone; and in its frowzy stead were tiers of warehouses, crammed with rich goods and costly merchandise. The old by-streets now swarmed with passengers and vehicles of every kind: the new streets that had stopped disheartened in the mud and waggon ruts, formed towns within themselves, originating wholesome comforts and conveniences belonging to themselves, and never tried nor thought of until they sprung into existence. Bridges that had led to nothing, led to villas, gardens, churches, healthy public walks. The carcasses of houses, and beginnings of new thoroughfares, had started off upon the line at steam's own speed, and shot away into the country in a monster train.
>
> As to the neighbourhood which had hesitated to acknowledge the railroad in its straggling days, that had grown wise and penitent, as any Christian might in such a case, and now boasted of its powerful and prosperous relation. There were railway patterns in its drapers' shops, and railway journals in the windows of its newsmen. There were railway hotels, office-houses, lodging houses, boarding houses; railway plans, maps, views, wrappers, bottles, sandwich-boxes, and time-tables; railway hackney-coach and cab-stands; railway omnibuses, railway streets and buildings, railway hangers-on and parasites, and flatterers out of all calculation. There was even railway time observed in its clocks, as if the sun itself had given in. Among the vanquished was the master chimney-sweeper, whilom incredulous at Staggs's Gardens, who now lived in a stuccoed house three stories high, and gave himself out, with golden flourishes upon a varnished board, as contractor for the cleansing of railway chimneys by machinery. (pp. 289–90)

Again, I do not want to overstate my case: this is not the 'Dickens' mode, as opposed to the 'Boz' mode, at its best – say as it appears in the great opening to *Bleak House* or even in the grandiloquent 'monster Death' passage elsewhere in *Dombey* itself. But we can see that mode emerging: the increasing tendency to modulate into a kind of highly rhythmical blank verse – 'granite columns of gigantic girth', 'crammed with rich goods and costly merchandise', 'with golden flourishes upon a varnished board'; the employment of a much more intricate syntax, with principal and subordinate clauses, sentences embedded one within another, the use of participle phrases and, oddly enough when one has been led to think that this is the 'new' Dickens, the frequent recourse to a slightly archaic vocabulary and turn of phrase – 'yore', 'tiers', 'whilom', 'costly merchandise'. It is true that the second paragraph here seems to be employing an accumulatively aggregative strategy – 'railway hotels . . . railway plans . . . railway [etc.]' – but this is very different from the nomadic, multiperspectived aggregations of, for example, the *Sketches*. Everything is subordinate to the dominant function of the railway. The language itself is being rail-roaded.

What has been lost is a capacity for seeing society as a massively heterogeneous and pulsatingly vital assemblage of discrete and inter-related clusters. Instead a homogenizing process is taking place: the crowdedness of the early works has become an amorphous mass. Now you may have the best of all intentions towards the 'masses' but the politically debilitating fact is that you are still treating them as a 'mass'. This is why I hesitate to share Raymond Williams's rather over-enthusiastic claims for those passages in Chapter 47 (pp. 737–9) where Dickens laments over the plight of the urban masses and calls for 'a good spirit to take the house-tops off'. Williams writes:

> It is not generalizing but general: a way of seeing beyond the isolated errors and vices, to their breeding-ground in society. It is indeed one of the classic moments in which a particular moral and philosophical tradition is challenged and transcended by another, in an experience which is the great creative achievement of the nineteenth century: a way of learning to see general social causes behind and beyond individual failures and weaknesses.[77]

Now it is to Williams's credit that he recognizes how easily we could describe the passages he quotes as 'preaching, moralizing or even rant' for this is, unquestionably, what they are. And I do not say that from 'dainty delicacy', as Williams would put it, but from the conviction that this 'new way of seeing' is effectively a way of constructing the dynamic energies of an urban and industrial populace as no more than a passive, pitiful, mass. The bad writing – even if it is well written, indeed *because* it is well written – is open to appropriation by a profoundly reactionary politics.

Interestingly, if this is the 'new' way of seeing, then the 'old' way of seeing – that of Boz – haunts the text like a bad dream: literally, like a bad dream. It is to be glimpsed in that frenzied, half-crazed, flight of Carker from Dijon:

> It was a vision of long roads, that stretched away to an horizon, always receding and never gained. . . . Of morning, noon and sunset; night, and the rising of an early moon. Of long roads temporarily left behind, and a rough pavement reached; of battering and clattering over it, and looking up, among house-roofs, at a great church-tower; of getting out and eating hastily, and drinking draughts of wine that had no cheering influence; of coming forth afoot, among a host of beggars – blind men with quivering eyelids, led by old women holding candles to their faces; idiot girls; the lame, the epileptic, and the palsied – of passing through the clamour, and looking from his seat at the upturned countenances and outstretching hands. . . . A troubled vision, then, of bridges, quays, interminable streets; of wine-shops, water-carriers, great crowds of people, soldiers, coaches, military drums, arcades. (pp. 868–9)

It is only here, in Carker's delirium, that we find the horror – 'the lame, the epileptic, and the palsied' – and the exhilaration – 'great crowds of people, soldiers, coaches, military drums, arcades' – that, as we have seen earlier, were the inspiration and the source of the buz of Boz.

It is, of course, Carker that is the real sacrifice that is made in *Dombey and Son*, for if there is anything left in the novel of Boz's particular gift for migratory wandering about the metropolis or of his ubiquitous vision and dispersed presence, it is embodied in Carker. Again and again we are shown Carker 'picking his dainty way' among the detritus, human as well as non-human, of the capital or 'gliding . . . threading . . . weaving' his way amongst the trees at Leamington. Carker, in a peculiar way, 'merges' with his background rather in that mode of spread-out display we have associated with Boz: he is dappled against a dappled background. Here we have him in his office, characteristically managing and manipulating – very much like the computer

register I referred to in attempting to characterize Boz's style – a whole
heap of permutable and heterogeneous materials:

> The letters were in various languages, but Mr. Carker the man-
> ager read them all. If there had been anything in the offices of
> Dombey and Son that he could *not* read, there would have been a
> card wanting in the pack. He read almost at a glance, and made
> combinations of one letter with another and one business with
> another as he went on, adding new matter to the heaps – much as a
> man would know the cards at sight, and work out their combina-
> tions in his mind after they were turned. Something too deep for a
> partner, and much too deep for an adversary, Mr. Carker sat in the
> rays of the sun that came down slanting on him through the
> skylight, playing his game alone.
>
> And although it is not among the instincts wild or domestic of
> the cat tribe to play at cards, feline from sole to crown was Mr.
> Carker the Manager, as he basked in the strip of summer-light and
> warmth that shone upon his table and the ground as if they were a
> crooked dial-plate, and himself the only figure on it. With hair and
> whiskers deficient in colour at all times, but feebler than common
> in the rich sunshine, and more like the coat of a sandy tortoise-
> shell cat; with long nails, nicely pared and sharpened; with a
> natural antipathy to any speck of dirt, which made him pause
> sometimes and watch the falling motes of dust, and rub them off
> his smooth white hand or glossy linen: Mr. Carker the Manager,
> sly of manner, sharp of tooth, soft of foot, watchful of eye, oily of
> tongue, cruel of heart, nice of habit, sat with a dainty steadfastness
> and patience at his work, as if he were waiting at a mouse's hole.
> (pp. 373–4)

Carker, we find, is a chimerical compound of discrete and distinctive
faculties and attributes. To compare him to a 'sandy tortoise-shell cat'
is to describe as well as possible his almost osmotic blending with his
environing space. And it is, of course, the mode of an almost perverse
mimicry that characterizes his relationship to Dombey himself:

> He affected a stiff white cravat, after the example of his principal,
> and was always closely buttoned up and tightly dressed. His
> manner towards Mr. Dombey was deeply conceived and perfectly
> expressed. He was familiar with him, in the very extremity of his
> sense of the distance between them. . . . The stiffness and nicety

of Mr. Carker's dress, and certain arrogance of manner, either natural to him or imitated from a pattern not far off, gave great additional effect to his humility. . . . That gentleman was standing with his back to the fire, and his hands under his coat-tails, looking over his white cravat, as uncompromisingly as Mr. Dombey himself could have looked. (pp. 239–44)

It is too simple just to recognize, as many have done, that in many ways Carker is Dombey's double, the repressed sexuality that lies buried beneath the latter's frigid exterior. The notion of the 'double' gives the relationship too theatrical a cast. Indeed I think this resort to the device of the 'double' – which I would want to argue is a compromise between the apprehension of molecular intensities and the constitution of a molar identity – is what makes the whole Alice/Edith parallel such an unconvincing narrative experience.

Earlier, when we began to examine the nature of the crisis that *Dombey* is both the product and symptom of, we suggested that the true nature of that crisis was to be found in the Toots/Nipper and Bunsby/MacStinger relationships: between inert heads and a quantum of energy that was mobile, nomadic and anarchic but which, above all, *marked* the body, incised it, machined it, if you like. The name 'Carker' like Nipper and MacStinger suggests again this process by which the relation between desire and the body is one of actual marking, scoring, inscribing – 'carking' in the sense that Dick Swiveller uses it in referring to 'carking care'. 'Carker' is the inscription of desire that Dombey refuses to negotiate. His loss is the shedding, in a sense, of a highly charged skin, a sensitized surface, like a photographic film, an openness to the world and its thrills and pains. It is not the loss of an interiority but of an exteriority (interiority comes by way of compensation), of a capacity for display. And this explains what Dombey's 'master vice' is: it is not Pride at all, but Envy. To have confused the two, as critics and readers have done for so long, is to do no more than share Dombey's own complete self-delusion. No, his master vice is envy, sheer envy, that Florence wins the adoration and acclaim and love that he so longs for. It is time now to recall that 'there was no envy in all this' of the 'Autobiographical Fragment': the casual disavowal did, indeed, disguise a terrible distress.

Dombey's loss, or anaesthetization, of his surface is connected, of course, to Dickens's own shift from the *flâneur*'s capacity for display to

the punctual identity of the 'purposive architect of a unique destiny'.
Dombey is still transitional, of course, the process is still taking place.
We do not yet have the authorial 'I' or 'eye' – the 'I observe'
emblazoned across the second chapter of *David Copperfield*. I think this
process of reduction from the Argos, or peacock, eye of display to the
single perspective of the observing eye accounts for the particular
structures of looking and overlooking, of 'askanceness' that occurs so
frequently in the novel – someone looking at someone looking at
someone (see the illustrations on pp. 685, 725, 823) – as well as the
frequent occurrence of anamorphic shapes – the shrouded furniture in
the Dombey household, the grotesque projection of the shadow of
'good' Mrs Brown on the wall, the late shadow of the returning Walter.
The dispersed eye is becoming caught in sets of rectangular, triangular,
networks while the anamorphic shapes are as if the spread-out mode of
display is curling up at the edges and folding in on itself, like paper
peeling off a wall.

Though it means another long quotation I think the process I am
trying to describe is very well illustrated in the description of Carker's
house:

> It is not a mansion; it is of no pretensions as to size; but it is
> beautifully arranged, and tastefully kept. The lawn, the soft,
> smooth slope, the flower-garden, the clumps of trees where
> graceful forms of ash and willow are not wanting, the conserva-
> tory, the rustic verandah with sweet-smelling creeping plants
> entwined about pillars, the simple exterior of the house, the well
> ordered offices, though all upon a diminutive scale proper to a
> mere cottage, bespeak an amount of elegant comfort within, that
> might serve for a palace. This indication is not without warrant;
> for, within, it is a house of refinement and luxury. Rich colours,
> excellently blended, meet the eye at every turn; in the furniture –
> its proportions admirably devised to suit the shapes and sizes of
> the small rooms; on the walls; upon the floors; tingeing and
> subduing the light that comes in through the odd glass doors
> and windows here and there. There are a few choice prints and
> pictures, too; in quaint nooks and recesses there is no want of
> books; and there are games of skill and chance set forth on tables –
> fantastic chessmen, dice, backgammon, cards and billiards.
>
> And yet amidst this opulence of comfort, there is something in
> the general air that is not well. Is it that the carpets and the

cushions are too soft and noiseless, so that those who move or
repose among them seem to act by stealth? Is it that the prints and
pictures do not commemorate great thoughts or deeds, or render
nature in the poetry of landscape, hall or hut, but are of one
voluptuous cast – mere shows of forms and colour – and no more?
Is it that all the books have all their gold outside, and that the titles
of the greater part qualify them to be companions of the prints and
pictures? Is it that the completeness and beauty of the place are
here and there belied by an affectation of humility, in some
unimportant and inexpensive regard, which is as false as the face
of the too truly painted portrait hanging yonder, or its original at
breakfast in his easy chair below it? Or is it that, with the daily
breath of that original master of all here, there issues forth some
subtle portion of himself, which gives a vague expression of
himself to everything about him?

   It is Mr. Carker the Manager who sits in the easy chair. A
gaudy parrot in a burnished cage upon the table tears at the wires
with her beak, and goes walking, upside down, in its dome-top,
shaking her house and screeching; but Mr. Carker is indifferent to
the bird, and looks with a musing smile at a picture on the opposite
wall. (pp. 553–4)

It is a passage that invites extensive commentary but I will try to make
the main points as briefly as possible. First, it is heavily 'loaded' by
Dickens himself against Carker and this loading is achieved by the
rather indirect and even slightly discreditable strategy of innuendo
through the use of those several questions – 'Is it that. . . . Is it
that. . . . Is it that. . . ?' If we take out the moral loading what we find
is a movement away from surfaces and textures towards a concentration on the inner malignity of Carker himself. And yet Carker's own
relation to his surroundings, as described by Dickens, is the reverse: an
'issuing-forth' of himself, the dispersal of his 'self' within and across
his milieu. The detail of the games is worthy of note: 'fantastic
chessmen, dice, backgammon, cards and billiards'. The 'game' is
always somewhere between the dispersal of a spectacle and the concentration of a rivalry. We know from elsewhere in the book (p. 456) that
Carker can play chess blindfolded. The space of display which requires
being seen, has become reduced to a geometrical perspective which can
be imagined even by the blind.[78] This severely geometrical space,
where all lines meet in one point, is well imaged in the bird cage

which, apart from appearing here, strangely roams the text and its illustrations. It is the image of a control within which madness rages.

Carker, of course, is a thoroughly nasty piece of work – a delinquent, just like Rob the Grinder: another name denoting a facility for marking and roughing up. Delinquent, but still desire, mobility, force, and delinquent, therefore, because repressed. Carker, in a sense, suffers two 'deaths' in the novel: he is manœuvred into the extraordinarily theatrical denouement in Dijon – the machinic inscription of desire is reduced to tawdry theatre. And, secondly, his actual death when his body is shredded by the train at the end. He becomes, so literally that it seems a sardonic joke, a 'corps morcelé' – that is that body in pieces, that aggregation of parts and organs and faculties – that Dombey refuses and paranoiacally dreads and desires.

And all in the interests of what: for the sake of 'a new departure for Dickens – a novel founded upon a relation, and upon a character's inner conflict'.[79] In the interests, that is, of collapsing what I hope I have shown to be a radically subversive talent for exploring and registering the varied and variegated complexities, human and social, of a society at a critical moment of development and change, to a lamentable obsession with familial strains and neurotic introspection. At the end it may be Diogenes barking on the beach, but it is Oedipus that the tide is bringing in.

VIII

It seems to me, at this point, that we should briefly trace and recapitulate a number of the interrelated processes that we have seen to be involved in the gradual transition from 'Boz' to 'Dickens' which reaches its climax in *Dombey and Son*.

First, there has been an increasing loss of the rhizomic flexibility of the 'Boz' register that could weave and thread its way through the heterogeneous groupings and contexts of a burgeoning metropolitan and industrial society. In its place we find an increasing hardening of style and an increasingly rigid authorial stance. Instead of the molecular, collectivist, nomadic dispersal of the subject across its circumambient field we find emerging a concentrated and privileged identity that orders its material from on high. The nomadic 'Boz' has given way to the despotic 'Dickens'.

The second process that we have traced is the gradual loss of hold on the social field – on the aggregates of micro-economies and the material complexities of 'sub-cultures' – and the increasing obsession, instead, with psychological states and inward processes. Coupled with this is the increasing reduction of the social context to the familial round and it is with this concentration on the determinations effected by the family to the exclusion of any consideration of the wider social and political milieu that Dickens seems, in many ways, to be anticipating the Oedipal ploy.

A third process – though at first it seems paradoxical – entails a certain loss of 'seriousness' and an increasing dependence, instead, on purely 'comic' effects. I think it is very important to understand this. 'Boz' was, in many ways, a very 'serious' writer and we can cite again in evidence of this the 'Fleet' episode in *Pickwick*, the 'Jacob's Island' passage in *Oliver Twist* and the 'Dotheboys Hall' episode in *Nickleby*. When this powerful engagement with social conditions gives way to the preoccupation with the inward and the psychological the rhizomic energy of 'Boz' is left no outlet but that of a manic comic twitch – the Mantalinis of *Nickleby*, Swiveller in *The Old Curiosity Shop*, Montague Tigg in *Chuzzlewit*, Captain Cuttle in *Dombey*. In other words, the 'showman's gusto, the ring-side intimacy, and the mountebank's creative mendacity' is not what Dickens escaped from but what, in fact, he resorted to when he reneged upon the major source of his own original genius. It is 'Dickens' who is the 'mountebank', not 'Boz'. 'Creative mendacity' and 'inwardness' are the correlatives one of the other that are all that are left when the surface and display collapse.

The fourth, again closely related, process involved in the shift from 'Boz' to 'Dickens' is the increasing loss of confidence in and celebration of the crowd, of groups, of collectivities of people. The stages can be marked by recalling the robust banter of the women in 'The Pawn-broker's' essay in the *Sketches* and the moving account of the inmates of the Fleet in *Pickwick*. Next we have the highly ambiguous fascina-tion with Fagin's gang in *Oliver Twist*. We saw the major break occur in *Nickleby* where the radical mode of the Dotheboys Hall episode fails to be carried through in the descriptions of the milliners' trade; in *The Old Curiosity Shop* interest 'jumps' from the massive broodingness of the city and the threat of the industrial landscape to a familial complex which enjoys – and that is probably the right word – albeit before its time, all the insignia of Oedipus. In *Chuzzlewit* the familial structure predominates – indeed it is almost a saga – and the groups that are left are mere spectres of what has gone before. Now, in *Dombey* the group itself is present only as a patronizingly fetishized token – the 'oodles of Toodles' as Pearson describes them – or in the even more patronizing, homogenizing mode of the urban masses. The geniality of Sam Weller and the effrontery of the Artful Doger have become reduced to the sullen loutishness of Rob the Grinder whose dreadful fate it is to have been cajoled from being a 'cove' to an 'indiwiddle' (p. 942).

It might be helpful, now, if I brought this account of the change marked most crucially by *Dombey* to a close by looking, albeit briefly and summarily, at two of the later novels to see how the processes we have described above develop further.

IX

David Copperfield, despite the fact that it is the barely disguised account of Dickens's own 'tragedy and triumph' – to use Edgar Johnston's phrase – is an incredibly sad book, not just in the record of Dickens's childhood sufferings which we have argued are, in any case, more mythical than true, but as a whole, as – to use what is by now a somewhat old-fashioned phrase – a structure of feeling, as a structure of relationships.

I think that, in a curious way, the unease is first triggered by the very confidence of the opening:

> Whether I shall turn out to be the hero of my own life, or whether that station will be held by anybody else, these pages must show. To begin my life with the beginning of my life, I record that I was born (as I have been informed and believe) on a Friday, at twelve o'clock at night. It was remarkable that the clock began to strike, and I began to cry, simultaneously. (p. 1)[80]

No one can read this without sensing its slightly mannered archness, the adoption of a narrative pose, even persona, that had already been ridiculed by Sterne. The birth, midnight and the clock striking, all amount to a little label saying 'This is a novel.' This very early assumption of a style not his own, the adoption, that is of a mask – and that a very thin one – is the first clue as to the peculiar friability, a certain lack of conviction, that seems to threaten almost every line of the text.

We find it again at the beginning of the second chapter where the uncompromising 'I observe' of the chapter title quickly gives way to the fear that he might be 'meandering' (the commas around this, in fact, are to be found in the original): what might 'meandering' mean – could it not be a dim trace of the 'Boz' mode of 'me-andering' the world, the world as *me-and*-the world' in a plane where an 'I observe' is impossible? It is the same hesitation in what he recalls as his first objects of view: on the one hand the molar figures of his mother and Peggotty, while, on the other, a whole gaggle of heterogeneous partial objects, sensations, sights and smells and textures:

> Here is a long passage – what an enormous perspective I make of it! – leading from Peggotty's kitchen to the front door. A dark store-room opens out of it, and that is the place to be run past at night; for I don't know what may be among those tubs and jars and old tea-chests, when there is nobody in there with a dimly burning light, letting a mouldy air come out at the door, in which there is the smell of soap, pickles, pepper, candles, and coffee, all at one whiff. (p. 14)

The most obvious image in the book of this self division is poor Mr Dick ('Dixon' to Mr Micawber) whose 'memorial' (an 'autobiography'?) is perpetually haunted by the head of Charles I – as if 'Dickens' himself was perpetually haunted by a former 'Charles'. Dick, in a sense, is the 'blown head' of Toots in a new guise, and while he is not redeemed by a Susan Nipper it is not without point to notice how surprisingly skilful he is in putting together odd bits and pieces to create the most astonishing results:

> He could cut oranges into such devices as none of us had an idea of. He could make a boat out of anything, from a skewer upwards. He could turn crampbones into chessmen; fashion Roman chariots from old court cards; make spoked wheels out of cotton reels, and birdcages of old wire. But he was greatest of all, perhaps, in the articles of string and straw; with which we were all persuaded he could do anything that could be done by hands. (p. 252)

For Dick desire remains molecular, aggregative, touchingly partial – the last in both senses of the term.

Still, *Copperfield* abounds in 'characters' in a way that none of his previous books have done. It is, in a way, a study in relationships: David and Dora, David and Steerforth, David and Agnes, Agnes and her father, Steerforth and his mother, Mr and Mrs Micawber, Peggotty and Barkis, Ham and Little Em'ly, Dr Strong and his wife Annie, Betsy Trotwood and her wretched husband, Mr and Miss Murdstone. This privileging of 'named', 'individualized' characters over aggregative subjects such as we find in the earlier works is nowhere better indicated than in comparing David's introduction to the boys under Creakle's care with Nicholas's introduction to his charges at Dotheboys Hall. In the latter instance, as we have seen, we are confronted by an indiscriminate heap of symptoms of a collective plight with no concentration on any particular individual. In the Salem House episode it is to be first noted that we have that 'seeing oneself seeing oneself' mode of narrative the inauthenticity of which we have commented on in the 'Autobiographical Fragment' – 'I picture my small self. . . . I picture myself. . . . I picture myself . . .' (p. 79) – and this self-individuation can relate only to other individuals – not to collectives. The boys at Salem Hall, therefore, are first and foremost to David a collection of *names*:

> There was an old door in this playground, on which the boys had the custom of carving their names. It was completely covered with inscriptions. . . . There was one boy – a certain J. Steerforth – who cut his name very deep and very often, who, I conceived, would read it in a rather strong voice and afterwards pull my hair. There was another boy, one Tommy Traddles, who I dreaded would make a game of it and pretend to to be dreadfully frightened of me. There was a third, George Demple, who I fancied would sing it. (p. 78)

What we have, then, unlike the Dotheboys Hall situation, is a set of specific individuals whose names are taken to designate their characters and the relationship David will have with them. Indeed, much of *Copperfield* is taken up with the relation between persons and their names and addresses.

Even so, the split that was so traumatic in *Dombey*, between the molar body and the molecular, rhizomic, patterns of desire, is still to be found in *Copperfield*. In the early part of the book it is to be found figured in some ways in Steerforth and Traddles, who are the two irreconcilable parts of David/Dickens's self – the purposive architect, if you like, and the skeletal collectives of desire. On the one hand Steerforth's overreaching self-confidence and manic-depressive exuberance; on the other Traddles's compulsive carving of myriads of little skeletons on his desk and elsewhere.

The really tragic mistake in Steerforth's life is not his seduction of Little Em'ly but his refusal to come to terms with the passionate intensity of Rosa Dartle. Her name, Rosa Dart-le, could not be more emblematic of the mystical intensity of an embrace that would leave the body marked with the stigmata of desire. Smothered by his mother's love Steerforth consigns Rosa to the hell of being a wound that has nowhere to register itself.

But the Steerforth/Traddles split is to be found repeated later in the novel in what we could describe as the Dr Strong/Traddles split. The relationship between Dr Strong and his young wife, Annie, is given a strong – one can hardly avoid the pun for it is the very point that is being made – homilectic value in the narrative. It is in Annie's profession of her love for her husband that David learns the mistake of his relation to Dora. The Strongs, that is, are presented as in some ways a model of what marriage ought to be. But Dr Strong is also engaged in another project the very purpose of which is to set standards, the compilation of his Dictionary. And it is of Dr Strong that David first seeks employment – helping with the Dictionary – when his Aunt loses her fortune.

At the same time, however, he decides to take up reporting debates in Parliament and to this end seeks help of Traddles in the learning of shorthand. Now shorthand – can we recall at this stage the 'stenographic' style of Jingle? – is very different from the kind of script that can be checked by a Dictionary. David describes his efforts to acquire his new skill:

> I bought an approved scheme of the noble art and mystery of stenography (which cost me ten and sixpence), and plunged into a sea of perplexity that brought me, in a few weeks, to the confines of distraction. The changes that were rung upon dots, which in such a position meant such a thing, and in such another position something else, entirely different; the wonderful vagaries that were played by circles; the unaccountable consequences that resulted from marks like flies' legs: the tremendous effects of a curve in the wrong place; not only troubled my waking hours, but reappeared before me in my sleep. When I had groped my way, blindly, through these difficulties, and had mastered the alphabet,

which was an Egyptian temple in itself, there then appeared a procession of new horrors called arbitrary characters; the most despotic characters I have ever known; who insisted, for instance, that a thing like the beginning of a cobweb, meant expectation, and that a pen-and-ink sky-rocket stood for disadvantageous. When I had fixed these wretches in my mind, I found that they had driven everything else out of it; then, beginning again, I forgot them; while I was picking them up, I dropped the other fragments of the system; in short it was almost heart-breaking. (pp. 537–8)

It would hardly be possible for Dickens to so clearly illustrate the two radically opposed tendencies of his own work: on the one hand the determination to attain a 'classic' status, to set a standard that others would be judged by, to encode as systematically as possible the proprieties of his reading public; on the other hand the manic flair for multiple and arbitrary connections, a rhizomic delight in dispersal and polyvalency, a writing that is hieroglyphic and rebus-like rather than linear and unidirectional.

But, sadly, in *Copperfield* these diametrically opposed tendencies can be presented only, as here, in schematic form. The groups and the crowds have gone. If, with the Toodles, the group has become fetishized and ideal, with the Micawbers it has become alcoholic and boorish – for this is what they are in spite of their acclaimed comic celebrity. Any bite or presence that the collective register that we have found in Dickens's early work might have had has dwindled here to literally dwarfish proportions in the astonishingly nomadic Miss Mowcher.

It's worse than that. Much earlier we have seen how the phrase 'the attraction of repulsion' was first used by Dickens to describe his fascination with the city, particularly with that particularly shady area – as it was then – around 'Seven Dials'. In *Copperfield* who should elicit that very response, the response, that is, to a collective entity, but none other than Uriah Heep:

I was attracted to him in very repulsion. (p. 379)

Now, Heep is execrated in the novel but the very revulsion he is made to evoke suggests a strong empathetic charge. And what his name evokes, of course, is precisely the accumulated, collective, thing that is a 'heap'; and in case we miss the point we have Micawber's description of him as a 'Heep of infamy' (p. 741).

There are two more things that need to be said about Heep. The first is that, perverted as in many ways it seems to be, the bond between him and his mother is as close to, even more close to, a real passionate love as that to be found in any of the other relationships in the novel. These people are vile, but they *feel* and there is a great deal in the treatment of them that derives from little else than pure class snobbery.

Which brings me to the second point. After naming Oliver 'Twist', the Beadle Bumble's next name will have to begin with a 'U': he has in mind 'Unwin', but he might well have chosen 'Uriah'. For Heep is the very mirror image of Twist – and it is not an accident that Uriah is so often described as 'twisting': while Oliver 'twists' an identity out of the collective that is the gang, Heep is the pathetic 'heap' that is left. Heep has had as hard a start in life as did the young Oliver. When David admonishes him with really grotesque hauteur that it is as 'certain as death' that cunning will always overreach itself, Heep replies with some justification:

> 'Or as certain as they used to say at school (the same school where I picked up so much umbleness), from nine o'clock to eleven, that labour was a curse; and from eleven o'clock to one, that it was a blessing and a cheerfulness, and a dignity, and I don't know what all, eh?' said he with a sneer. 'You preach, about as consistent as they did. Won't umbleness go down? I shouldn't have got round my gentleman fellow partner without it, I think.' (pp. 750–1)

Heep's 'crime' is that, not being a 'gentleman', he has beaten the system at its own game of hypocrisy, double standards, treachery and deceit.

In the end, as always, the 'system' wins. The last time we see Heep it is, with Littimore, as prisoners in a new model prison (clearly Pentonville[81]) – presided over by the highly improbable Creakle. Now, most commentators find this whole episode highly contrived, not to say positively wayward. Collins, for example, considers that 'it is introduced quite unnecessarily'[82] while Butt and Tillotson regard it as an 'irrelevant excursion into sociology'.[83] It always amazes me how commentators on an author find aberrant those very passages that strike at the very heart of the issues at stake. Dickens has David describe what is the distinctive feature of the new 'system':

As we were going through some magnificent passages, I enquired of Mr. Creakle and his friends what were supposed to be the main advantages of this all-governing and universally over-riding system. I found them to be the perfect isolation of prisoners – so that no one man in confinement there, knew anything about another; and the reduction of prisoners to a wholesome state of mind, leading to sincere contrition and repentance. (p. 841)

Dickens then goes on to make a mockery of the whole thing: it is the very environment in which the humble contriteness of a Heep would be most at home. But that is to miss the point, and Dickens seems to miss it too. Just as the Fleet episode in *Pickwick* is the very embodiment of the best values of the 'Boz' mode, here the Pentonville 'system' is the very model of the structure of relationships that constitute *Copperfield*. The book is like a panopticon with the magisterial 'I observe' at the centre surrounded by sets of relationships which exist in forlornly separate cells: Mr and Miss Murdstone, Betsy Trotwood and her husband, Agnes and her father, Rosa Dartle and Mrs Steerforth, Peggotty and Barkis, David and Dora – even David and Agnes. The 'system' is bourgeois society itself, with all its loneliness, its indulgences, its waste and its complete lack of self-awareness, its pious cynicism. Cannot Dickens *see* the double-edgedness of the following?:

I said aside, to Traddles, that I wondered whether it occurred to anybody, that there was a striking contrast between these plentiful repasts of choice quality, and the dinners, not to say of paupers, but of soldiers, sailors, labourers, the great bulk of the honest, working community; of whom not one man in a five hundred ever dined half so well. But I learned that the 'system' required high living; and, in short, to dispose of the system, once for all, I found that on that head and all others, 'the system' put an end to all doubts, and disposed of all anomalies. Nobody appeared to have the least idea that there was any other system but *the* system, to be considered. (p. 841)

Dickens could hardly have better described the system of class society, where those that labour least have everything while those that produce most have least. Dickens is, by this time, locked in his own class 'system'.

X

If it is Dickens that is trapped in *Copperfield* then in *Bleak House* it is the reader. Reading *Bleak House* is an extraordinarily claustrophobic and scary experience. Throughout the reader is seduced and flattered and cajoled into a complicit indulgence in a hermeneutic delirium. In a way it is a magnificent achievement for, as Hillis Miller so shrewdly points out in his introduction to the novel,[84] in joining in the perfervid decipherment of the text the reader himself becomes tainted by the very processes of quibble and query that bedevil the case of Jarndyce v. Jarndyce, by the very disease that is the system itself. The plague that haunts *Bleak House* is literature itself and the reader, caught by the prevailing jaundice, is almost the last to realize that everything he/she sees is yellow. The only hope – as Benjamin remarked of Kafka – lies in the very rottenness of the achievement, the virulence of the disease, the sickness that might, just, cure. Not Jarndyce v. Jarndyce, but jaundice v. jaundice.

In *Bleak House* the increasing reification and thickening of language and style that we have noticed earlier become so uncompromisingly compacted and set that any prize upon it, any opening up of it, becomes virtually impossible. Compare, for example, the description of Krook's premises with the accounts of 'The Pawnbroker's Shop' and the passages from *Dombey* describing The Little Midshipman and Brogley's brokerage:

> She (Miss Flite) had stopped at a shop, over which was written, KROOK, RAG AND BOTTLE WAREHOUSE. Also, in long thin letters, KROOK, DEALER IN MARINE STORES. In one part of the window was a picture of a red paper mill, at which a cart was unloading a quantity of sacks of old rags. In another, was the inscription, BONES BOUGHT. In another, KITCHEN-STUFF BOUGHT. In another, OLD IRON BOUGHT. In another, WASTE-PAPER BOUGHT. In another, LADIES' AND GENT-LEMEN'S WARDROBES BOUGHT. Everything seemed to be bought, and nothing to be sold there. In all parts of the window, were quantities of dirty bottles: blacking bottles, medicine bottles, ginger-beer and soda-water bottles, pickle bottles, wine bottles, ink bottles: I am reminded by mentioning the latter, that the shop had, in several particulars, the air of being in a legal neighbour-hood, and of being, as it were, a dirty hanger on and disowned

relation of the law. There were a great many ink bottles. There was a little tottering bench of shabby old volumes, outside the door, labelled 'Law Books, all at 9d.' Some of the inscriptions I have enumerated were written in law-hand, like I had seen in Kenge and Carboy's office, and the letters I had so long received from the firm. Among them was one, in the same writing, having nothing to do with the business of the shop, but announcing that a respectable man aged forty-five wanted engrossing or copying to execute with neatness and dispatch; Address to Nemo, care of Mr. Krook within. There were several second-hand bags, blue and red, hanging up. A little way within the shop-door, lay heaps of old cracked parchment scrolls, and discoloured and dog's-eared law-papers. I could have fancied that all the rusty keys, of which there must have been hundreds huddled together as old iron, had once belonged to doors of rooms or strong chests in lawyers' offices. The litter of rags tumbled partly into and partly out of a one-legged wooden scale, hanging without any counterpoise from a beam, might have been counsellors' bands and gowns torn up. One had only to fancy, as Richard whispered to Ada and me while we stood looking in, that yonder bones in a corner, piled together and picked very clean, were the bones of clients, to make the picture complete. (pp. 98–9)

This is now a stage further than that de-historicizing and de-socialization of objects, their fetishization and commodification, that we found in Sol's and Brogley's shops. Now everything is de-materialized, transubstantiated, into the symbolic structure of the novel itself. Krook's is not just a textual construct but is, itself, *text* – ink, paper, handwriting, labels, law-books and so on. There is a great danger here, surely, of literature disappearing up its own articles.

I think it is this withdrawal of language within itself, its disengagement from the environment, that explains the necessary horror of the night of Krook's death. No longer negotiated by language the environment becomes a kind of thickly repellent stew, nauseously palpable, alien and threatening:

> A thick, yellow liquor defiles them, which is offensive to the touch and sight and more offensive to the smell. A stagnant, sickening oil, with some natural repulsion in it that makes them both shudder. (p. 509)

Krook's 'spontaneous combustion' – unlikely though it be – effectively plasters him across his environment – surely a desperate strategy of display – but also marks the return of the environment on a language that would dispense with it.

How far from 'The Dials' are we, too, in the following description of Bleak House itself:

> The furniture, old-fashioned rather than old, like the house, was all pleasantly irregular. Ada's sleeping-room was all flowers – in chintz and paper, in velvet, in needlework, in the brocade of two stiff courtly chairs, which stood, each attended by a little page of a stool for greater state, on either side of the fire-place. Our sitting-room was green; and had, framed and glazed, upon the walls, numbers of surprising and surprised birds, staring out of pictures at a real trout in a case, as brown and shining as if it had been served with gravy; at the death of Captain Cook; and at the whole process of preparing tea in China, as depicted by Chinese artists. In my room there were oval engravings of the months – ladies haymaking, in short waists, and large hats tied under the chin, for June, smooth-legged noblemen, pointing, with cocked hats, to village steeples, for October. Half-length portraits, in crayons, abounded all through the house; but were so dispersed that I found the brother of a youthful officer of mine in the china closet, and the grey old age of my pretty young bride, with a flower in her bodice, in the breakfast room. As substitutes, I had four angels, of Queen Anne's reign, taking a complacent gentleman to heaven, in festoons, with some difficulty; and a composition in needlework, representing fruit, a kettle, and an alphabet. All the movables, from the wardrobes to the chairs and tables, hangings, glasses, even to the pincushions and scent-bottles on the dressing-tables, displayed the same quaint variety. They agreed in nothing but their perfect neatness, their display of the whitest linen, and their storing-up, wheresoever the existence of a drawer, small or large, rendered it possible, of quantities of rose-leaves and sweet lavender. Such, with its illuminated windows, softened here and there by shadows of curtains, shining out upon the starlight night; with its light and warmth, and comfort; with its hospitable jingle, at a distance, of preparations for dinner; with the face of its generous master brightening everything we

saw; and just enough wind without to sound a low accompaniment to everything we heard; were our first impressions of Bleak House. (pp. 116–17) (see also pp. 142–3)

or in the following account of the 'new' Bleak House towards the end of the book:

We went on by a pretty little orchard, where cherries were nestling among the green leaves, and the shadows of the apple-trees were sporting on the grass, to the house itself – a cottage, quite a rustic cottage of doll's rooms; but such a lovely place, so tranquil and so beautiful, with such a rich and smiling country spread around it; with water sparkling away into the distance, here all overhung with summer-growth, there turning a humming mill; at its nearest point glancing through a meadow by a cheerful town, where cricket players were assembling in bright groups, and a flag was flying from a white tent that rippled in the sweet west wind. And still, as we went through the pretty rooms, out at the little verandah doors, and underneath the tiny wooden colonnades, garlanded with woodbine, jasmine, and honey suckle, I saw, in the papering on the walls, in the colours of the furniture, in the arrangement of all the pretty objects, *my* little tastes and fancies, *my* little methods and inventions which they used to laugh at while they praised them, my odd ways everywhere. (p. 912)

The question must arise as to which one of these passages is describing a wall-paper. There is nothing here but the most trivial kind of banal artifice. It is not just that these descriptions as a whole describe something that is chintzy and toy-like but that the very language itself seems to be enjoying some kind of rarified playing with itself.

Nor do I think it is enough to recall that all these passages are mediated through Esther's consciousness. Certainly there is an almost malicious deployment of irony here as the very name 'Bleak House' perhaps best indicates. But the question I want to ask is just who notices this irony? It's all very well for us so-called 'experts', the literary critics, who have the time and skill to tease these things out, but just how many of Dickens's readers, then and now, remain quite content with lapping up this kind of Mills & Boon – Alan Woodcourt, for example, could be straight out of a Mills & Boon romance – wish-fulfilment?

Or, again, elsewhere, how are we to take Esther's commendation of domestic duty before all else – certainly before Mrs Jellyby's interest in Africa?:

> 'We thought that, perhaps,' said I, hesitating, 'it is right to begin with the obligations of home, sir; and that, perhaps, while those are overlooked and neglected, no other duties can possibly be substituted for them.' (p. 113)

Is this ironical or not? Possibly not, but it is difficult to be sure. If it's not ironical then there is something rather nasty about the sustained attack on people devoted to charity work or to missionary work or to womens' rights in the rest of the novel. If it is ironical then these attacks also have to be reconsidered: is there an irony of irony here?

We face the same difficulty with Esther's reflections on the plight of the brick-makers:

> We both felt painfully sensible that between us and these people there was an iron barrier. . . .
>
> I thought it very touching to see these two women, coarse and shabby and beaten, so united; to see what they could be to one another, to see how they felt for one another; how the heart of each to each was softened by the hard trials of their lives. I think the best side of such people is almost hidden from us. What the poor are to the poor is little known, excepting to themselves and GOD. (pp. 159, 160–1)

I find this ironic: Esther is abysmally unaware of her own limited consciousness and class prejudices – but how many readers would have read and would still read this 'straight'?

The trouble is, surely, that we are so trapped in Esther's consciousness that it is almost impossible to find a vantage point from which we might be in a position accurately to 'place' it. The effect of this, it seems to me, is to make us feel all the time that we are being taken for a ride, that somewhere someone is indulging in a great laugh at our expense. I think this explains, in part, the role of Skimpole in the novel. His disingenuous cynicism is thoroughly unlovable but his smirk never ceases to be disconcerting. Maybe he knows something we don't know. Isn't his appraisal of the mixture of good and evil in the world, after all, very much a laying bare of the emotional complex that contributes so much to Esther's sense of being useful?:

> [he] began to understand the mixture of good and evil in the world now; felt that he appreciated health the more, when somebody else was ill; didn't know but what it might be in the scheme of things that A should squint to make B happier in looking straight; or that C should carry a wooden leg, to make D better satisfied with his flesh and blood in a silk stocking. (p. 577)

Indeed, for far too much of the novel the 'poor' and the 'oppressed' seem to exist for no other reason than to be the objects of middle-class charity and the occasion for middle-class complacency.

Already we have seen in the novels prior to *Bleak House* the increasingly meagre attribution of initiative and drive to those groups and collectivities that so swarmed through the earlier works. Here that process reaches its nadir in the depiction of Jo, the crossing sweeper, who 'don't know nothink' (p. 199):

> Jo lives – that is to say, Jo has not yet died – in a ruinous place, known to the like of him by the name of Tom-all-Alone's. It is a black, dilapidated street, avoided by all decent people; where the crazy houses were seized upon, when the decay was far advanced, by some bold vagrants, who, after establishing their own possessions, took to letting them out as lodgings. Now, these tumbling tenements contain, by night, a swarm of misery. As on the ruined human wretch, vermin parasites appear, so, these ruined shelters have bred a crowd of foul existence that crawls in and out of gaps in walls and boards; and coils itself to sleep, in maggot numbers, where the rain drips in; and comes and goes, fetching and carrying fever, and sowing more evil in its every footprint than Lord Coodle and Sir Thomas Doodle, and the Duke of Foodle, and all the fine gentlemen in office, down to Zoodle, shall set right in five hundred years – though born expressly to do it. (pp. 272–3)

Of course Jo 'stands for' the 'inarticulate' masses – indeed, a couple of pages later his plight is closely related to his inability to read (p. 274) – and Tom-all-Alone's 'stands for' the appalling living conditions endured by the London poor and this is, no doubt, very comforting, underwriting Dickens's essential seriousness and concern. But I think this is shabby consolation, that the Dodger should be reduced to Jo, or that the 'Dials' with all its 'fascination of repulsion', with all its human variety, should be reduced to the amorphic maggot heap of Tom-all-

Alone's. Or that, elsewhere in the novel, the sparring wit of the women in the Pawnbroker's shop, or even the sparky energy of Susan Nipper, should become so inneffectual in a creature like Charlie that she could become a mere 'present' for Esther (p. 389). The fact is I don't think Dickens *is* being serious any more: all that Coodle, Doodle, Foodle and Buffy, Cuffy, Duffy stuff is just very silly.

If there is a group left in *Bleak House* it consists of the forlorn apprentices of Caddy and Turveydrop:

> The apprentices were the queerest little people. Beside the melancholy boy, who, I hoped, had not been made so by waltzing alone in the empty kitchen, there were two other boys, and one dirty little limp girl in a gauzy dress. Such a precocious little girl, with such a dowdy bonnet on (that, too, of a gauzy texture), who brought her sandalled shoes in an old threadbare velvet reticule. Such mean little boys, when they were not dancing, with string, and marbles, and cramp-bones in their pockets, and the most untidy legs and feet – and heels particularly. (p. 595)

What a long way we are now from the gang of *Oliver Twist* or the Crummles troupe in *Nickleby*. These little, pathetic, apprentices invite the label of 'Turveydroppings' and I am not too sure that this does not to a very large extent describe what Dickens, in the closet of his irony, is doing to his readers: shitting on us. We would do well to watch our step, to tread very warily.

Watch your step; tread warily. It seems to me that in addition to the increasing reification of style, to the increasing insistence on inwardness and to the increasing marginalization of a collective or group consciousness we need to draw attention to a fourth process that can be traced in Dickens's work and which reaches its climax in *Bleak House*. This is an obsession with policing, both with self-policing and with policing by the state. With the increasing obsession with mental states and psychological processes – beginning, perhaps, with Martin Chuzzlewit's breakdown in Eden and proceeding with the inner torments of Dombey and Edith in *Dombey and Son* and culminating in Lady Dedlock's desperate self-control in *Bleak House* – it is almost as if the nomadic, multiperspectived, argos-eyed, aggregate consciousness of the *Sketches* which had been open to the variegated heterogeneity of the popular scene has now become an essentially introspective process of double-takes, self-monitoring and self-watching. Lady Dedlock, like Dombey and Edith before her, virtually imprisons herself in her own guilt, pride and remorse.

This is bad enough but at another level it is possible to note that as the vital energy that characterized the group consciousnesses of the early works gradually dwindles to Jo's pathetic inertia, it is to be found resurgent elsewhere in the increasing importance and authority that Dickens gives to that novel figure of the period, the detective. From the marginal position occupied by such figures as Fang, the magistrate, and by the Bow Street runners, Blathers and Duff in *Oliver Twist*, through Newman Noggs in *Nickleby* and the unforgettable Nadget of *Chuzzle-wit* – and, perhaps too, the shadowy but effective figure of Morfin in *Dombey* – the role of the investigative detective has gradually come to assume a central place until it assumes its first major apotheosis in Inspector Bucket in *Bleak House.*

Dickens's fascination with the detective figure and the professional camaraderie of the police force has been well described elsewhere[85] and it will suffice here to make the following points. The first is that it would appear that Dickens's early fascination with groups and collectives and their respective jargons and clan ideolects has now shifted to the newly constituted police force and the new 'in'-language of forensic science. The second thing to notice is that, in many ways, this new police force with its massive apparatus of surveillance takes upon itself that capacity for collective and dispersed observation that was one of the chief characteristics of the 'Boz' mode. Thirdly, as is well exemplified by Inspector Bucket, the detective figure shares with Boz an absolute relish for disguise and dissimulation, for becoming by some kind of mimicry part and parcel of the scene about him. The name 'Bucket', of course, suggests 'depth' and Bucket is, indeed, 'deep' (see p. 362) but Bucket's principal characteristic is to appear to be everywhere (see p. 769) – to be, that is, u-bucket-ous.

It is Bucket, of course, who, by dint of scrupulous attention to detail, by brilliant acts of deduction and observation, by profound psychological insight, by a mastery of his terrain, by the deployment of the myriad eyes of the force at his disposal, solves the mystery of Tulkinghorn's murder and pieces together for himself the fabric of the novel as a whole. This, in a sense, is the final betrayal of 'Boz': that his anarchic flair, his nomadic ranging, his mercurial affinity with the life of the great city around him, have all been handed over to an agent of the state – for that, and that alone, as Skimpole shrewdly notes, is what Bucket represents:

> The State expressly asks him to trust Bucket. And he does. And that's all he does. (p. 886)

Bleak House is, then, a dreadful prison – a prison house of language, a prison house of the soul, a prison house of genius. There is no real way out. Perhaps there is a trace of hope in the North, in Rouncewell's factory where a new economic order seems to be in the making (see p. 902) but the option hardly seems open to us. Perhaps there is a desperate hope in the half-crazed Miss Flite who, alone, seems to recognize the apocalyptic moment that she is living, and whose weirdly named birds –

> Hope, Joy, Youth, Peace, Rest, Life, Dust, Ashes, Waste, Want, Ruin, Despair, Madness, Death, Cunning, Folly, Words, Wigs, Rags, Sheepskin, Plunder, Precedent, Jargon, Gammon, and Spinach. (p. 875)

– take flight in the dusk of the novel – a winging into the darkness of the variegated and volatile moods of our existence, our glory and our pettiness, the sheer insanity that might save us. Or there is the very last hope – *in extremis* – of silence. On almost the last page of the novel Esther remembers Caddy's 'poor little girl':

> She is not such a mite now; but she is deaf and dumb. I believe there never was a better mother than Caddy, who learns, in her scanty intervals of leisure, innumerable deaf and dumb arts, to soften the affliction of her child. (p. 933)

In a novel as highly wrought as is *Bleak House* that late invitation to consider the possibility of a language that is deaf and dumb is no accident.

Still, these are all but feeble consolations in the shadow of the massively closed edifice that is *Bleak House*. Perhaps, in the end, when the liberal consciousness withdraws into the keep of its own language and its own self-engrossed obsessions and hands the keys of its soul to the state there is really only one language left and that is the sullen defiance of the lout. In the *Sketches* we saw how the loutish carpenter of 'The Pawnbroker's' essay was shouted down by the women around him. In *Bleak House*, when the drunken brick-maker shouts out there

is nothing and no one left to restrain him. In many ways his outburst is
the most authentic cry of the novel. He is certainly not trying to kid
anybody:

> 'I wants a end of these liberties took with my place. I wants an end
> of being drawed like a badger. Now you're a-going to poll-pry and
> question according to custom – I know what you're a-going to be
> up to. Well! You haven't got no occasion to be up to it. I'll save
> you the trouble. Is my daughter a-washin? Yes, she *is* a-washing.
> Look at the water. Smell it! That's wot we drinks. How do you like
> it? Yes, it's dirty – it's nat'rally dirty, and it's nat'rally onwhole-
> some; and we've had five dirty and onwholesome children, as is all
> dead infants, and so much the better for them, and for us besides.
> Have I read the little book wot you left? No, I an't read the little
> book wot you left. There an't nobody here as knows how to read
> it; and if there wos, it wouldn't be suitable to me. It's a book fit for
> a babby, and I'm not a babby. If you wos to leave me a doll, I
> shouldn't nuss it. How have I been conducting myself? Why, I've
> been drunk for three days; and I'd a been drunk four, if I'd a had
> the money. Don't I never mean to go to church? No, I don't never
> mean to go to church. I shouldn't be expected there, if I did; the
> beadle's too gen-teel for me. And how did my wife get that black
> eye? Why, I give it her; and if she says I didn't, she's a Lie!'
> (p. 158)

Here we go! Here we go! Here we go!

Appendix I

Deleuze and Guattari

The influence of the work of Gilles Deleuze and Felix Guattari, principally their *Anti-Oedipus* and *Mille Plateaux*, on the essays in this volume is enormous but, sadly, there is little evidence that they have as yet received the attention here that I think they deserve. Because I have drawn so extensively on their work and used so many of their ideas and concepts which may be unfamiliar to some readers, it might be helpful if I attempt to give a brief introduction to their principal notions and themes. I do this with some diffidence for their work is extraordinarily wide-ranging and, at times, incredibly complex. What follows must inevitably do less than justice to them. I will not quote much, but try, instead, to paraphrase their ideas as clearly as possible. I have said they are wide-ranging and complex: but I hope this is not a deterrent. Practically anyone who makes the attempt to read their work will find themselves (and in the context of Deleuze and Guattari that is not a solecism) seduced, delighted, baffled and thrilled.

One of the difficulties of Deleuze and Guattari is that they throw out and deploy a whole mass of terms and notions that are not so much concepts as provocative metaphors for states of feeling: flows, the body-without-organs, the 'corps morcelé', rhizome, plateau, noma-dology, the war machine and so on. This capriciousness is, in many ways, deliberate – if the paradox be allowed – and Deleuze and Guattari work much with paradoxes – for what they are attempting to do is completely to outflank our conventional conceptual frameworks whether those of traditional academic disciplines or of more 'radical' approaches such as psychoanalysis and marxism. The principal target of their two books is conventional psychoanalysis, particularly its obsession with the 'Oedipus complex'. For Deleuze and Guattari the invention of the Oedipus complex – or its 'discovery' – was the original sin of psychoanalysis for what 'Oedipus' does is encode the massive productive energies of desire, which are im-personal and extra-per-sonal, within the personalized apparatus of a theatre. It is this trans-lating of the *factory* of the unconscious into a 'theatre' that Deleuze and Guattari lampoon and deplore (in the essays here this conver-sion of the threat of an area of production into a fear provoked by a priv-ate theatre is to be found in the essay on *Mansfield Park* and, again, in what happens to Carker in *Dombey and Son*). I will say more about Deleuze and Guattari's own model (a word they don't like – for all their wordplay Deleuze and Guattari want to be taken very literally: models, like metaphors, *work*) of the unconscious and desire in a moment.

The attack on conventional marxism is more oblique but far more far-reaching. In the course of their work they dispense with practically every major concept that most 'marxists' (and here the work of Jameson, which I shall turn to later, is exemplary) find to be of the very essence of their orthodoxy: mediation, ideology, contradiction, total-ity, history, class. In their place we find, instead, notions of mixed semiotic chains and the reciprocal purchases of codes upon one another (what I have described as 'pilgrim-crabbing' in the chapter on Dickens; see also below, pp. 248 ff. on Caduveo markings). For Deleuze and Guattari a text does not work through ideology; the process is more direct – what they call the 'agencement' (there is no real English equivalent – the 'arrangement' used by John Johnston is far from satisfactory; we need something like a 'working') of a text – as for example when Deleuze and Guattari proclaim:

Literature is an 'agencement'; it has nothing to do with ideology. There is no ideology and there never has been.[1]

Instead of 'contradiction', Deleuze and Guattari speak of 'flights' (by which I take them to mean those excesses and unpredictabilities that cannot be contained within the logic of 'contradiction', not even with the ruses of the 'dialectic') or of 'lesions' and 'humors' (which I want to write also as 'legions' and 'humours' – the effects are multiple and how often does a joke work at a distance) by which they attempt to describe 'effects at a distance', dissonances, consonances, echos, fissures – the way a windscreen shatters when hit by a stone – becoming, indeed, *crazed*. Deleuze and Guattari don't completely dispense with the notion of 'totality' but they do not see it as a 'totalizing' or unifying, or transcending phenomenon but rather as one more element to be added to what one usually regards it as totalizing. A 'totality' is, in this sense, peripheral to all non-totalized and heterogeneous clusters. For 'history' – which they regard as the product of the sedentary state – Deleuze and Guattari propose, instead, a 'nomadology', the study of the migrant, the contingent, the 'guerrilla', all that conjures the very formation of the 'state'.[2] 'Class' Deleuze and Guattari regard as a concept which serves only to perpetuate 'class' society, that is as an essentially bourgeois category (I have made the same point towards the end of the essay on *Frankenstein*). What Deleuze and Guattari address rather than 'classes' are groups, gangs, clusters, multiplicities, non-hierarchized conglomerates that are fluid, molecular volatile, nomadic – all that is opposed to what is static, molar, stable and sedentary.

At the basis of Deleuze and Guattari's whole project is their theory of desire as a process of 'flows': everything is a matter of 'flows' – milk, urine, shit, blood, menstrual flows, spermatozoa – but also flows of money, goods, organs, words, sunshine, plants, minerals. These flows criss-cross each other and in the process cut into each other, articulate each other, appropriate bits and pieces from each other, so that each code becomes a composite of many, quite heterogeneous, codes. The processes, therefore, are at one and the same time processes of production, of dividing up, and of consumption. The unconscious itself is such a field of germinative, articulating and consuming flows of desire, of attraction and repulsion, love and hate, joining and division, dissolution and separation. The unconscious is, therefore, molecular, larval, productive – but it is also apersonal, indifferent and capricious. The 'molecular' unconscious knows nothing of 'molar' persons, it is indifferent as to what it connects with or is traversed by, and it is capable of conjugations and permutations of the most extraordinary kind. This molecular, flowing, productive unconscious knows absolutely nothing about persons – parental or otherwise: or lack – what is lacking in the unconscious is the notion of the 'subject'; or about 'meanings' – the unconscious *works* rather than 'means', whence Deleuze and Guattari's whole impatience with psychoanalytical 'interpretation' – in fact with 'interpretation' in general. Finally what this a-signifying, a-personal, productive process of desire produces is the 'real' – for Deleuze and Guattari,

> The real is not impossible; on the contrary, within the real everything is possible, everything becomes possible. Desire does not express a molar lack within the subject; rather, the molar organization deprives desire of its objective meaning.[3]

In other words, desire produces, knows nothing of lack, that lack which is instituted, which is constructed, for and within the molar subject by a social formation that works through the engineering of scarcity. It is in this sense that the 'Oedipus complex' exists to the extent that its whole paraphernalia, the familial triangle of 'mummy, daddy and me', centred upon lack, upon castration and envy, is the engineered internalization of the basic problematic of a capitalism that works in terms of 'stock' (capital/phallus) and 'lack' (scarcity/envy). Deleuze and Guattari remind us, incidentally, that this was D. H. Lawrence's early insight as to what 'oedipus' really meant: not something inherent to the child, but the foisting upon the child of the guilt of a social formation – and Lawrence's brilliant essay on 'Fantasia and the Unconscious'[4] is possibly the best possible introduction to the kind of account of libidinal energy that Deleuze and Guattari are elaborating in their work.

What these flows of desire require now is a surface of inscription, that is, somewhere where they can be registered, encoded, 'written'. It is at this point that Deleuze and Guattari introduce their concept of 'the body without organs'. It is a complex notion and, again, I must simplify drastically. Many surfaces can supply this 'body without organs' – first and foremost (at least for the sake of my present exposition, for it is precisely Deleuze and Guattari's point that this most obvious case is by no means a privileged one) is the 'human body' itself. As I say in my chapter on *Vanity Fair*, 'desire is written on the body, it maps its erogeneous zones, allocates points of intensity, articulates lines of force' (see above, p. 135) but this mapping does not coincide with anatomical locations. We have to understand that the 'organs' of desire do not necessarily coincide with anatomical 'organs'. This means that the 'organs' can be distributed quite randomly about the body so that, for example, a body might be registered with any number of phalluses or vaginas, any number of ears or mouths, any number of eyes or anuses, each and all effecting their flows of repulsion and attraction, of interaction and production. It is in this sense that desire is molecular and volatile, indifferent to anatomy and to the 'molar' organization of a discrete, exclusively gendered, 'individual' 'subject'.

There can be a number of relationships between the 'corps morcelé' – 'the body in pieces' – that is the assemblage of the organs/drives – and the 'body without organs'. The first of these might be 'paranoia', that is, the 'body without organs' regards the 'corps morcelé' (organs/ desires) as a threat to its self, as alien barbs and tools of pain – perhaps the most powerful images of this are those late medieval paintings of the Crucifixion with the bleeding body of Christ surrounded by the instruments of torture. A more familiar example that I frequently use is the dread of Robinson Crusoe, so dressed in skins as to become virtually a drum, of the 'bodies in pieces' of the cannibals' feast – Crusoe, more than anyone, fears his own desires. In the present volume the best illustration (literally that) is perhaps that of the inert George Osborne surrounded by miscellaneous limbs, weapons, and torsos (see p. 131 and Plate 3). It is the fear of Jos Sedley of Becky Sharp, of Dombey of Carker, of Steerforth of Rosa Dartle, of Dickens of 'Boz'.

The second possible relationship between the organs of desire and the 'body without organs' is, in many ways, the opposite of the first. Now the 'body without organs' positively attracts the distribution of intensities which it had once found such a threat, like a general of a decadent state bedecking himself with medals. Deleuze and Guattari use a coinage for this: the body without organs 'miraculates' the intensities, allocating them to itself with sovereign dictate and, in this sense, it is a despotic, arbitrary gesture of power and decision. Here the migratory and capricious energies of the earlier moment become fixed and put in place once and for all. It is thus something like the erection – I choose the word deliberately – of a despotic and patriarchal law which works by assigning power and impotence, division and classifications, that encode within strict bounds all the vagaries of desire. It is this that

Quilp so frenziedly resists in *The Old Curiosity Shop* (see above, pp. 195–6). It is also the manic-depressive condition that we find in Emily Brontë's Gondal legend, with the manic A.G.A. ruling by sovereign whim and caprice – A.G.A. is a 'miraculation' of desire.

The third relation of desire to the body without organs transcends both the paranoiac moment and the manic-depressive moment to establish what Deleuze and Guattari describe as the 'celibate machine' – so inadequately translated as it has been, by Jameson among others, as a 'bachelor machine'. With the establishment of the 'celibate machine' the body without organs loosens the controls established in the 'miraculous' moment and allows once again all the permutations and peregrinations of the paranoiac moment but without itself falling back into catatonic paralysis. The 'celibate machine' is magnificently and resplendently impersonal, transcending genders and codings and making available intolerable but ineffable intensities. It is here that a new subject can appear that is quite peripheral to identity – which belongs to the manic-depressive moment – a new subject that can roam at will all the intensities, all the genders, all the histories, all the names, all the conditions that are available to it. It is this that I have called in the essay on Emily Brontë – half in an effort to stop frightening people – the 'Keegan effect' (see above, p. 85) (maybe I should now update this to the 'Maradona effect'). It is a state, I suppose, that is close to that attained by a mystic but it seems to me that it becomes available to us also in moments of joy and illumination, in moments of grief and love, in all those moments of intensity that offer multiple entrances and positions. The bliss and the pain of such moments is that they do not belong to 'us' – to a 'me'.

To each of the three 'stages' described above Deleuze and Guattari have ascribed specific forms of combination to the flows of desire. In the first stage the connections are simply aggregative – one connected to one connected to one – with little or no pattern or organization; it is the mode, perhaps, that can be described as one of 'polymorphous perversity' where any connections will do, any combinations, any substitutions or permutations. Here I have ascribed such arbitrary and capricious connections and codings to the titles Emily Brontë gives to her Gondal poems and I make there the significant point: there are no 'stories' at this level, no heroes, no persons, no molar identities as such – just molecular clusters and brownoidian movements, spirals of repulsion and attraction, larval intensities. It is such a 'larval' moment that I have suggested is being dug up at the beginning of Dickens's *The Battle of Life* (see above, pp. 152–3).

The characteristic connections of the second moment, the manic-depressive, are what Deleuze and Guattari characterize as 'exclusive disjunctions' – a pattern of 'either . . . or'. This we may say simply is the 'normal' phase: here we are either male or female, parent or child, alive or dead – always gendered, affiliated, identified. Here we are on familiar – and familial – territory with securities that make 'narratives' possible. It is this level, which 'the state' requires so desperately, that the novel form has so successfully 'agenced'. It is this level and its operations of power that the Monster in *Frankenstein* so spectacularly threatens – it significantly does not see its life as a 'narrative' but as a 'series of being'[5] – a migration, that is, of discrete but not exclusive intensities.

It is this establishment of discrete but not exclusive intensities that is the characteristic mode of connection of the last, 'celibate' stage where the subject can experience a 'commingling' of roles and statuses, of genders and conditions. The mode of 'either . . . or . . . or' all at once. Here one can be male because female, father because child, alive because dead, human because animal, vegetable because mineral. I have illustrated this condition as best I can in my comments on the Monster in the *Frankenstein* chapter and in the essay on Emily Brontë.

Perhaps the most speculative feature of Deleuze and Guattari's work is the extension of the three 'stages' outlined above to the problematical area of the categorization of 'modes of production'. This is a tricky issue at the best of times but some account of their contribution to this debate is required for a fuller understanding of some of the arguments I am trying to advance in the individual essays of this volume.

The classical excursion into the question of the categorization of 'modes of production' is Marx's notes on 'Pre-capitalist economic formations' in the *Grundrisse*, that compilation of notes of work in progress that Marx undertook before launching upon the writing of *Capital* itself. Briefly, what Marx proposes in the *Grundrisse* is that there were three or four modes of production prior to the capitalist mode itself: the Ancient mode of production, the Asiatic mode of production and the Feudal mode of production – the fourth mode of production being what he calls the 'German' mode of production. Attention on the whole, however, has usually, in marxist debate, been concentrated principally on the following three: the Asiatic mode of production, the Feudal mode of production, and capitalism itself – a tripartite division that goes back at least as far as Vico and Montesquieu. In Deleuze and Guattari's work these three have been replaced by what they call 'territorial' societies, 'despotic' societies and 'capitalist' societies. Each of these correspond in some ways with the series of stages of consciousness we have described above.

According to Deleuze and Guattari it is the prime requirement of every social formation that it should 'code' the flows of desire. In a 'territorial' society this coding is achieved, is inscribed, on the 'body without organs' of the earth. That is, all the energy and productivity of desire is engineered by, coupled to, canalized by, registered on the body of the earth. Here, the body without organs plus its codings constitutes what they call the 'socius': a 'socius' that loses its codings reverts to the condition of being a desert – the equivalent of the catatonic body in our earlier series. The 'territorial' society, then, exists in and through its codings, its marks. The fear that haunts every territorial society is that it should lose its codes and this is why territorial societies marginalize those activities – like metallurgy and trade – that by making something like coinage and exchange possible threaten to convert the vital marks of the body of the socius into abstract and convertible quantities. A territorial society does not work by exchange but by inscription, the marking of bodies in a festival of cruelty that allocate them as organs and appendages of the earth itself. In many ways – and I hope specialists will forgive what is certainly a simplification – the Mexico of the Aztecs, before the coming of Cortés, was such a society: the mutilations of the priests, the wars of flowers, the celebration of the intoxicative values of plants, the sacrifices on the temple steps, the communal latrines, the volatile geometry traced by a rubber ball – were all characteristic of a society inscribed on, stapled into, the earth.

With the arrival of the Despot – to continue our example of Mexico, with the arrival of Cortés – everything changes. The Despot works by 'over-coding', that is, vesting all the pre-existent codings and canalizations of power in his own person. A terrible process of deterritorialization takes place, takes place, ironically, by the settling of the Indians in fixed residences: the former *calpullis* based upon the configuration of groups, gives way to the bureaucratically policed *barrio*.[6] Nowhere is the 'overcoding' more manifest than in the whitewashing of the Aztec temples to turn them into shrines for the Virgin Mary. Barter, which depends upon the evaluative eye, gives way to the exact quantifications of a stamped currency, the treasures of the Aztec temples are rendered down into naked bullion. Divination and the marking of bodies give way to the decree. In place of the festival of cruelty we have the branding of slaves and the calculated deployment of terror (the massacre at Cholula). The connection with the germinal flows of the body of the earth is broken and replaced, instead, by the establishment of an imperial hierarchy.

Whereas territorial societies work by codings and despotic societies work by over-codings, capitalism itself operates through the scrambling of all codings. Requiring as it does the free flows of money and the free-flows of labour and their unregulated meeting in the market place, capitalism is that thing that haunts all societies: the loss of its inscriptions, its codings, its markings. The enormous energy of capitalism is at one with the madness it inflicts upon the world and at one, too, with the waste it creates. For where the codes of the socius become scrambled only a desert remains. Here Deleuze and Guattari remind us that capitalism doesn't only create ravages elsewhere but also in the very dustbowls and derelict communities of its heartlands. Capitalism 'lays' waste just as it 'lays' golden eggs: its motor is stupidity as much as it is ingenuity. Caught in this schizophrenic delirium, capitalism, if it is to stop blowing itself apart, must have urgent recourse to strategies that will, at least for a time, contain, constrain, control its own insanity. This is achieved, according to Deleuze and Guattari, by processes of what they term 're-axiomatization', of elaborating new social equations, new statistical models, ever fresh theorems and axioms with which to formulate its own exorbitant energies – the New Deal, Keynesianism, monetarism, corporatism. But it works also by creating *artificial* territories – anachronisms, throw-backs, archaisms, atavisms: this is why Schumpeter can argue that 'imperialism' is not the expression of monopoly capitalism but an atavistic residue of feudalism. There is no contradiction here: capitalism works by means of these atavisms, they are the conditions of its survival.

It is here that 'Oedipus' appears at last. One of the effects of capitalism is to marginalize the family from the processes of production and this makes the family available as a point of application of control. It is in the family that the flows of desire set free by the social formation at large can be 're-axiomatized', re-bundled as it were, about a non-socialized, non-politicized, nucleus. The family in this sense is the most artifical and atavistic of all re-territorializations for in it, through Oedipus, return the taboos and fetishes of the territorial regime and the imperium of the Despot. In the essays of this volume I have tried to show how threatening can be the real energies that threatened the social formation in the nineteenth century when capitalism was in its most revolutionary phase – the exorbitance of the Monster, the visionary intensities of Emily Brontë, the mercurial irreverence of Becky Sharp, the swarming vitality of Boz's London – and to trace also some of the strategies – particularly the construction of the oedipalized family, achieved through a whole apparatus of character, narrative, grammar – resorted to to contain them. I know there is a lot more to be done but, again, I appeal to my title – 'Partings. . . .'

Deleuze and Guattari's conception of desire as a series of molecular flows and breaks rather than a theatre centred around molar identities leads directly to the distinction they make between what they call 'rhizomic' structures and 'tree' structures.

For Deleuze and Guattari rhizomic structures are hardly structures at all: they resist totalizations. Instead they are essentially conglomerates and aggregates of molecular, heterogeneous multiplicities whose relationships with each other are poly- and multivalent, arbitrary and volatile, provisional and unstable. What the rhizome dispenses with and outflanks are molar, that is totalized, identities and unities. The rhizome is nomadic and multiple rather than sedentary and fixed. It is the tribe versus the state, 'Go' as opposed to chess, the pack as opposed to the individual, the negotiation of borders rather than the focusing of centres. For Deleuze and Guattari what meet are not molar individuals but heterogeneous clusters and each cluster will be a composite of molecular inconsistencies, pieces of this and pieces of that, vegetable and animal, mineral and organic, alive and dead. So that between clusters all sorts of permutations and combinations may take place or may not take place, connections and disconnections, feints and parries, assaults and repulses, and so on. For Deleuze and Guattari we are all such clusters: we are not molar identities but congeries of partial objects and molecular intensities, all of which are capable of multiple imbrications with all other congeries, groups, composites. The 'individual' is an arbitrary construct on a field of intensities, like a biscuit shape on a field of pastry. The field extends far beyond the individual and meets up with other fields – what Deleuze and Guattari call 'plateaux' or 'planes' – of consistency with which it overlaps, merges with, slips under. In this sense the shimmering field that is 'me' flows far beyond me and makes all sorts of breaks and connections with the many other fields that surround it – with the office, the kitchen, the street – all these not so much designations of places as of affective spaces. We are plugged in, then, to the world around us by all manner of cables and currents. Here there are no 'mediations', just a complexity of connections and disconnections. This is how love works – through multiple connections and disconnections – and also how power works: political repression works not through 'ideology' or 'mediations' but through pot-holes in the street, through queues, through dirty and unpunctual trains, through baton charges and tapped telephones. We are all 'tapped': clipped onto and drained.

Less needs to be said about 'tree' structures for it is with a whole arborescent culture that we are too sadly familiar. So many disciplines, from biology to linguistics are structured on trees.

> It is curious how the tree has dominated Western reality, and all of Western thought, from botany to biology and anatomy, and also gnosticism, theology, ontology, all of philosophy. . . .[7]

The 'tree' is that hierarchical organization of separate and individual identities which is best illustrated by the genealogical 'tree': it arranges and distributes molar figures in fixed locations that are the co-ordinates of power and domination. The tree allocates designations of gender, descent and vital state and is allied to and underwrites the despotic power of the state. It is all this that the notion of the rhizome threatens: the rhizome is anti-genealogical and anarchic, essentially subversive and revolutionary.

Perhaps the most difficult aspect of the work of Deleuze and Guattari[8] is their theory of language but I have drawn on it extensively in the essays in this volume and some attempt, albeit very brief, must be made to explain it.

The most important thing for Deleuze and Guattari is that language, its meaning or sense, is first and foremost an *event*. The meaning or sense of a language does not reside in signification (its systems of concepts), or in its expressiveness (grounded in the speaking subject) or in its designations (the things it refers to). For all of these to be operative at all we first need to be somehow or other already installed in the meaningfulness of language itself. This meaningfulness (the French word is 'sens' – which is almost impossible to translate for neither 'meaning' nor 'sense' are really satisfactory and 'meaningfulness' is rather cumbersome) is above all an experience, something happening. This experience or event is at the frontier of words and bodies and much of the fascination of Deleuze and Guattari's theory of language lies in this interest in the relationship between words and the body. Let us take the example of the word 'grow': it has a dictionary meaning, it can be uttered by a subject, it can point to something. But 'growing' is none of these things: it is an event. Not just a physical event, the ageing of a body, but a real process of discovery and development. All people get old, but not all people 'grow'. Take another word: what is a 'party'? It is not a gathering of people with drinks in their hands for these alone by no means guarantee that a 'party' takes place whereas some of the best 'parties' I have ever attended have been entirely by myself. The 'party' therefore exists not in the collection of bodies nor in the word itself but in the strange and not always predictable alliance of the two. A 'party' is, therefore, something like a 'mood'. It is something in things and words yet not in them: in this sense the 'meaning' of an event is spectral and neutral. Two more examples: the first from Deleuze and Guattari. What does it mean to 'declare war': it is a 'declaration' but with that declaration the actual condition of a whole society can and does really change, what we mean by 'mobilization' – through just a simple utterance – what Deleuze and Guattari describe as a 'mot d'ordre'. The last example – one I frequently use in order to explain this notion of language as an event – is to be found in what happens to Adela in Forster's *Passage to India*. Where does the 'event' that is supposed to occur in the Marabar caves take place? Not in the caves at all, but elsewhere, in the court-room:

> But as soon as she rose to reply, and heard the sound of her own voice, she feared not even that. A new and unknown sensation protected her, like magnificent armour. She didn't think what had happened, or even remember in the ordinary way of memory, but she returned to the Marabar Hills, and spoke from them across a sort of darkness to Mr. McBryde. The fatal day recurred, in every detail, but now she was of it and not of it at the same time, and this double relation gave it indescribable splendour.[9]

It is this splendid double relation of the event that Deleuze and Guattari argue to be of the very essence of the meaning of language. The meaning is not in the physical constituents of an event (which is what constitutes a mere accident), nor in the mere description of it but in the experience of it, the event, in a sense, of the event. For this reason events are strangely ungrounded, atemporal, waiting to happen. It is this that leads Deleuze and Guattari to characterize 'events' as strangely pre-personal and impersonal, neutral. An event like a 'gift', for example, has what Deleuze and Guattari would describe as 'many entrances', like a warren, so that many positions can be occupied in it at once: the giver, the gift and what we might call the 'givee' can constantly change position – who gives what to whom?

It is thus with so many seeming names and designations: to be a father or a mother is not just to have a child – so many children, poor things, have to be the 'fathers' and 'mothers' of their 'parents'. But all the names of history can be such events or such effects: the Napoleon event/effect, the Joan of Arc event/effect, the Messiah event/effect. So that these events and effects are waiting there, always available, always capable of being potentialized. I have tried to give examples of such potentializations and mobilizations of name/effects in the essays on *Frankenstein* and *Wuthering Heights*. It means that many more 'names' are available to us than those inscribed on our birth-certificate – more names, more genders, more histories. All such names/effects are what Deleuze and Guattari term 'singularities', neither general nor specific, but somehow 'in between'. A singularity is the focus of its own specific field of intensity, or plane of consistency, which, as described above, connects up with, overlaps, creeps under other planes of consistency.

There is a lot more to be said about Deleuze and Guattari's theory of language (especially about the way in which language evolves out of the body) but, hopefully, I think that the above will be sufficient for the purposes of this collection of essays.

The above account of the work of Deleuze and Guattari has been necessarily simplified and compressed. There can be no substitute for grappling with the original works themselves and if I have encouraged some to do that then I am more than satisfied.

Appendix II

Fredric Jameson: *The Political Unconscious*

When I wrote the essays of this book, indeed even when I set about writing the 'Introduction' – that feature of a book which always comes last – I had no idea that I would find myself having to elaborate some sort of 'critique' of Jameson's *The Political Unconscious*. This has become necessary, however, for a number of reasons. The first and foremost is that Jameson's work has been seen by W. C. Dowling as a 'taking on'[1] of the work of Deleuze and Guattari (though Dowling himself also sees the encounter as something of a 'sidestep'.[2] As my own work has drawn so extensively on that of Deleuze and Guattari it follows that, given that the essays here are also concerned with something that might be termed 'the political unconscious' or, which places me even closer to Jameson, 'the construction of the bourgeois subject . . . and its schizophrenic disintegration'[3] my own position needs to be made clear *vis-à-vis* Jameson's project and methodology.

The second reason for wanting to make some comment on Jameson's work is that I feel that he has woefully misunderstood Deleuze and

Guattari's work and as this work is already so much the object of resistance in many quarters it seems to me a shame that the one encounter we find with it in a work regarded as being somehow 'seminal' is such a travesty. The shame is all the more to the extent that Jameson, again and again in his book, presses upon us the need for the elaboration of a body of concepts addressed to that 'untheorized object – the collective'.[4] He writes:

> What is wanted here – and it is one of the most urgent tasks for Marxist theory today – is a whole new logic of collective dynamics, with categories that escape the taint of some mere application of terms drawn from individual experience.[5]

Now it seems to me – and I hope this has been made clear both in the foregoing account of their work and in the essays in this volume – that it is precisely in Deleuze and Guattari that we find the most worked out and most extensive attempt to elaborate such a theory of collectives. That Jameson has totally misunderstood this is really quite extraordinary but that such a misunderstanding has occurred is evident from a remark such as the following which is, quite simply, wrong:

> The value of the molecular in Deleuze, for instance, depends structurally on the preexisting molar or unifying impulse against which its truth is read.[6]

The whole thrust of Deleuze and Guattari's work is to urge the irreducible primacy of the molecular and the wholly derivative status of the molar whole. It comes out most strongly in their criticisms of Melanie Klein whom they see as again and again forcing the child's play with discrete partial objects – trains and plugs and building bricks – into an interpretative framework based upon parental figures.[7]

The trouble with Jameson's book is that it remains fascinated with such totalities and molar wholes and there is something very disturbing in his resort to the work of such conservative theorists as Northrop Frye and Vladimir Propp. Jameson himself is all too aware that all methodologies perpetrate their respective ideologies[8] and so it should come as no surprise that when he himself, drawing on Propp, tries to describe Heathcliff in *Wuthering Heights* as occupying 'in some complicated way the place of the donor in this narrative system'[9] the reading that emerges is at once naïve and really rather banal:

The ageing of Heathcliff constitutes the narrative mechanism whereby the alien dynamism of capitalism is reconciled with the immemorial (and cyclical) time of the agricultural life of a country squiredom; and the salvational and wish fulfilling Utopian conclusion is bought at the price of transforming such an alien force which, eclipsing itself, permits the vision of some revitalization of the ever more marginalized countryside.[10]

Because Jameson is so concerned with interpretation rather than the way in which a novel 'works' (one of the specific points of contention between himself and Deleuze and Guattari)[11] this speculation on what Heathcliff 'means' – a 'proto-capitalist' we are told – he fails completely to see how the novel actually *operates* – the task which I address myself to both in this book and elsewhere. To respond to Jameson at his own level, I for my part just do not see the 'Utopian conclusion' that he describes – a kind of mixture of Dallas and Ambridge – for the whole thing seems to be one long anticlimax, a terrible aftermath, indeed, to use a word from the novel, a 'devastation'. Jameson's reading, that is, is, to use his own phrase, a 'strategy of containment' which completely fails to recognize the revolutionary provenance of the novel itself and its own 'strategies of containment'. Jameson colludes with the very project the novel set itself.

The nostalgia in Jameson for an almost religious conception of history – 'the mystery of the cultural past', 'the human adventure is one', 'a single great collective story', 'a single vast unfinished plot', 'that uninterrupted narrative'[12] is astonishing in someone who is heralded (Dowling's eulogy of Jameson is just too embarrassing to even quote here) as the most important American marxist critic now living. One can understand how this reputation can be gained in that Jameson deploys with some considerable dexterity many of the 'concepts' which mark, as it were, the 'marxist': ideology, class, contradiction, totality, mediation and so forth. Which brings me to the last reason why I have felt it necessary to comment on Jameson's work. My own work registers again and again a profound impatience with these very 'concepts' and this means that I want to call into question Jameson's whole theoretical – and, it becomes unavoidable, political – project. It might help to make my position clearer if we consider for a moment the very example that Jameson uses to explain the dialectical virtues of his own approach. This is his reading of Lévi-Strauss's account of the Caduveo facial and body paintings in *Tristes tropiques*.[13]

Lévi-Strauss's account of these paintings is long, complex and difficult to paraphrase so I shall quote from his work at length.

First it is important to know that the Caduveo were only one group of a much larger tribe known as the Mbaya-Guayguru, other members of which were the Guana and Bororo. All these tribes were divided into three hierarchical classes and marriage between them prohibited. The risk of excessive inbreeding that this system might incur was solved by the Guana and Bororo by dividing their societies also into two halves or moitiés so that any member of one moitié could marry any member of the other moitié, irrespective of class difference. There was, thus, a social solution to a specific contradiction – a hierarchical structure that prohibited marriage between classes and the social practice that never-theless was bound to occur. The contradiction was resolved by a combination of both a ternary structure (three classes) and a binary structure (two moitiés). The Caduveo, apparently, had not managed to organize such a solution. It is in this context that we can look at the account of the facial and body paintings.

> As I observed in my earlier study, Caduveo art is characterized by a male/female dualism – the men are sculptors, the women painters; the art of the former is figurative and naturalistic, in spite of its stylization, whereas the latter practise a non-figurative art. Restricting myself now to the consideration of this feminine art, I would like to emphasize that it exhibits a continuation of the dualism on several levels.
>
> The women employ two styles, both prompted by a sense of decoration and abstraction. One is angular and geometrical, the other, curvilinear and free-flowing. More often than not, the compositions are based on an orderly combination of the two styles. For instance, one is used for the edge or border, the other for the main pattern. In the case of pottery, the division is more striking: the geometrical pattern is usually found on the neck and the curvilinear pattern on the belly, or vice versa. The curvilinear style is more often used for facial paintings, and the geometrical style for body paintings; but sometimes, through an additional division, each area is patterned with a combination of the two styles.
>
> Whatever the mixture, the completed work expresses an urge to find a balance between other principles which also go in pairs: an originally linear pattern may be gone over again in the final phase

and partially changed into surfaces by the filling in of certain sections, as happens with us when we are doodling; most of the designs are based on alternating themes; and almost always the motif and the background occupy approximately the same amount of surface area, so that it is possible to interpret the design in two ways, by reversing their respective roles – each motif being read positively or negatively. Finally, the pattern obeys a twofold principle of simultaneous symmetry and asymmetry, and this produces contrasting registers which to use heraldic terms, are seldom parted or couped but more often parted per bend or parted per bend sinister, or even quartered or gyronny. I am using such terms deliberately, for all these rules inevitably remind one of the principles of heraldry.[14]

Lévi-Strauss then goes on to describe how one woman constructs her design:

She worked like a man laying paving stones, constructing success-ive rows by means of identical elements. Each element is com-posed of one section ribbon, formed by the concave part of one band and the convex part of the adjacent band, and a tapering field with a charge at the centre of it. These elements interlock with each other through dislocation and it is only at the end that the pattern achieves a stability which both confirms and belies the dynamic process according to which it has been carried out.[15]

and he concludes:

The Caduveo decorative style therefore presents us with a whole series of complexities. There is in the first place a dualism which is projected on to successive planes, as in a hall of mirrors: men and women, painting and sculpture, figurative drawing and abstrac-tion, angle and curve, geometry and arabesque, neck and belly, symmetry and asymmetry, line and surface, border and motif, piece and field, pattern and background. But these oppositions are only perceived retrospectively; they are static in character; the dynamic movement of the art, that is the ways in which the motifs are imagined and carried out, intersects the basic duality at all levels: the primary themes are first decomposed, then reconsti-tuted as secondary themes which use fragments taken from the first as elements of a provisional unity, and then these secondary themes are juxtaposed in such a way that the original unity re-emerges as if it had been conjured back into existence.[16]

Lévi-Strauss then proceeds to ask what is the purpose of this art and it is here that we can proceed to his conclusions:

> Although I have given only a brief description of the Guana and Bororo system . . . it is clear that, on the sociological level, it presents a structure analogous to the one worked out, on the stylistic level, in connexion with Caduveo art. We are dealing with a double opposition in both cases. In the first instance, it consists primarily in the opposition between a ternary and a binary organization, one symmetrical, the other asymmetrical; and in the second instance, in the opposition between social mechanisms, some of which are based on reciprococity, others on hierarchy. In its effort to remain faithful to these contradictory principles, the social group divides and subdivides into relating and opposed sub-groups. Just as a coat of arms unites within its field prerogatives deriving from several lines, this society could be said to be parted, parted per bend sinister and couped. We need only study a plan of a Bororo village . . . to see that it is organized in the same way as a Caduveo pattern.
>
> It would seem, then, that the Guana and the Bororo, having been faced with a contradiction in their social structure, had succeeded in resolving (or concealing) it by essentially sociological methods. . . . This solution never existed among the Mbaya [that is the Caduveo, D.M.]: either they did not know of it (which is unlikely), or, more probably, it was incompatible with their fanaticism. They therefore never had the opportunity of resolving their contradictions or of at least concealing them by means of artful institutions. But the remedy they failed to use on the social level, or which they refused to consider, could not elude them completely; it continued to haunt them in an insidious way. And since they could not become conscious of it and live it out in reality, they began to dream about it. Not in a direct form, which would have clashed with their prejudices, but in a transposed, seemingly innocuous, form: in their art. If my analysis is correct, in the last resort the graphic art of the Caduveo women is to be interpreted, and its mysterious appeal and seemingly gratuitous complexity to be explained, as the phantasm of a society ardently

and insatiably seeking a means of expressing symbolically the institutions it might have, if its interests and superstitions did not stand in the way. In this charming civilization, the female beauties trace the outlines of the collective dream with their make-up; their patterns are hieroglyphics describing an inaccessible golden age, which they extol in their ornamentation, since they have no code in which to express it, and whose mysteries they disclose as they reveal their nudity.[17]

For Jameson this is 'the model of . . . an interpretative operation':

the individual narrative, or the individual formal structure, is to be grasped as the imaginary resolution of a real contradiction.[18]

thus

the visual text of Caduveo facial art constitutes a symbolic act, whereby real social contradictions, insurmountable in their own terms, find a purely formal resolution in the aesthetic realm.[19]

This notion that the literary text is a 'socially symbolic act' which achieves aesthetic resolutions to real contradictions is the classic position of people like Althusser and Macherey but it is one which I now find totally inadequate for it fails to understand the real engineering undertaken by a literary work – a point I have already made in the current volume several times. The basic mistake of this position is to underestimate the real social efficacy of the 'aesthetic' itself: it is only bourgeois culture that has so stupidly and ineptly constructed a domain of 'aesthetics' extrinsic to the social itself. What Lévi-Strauss and Jameson are doing is attributing this essentially bourgeois function of the 'aesthetic' to the Caduveo painters. That the Caduveo would find the conception of the function of the aesthetic as totally bizarre is evident from an exchange recorded by Lévi-Strauss himself:

He [a missionary] condemned Indian men who, forgetful of hunting, fishing and their families, wasted whole days in having themselves painted. But they would ask the missionaries, 'Why are you so stupid?' 'In what way are we stupid?' the latter would reply. 'Because you do not paint yourselves like the Eyiguayeguis.' To be a man it was necessary to be painted; to remain in the natural state was to be no different from the beasts.[20]

The ethnocentricist prejudices of both Lévi-Strauss and Jameson emerge again and again with a lack of self-consciousness that is almost breathtaking. There is Lévi-Strauss's resort to the 'fanaticism' of the natives when the logic of their conduct escapes him; or there is that little exoticist touch of 'female beauties . . . reveal their nudity'. Coming from an older generation and writing very much in the genre of the travelogue Lévi-Strauss can be perhaps forgiven such little touches but when Jameson writes as follows it is much harder to find excuses. He suggests, for example, that Lévi-Strauss's work

> offers the spectacle of so-called primitive peoples perplexed enough by the dynamics and contradictions of their still relatively simple forms of tribal organization to project decorative or mythic resolutions of issues that they are unable to articulate conceptually.[21]

What's this being 'relatively simple' or 'unable to articulate conceptually', which echoes Lévi-Strauss's 'since they have no code'? This is why I have quoted Lévi-Strauss's text so extensively for what it shows beyond any shadow of doubt is that this 'so-called primitive people' has an extraordinarily complex social organization – that Lévi-Strauss cannot understand it[22] is not surprising – and what are these intricate markings and tracings of bodies other than a form of highly complex coding? of conceptual articulation? It is made clear again and again in Lévi-Strauss's account of the paintings that they are social markings, designating social positions and functions. He speaks of the society as

> absorbed in their cruel game of prestige and domination in a society which might be said to be doubly 'clear cut'[23]

and the translator explains what Lévi-Strauss evidently means by 'clear cut'; 'A l'emporte-piece, literally, tooled or punched out; metaphorically, clear-cut, trenchant. The author appears to be referring to the sharply defined social relations and to the clear-cut decorative motifs.' These markings are the codes and the concepts of this society and the fact that they are not subject to some phonetic signifier in the head simply means that there is not the alignment in these societies between speech and marking that there is in our own in our notion of writing. Surely Derrida made all this very clear a long time ago in his own paper on another of Lévi-Strauss's little stories, 'The Writing Lesson', found elsewhere in *Tristes tropiques*.[24] In this sense the facial and body markings of the Caduveo are as socially efficacious as those 'state-ments', those discursive machinations, exclusions, allocations of places – all those strategies discussed by Corrigan and Sayers in *The Great Arch* – that operate upon us. These markings are not 'dreams' of things that could not be made conscious, but reality itself. Without these markings, these codings, these concepts, there would be no reality, no society, nothing at all.

There is so much to be learned from these body markings for what can these tesselated patterns, this intricate setting of 'paving stones', these shimmering oscillations of patterns, of background and foreground, of border and motif, of line and plane be – if not the codings of desire, the establishment of discrete but mobile intensities, a distribution of partialities – in every sense of the term – about the body without organs – the very distribution that makes the socius possible. These bodies are molecular, clustered, myriad, with all the codes intermixing with, appropriating from, rendering up to other codes and patterns. All this is brilliantly described in Lévi-Strauss's text. It is important to note also what Lévi-Strauss records many times: the indifference of these designs to anatomy (the designs are as though composed on a totally flat surface[25]), to reference (i.e. to the locations of eyes, mouth, lips, nose, etc.[26]), to procreation (the tribe 'reproduced' itself by adoption[27]). Desire, the social person, is determined neither by his or her organs, nor by reference to some fixed signified, nor by his or her place in some genealogy.

In other words the very example that Jameson chooses to demonstrate the aesthetic as 'symbolic act' is precisely the illustration that might have been chosen to prove that this whole notion is profoundly ideological, a 'strategy of containment'. If the aesthetic as 'symbolic act' is the nonsense that I think it to be then the whole of Jameson's methodological structure crumbles – or, better, reveals itself to be what, in fact, it is: a theology of power. This is nowhere more apparent than when, at the end of *The Political Unconscious*, Jameson suggests that any attempt within a marxist framework to resolve the problem of the collective could do far worse than consider Marx's own approach to this problem in the *Grundrisse*, in his delineation of the *Asiatic* mode of production. Jameson quotes:

> In most Asiatic land-forms, the comprehensive unity standing above all these little communities appears as the higher proprietor

or as the sole proprietor . . . because the unity is the real proprietor and the real presupposition of communal property . . . the relation of the individual to the natural conditions of labour and of reproduction . . . appears mediated for him through a cession by the total unity – a unity realized in the form of the despot, the father of many communities – to the individual, through the mediation of the particular commune.[28]

I still find it hard to believe that Jameson is here being serious because what he is proposing is absolutely preposterous for it is nothing less than the model of the absolute state. We can see now how his mystique of narrative, which we referred to earlier, is at one with the celebration of the state.

It is all very bewildering. As in his choice of *Tristes tropiques*, Jameson's choice of the *Grundrisse* is uncannily helpful to the extent that the very material Jameson cites to support his argument affords even more compelling material for those who would contest it. To begin with, I should say that I am less ready than Jameson to share the, albeit orthodox, view that the *Grundrisse* should be classed amongst Marx's 'mature' works, if by that we understand it to represent any final or achieved moment of his thought. Its history is notorious: it consists largely of a vast quantity of notes and sketches of 'work in progress' in 1857–8 leading up to the writing and publication of *Capital* itself.[29] It was not published until 1939–41 and did not receive general attention until 1953. The point is that the *Grundrisse* is entirely and brilliantly speculative and it has the kind of excitement that Marx always generates when he is writing more or less off the top of his head. It seems to me that in one such passage, again in the section dedicated to 'Precapitalist economic formations', Marx does approach the problem of thinking the collective – but in sketching that mode of production which, as far as I know, has received very little attention in later marxist thinking – that is the 'Germanic' mode of production:

In the Germanic form the agriculturalist is not a citizen, i.e. not an inhabitant of cities, but its foundation is the isolated, independent family settlement, guaranteed by means of its association with other such settlements by men of the same tribe, and their occasional assembly for purposes of war, religion, the settlement of legal disputes etc., which established their mutual surety. Individual landed property does not here appear as a contradictory form of communal landed property, nor as mediated by the community, but the other way round. The community exists only in the mutual relation of the individual landowners as such. Communal property as such appears only as a communal accessory to the individual kin settlements and land appropriations. The community is neither the substance, of which the individual appears merely as the accident, nor is it the general, which exists and has its being as such in men's minds, and in the reality of the city and its urban requirements, distinct from the separate economic being of its members. It is rather on the one hand, the common elements in languages, blood, etc., which is the premise of the individual proprietor; but on the other hand it has its real being only in its actual assembly for communal purposes; and in so far as it has a separate economic existence, in the communally used hunting grounds, pastures, etc., it is used thus by every individual proprietor as such, and not in his capacity as the representative of the state (as in Rome). It is genuinely the common property of the individual owners, and not of the union of the owners, possessing an existence of its own in the city, distinct from that of the individual members.[30]

There is not space to go into it here but in many ways Marx's essay on 'Precapitalist economic organizations' is like a series of speculative geographies and one can almost sense him doodling with the various patterns on the sheet before him. Although Marx refers to the 'family' in the above passage the term he uses a little earlier is 'home', 'which itself appears merely as a point in the land belonging to it'. In this sense the 'home' seems like a point of intensity occupying its own mobile and fluidly defined affective field and as such it seems to me to be analogous to Deleuze and Guattari's account of a 'singularity' and its associated fields. The geographies that Marx describes in his essay are in many ways geographies of power and desire. The 'Germanic' model he sketches here can quite easily be seen as a model of Deleuze and Guattari's plateaux of desire or planes of consistency.

It is, of course, not fully worked out, but what is striking in the passage that I have quoted is the apparatus that is missing. The individual is not 'mediated' by the community, but the community exists in the 'mutual relation' of individuals – there are no mediations here. The community is not some ideal 'existing in men's minds' – the despotic 'symbolic enactment' of Jameson's preferred 'Asiatic' model: the community here is an 'actual assembly', it really exists. And it follows from this that there is no need here for the notion of 'the representative' and representation. Finally, where the communal exists, it doesn't exist as a 'totalization' of the collective but as the collective's collection of individual acts in hunting and pasturage. The 'totality' is adjacent to the 'fields' of the 'homes'. If Marx ever addressed the problem of the 'collective' and how it should be 'thought' it is surely here.

One final remark on Jameson's work. For all its 'marxist' orthodoxy and in spite of the flirtation with the 'Utopian' hopes he alleges to be part and parcel of class thought, *The Political Unconscious* is a terribly depressing and coercive book. What could be more defeatist than the following?

> History is what hurts, it is what refuses desire and sets inexorable limits to individual as well as collective praxis, which its 'ruses' turn into grisly and ironic reversals of overt intentions.[31]

Is it not rather the reverse? It is history that makes promises possible and the very field that desire produces. There are no inexorable limits, but an infinity of boundaries to be crossed. The 'ruses' are all on our side: they turn our disasters into triumphs, they laugh at our preconceptions and it is they that bide the fall of all our despots.

Notes

1 Introduction

1 Jacques Derrida, *Of Grammatology*, trans. G. C. Spivak, Johns Hopkins University Press, Baltimore, 1976.

2 Michel Foucault, *The Order of Things*, Vintage Books, New York, 1973; see especially chs 8 and 9.

3 Renée Balibar, *Les Français fictifs*, Hachette, Paris, 1974.

4 Gilles Deleuze and Felix Guattari, *Anti-Oedipus*, Viking Press, New York, 1977, and *Mille Plateaux*, Editions de Minuit, Paris, 1980.

5 Ernesto Laclau, *Politics and Ideology in Marxist Theory*, New Left Books, London, 1977.

6 J.-J. Lecercle, *Philosophy through the Looking-Glass*, Hutchinson, 1985.

7 *On the Line*, trans. John Johnston, Semiotext(e), New York, 1983.

8 Fredric Jameson, *The Political Unconscious*, Methuen, London, 1981.

9 W. C. Dowling, *Jameson, Althusser, Marx*, Methuen, London, 1984.

10 Philip Corrigan and Derek Sayer, *The Great Arch*, Basil Blackwell, Oxford, 1985.

11 That these are the more accurate designations of the strike is nowhere made more evident than in MacGregor's own account of the strike in his *The Enemies Within*, Collins, London, 1986; see *The Sunday Times*, 21 Sept. 1986.

12 See Jean-Pierre Faye, *Langages totalitaires*, Herman, Paris, 1972.

13 Deleuze and Guattari, *Anti-Oedipus*, p. 133.

14 Corrigan and Sayer, op. cit., p. 141.

15 ibid., p. 203.

16 ibid., p. 179.

17 ibid., p. 200.

18 ibid., p. 180.

19 ibid., p. 139.

20 Deleuze and Guattari, *Anti-Oedipus*, p. 265.

21 The phrase is from E. P. Thompson, *The Making of the English Working Class*, Penguin Books, Harmondsworth, 1968, p. 597.

22 Corrigan and Sayer, op. cit., pp. 5 and 7.

23 ibid., p. 198.

24 ibid., p. 205.

2 Return to *Mansfield Park*

1 Q. D. Leavis, 'The first modern novel in England', in *Casebook on 'Sense and Sensibility' and 'Mansfield Park'*, ed. B. C. Southam, Macmillan, London, 1976, p. 236.

2 T. Tanner, Introduction to *Mansfield Park*, Penguin Books, Harmondsworth, 1966, p. 32.

3 See *Jane Austen's Letters*, ed. R. W. Chapman, Oxford University Press, 2nd edn, 1952, p. 298.

4 *Letters*, p. 410.

5 Marvin Mudrick, *Jane Austen: Irony as Defence and Discovery*, Princeton University Press, Princeton, 1952, p. 173.

6 See Terry Lovell, 'Jane Austen and gentry society', in *Proceedings of the Essex Conference on 'Literature, Society and the Sociology of Literature'*, University of Essex, Colchester, 1977, pp. 118 ff.

7 *Letters*, p. 298.

8 ibid., p. 410.

9 ibid., p. 417.

10 ibid., pp. 299–300.

11 ibid., p. 317.

12 ibid., p. 411.

13 ibid., p. 419.

14 ibid., p. 340.

15 ibid.

16 See K. Moler, 'The two voices of Fanny Price' in *Jane Austen: Bicentenary Essays*, ed. J. Halpen, Cambridge University Press, Cambridge, 1975, pp. 172–9.

17 L. Trilling, 'Mansfield Park', in *Casebook on 'Sense and Sensibility' and 'Mansfield Park'*, pp. 216–35.

18 Tanner, op. cit., p. 27.

19 M. Butler, *Jane Austen and the War of Ideas*, Clarendon Press, Oxford, 1975, pp. 233–4.

20 W. Reitzal, 'Mansfield Park and Lovers Vows', in *Review of English Studies*, IX, Oct. 1933, pp. 451–6.

21 Butler, op. cit., p. 232.

22 Q. D. Leavis, 'A critical theory of Jane Austen's writings', in *Scrutiny*, X, 1–2, June and October 1941, pp. 61–87 and pp. 114–42.

23 ibid., p. 122.

24 *Lovers' Vows*, trans. Mrs Inchbald, London, 1808, p. 23.

25 ibid., p. 5.

26 ibid., p. 7.

27 E. P. Thompson, *The Making of the English Working Class*, Penguin Books, Harmondsworth, 1968, p. 497.

28 ibid., p. 499.

29 ibid., p. 497.

30 See Thompson, op. cit., p. 603, and H. Perkin, *The Origins of Modern English Society 1780–1880*, Routledge & Kegan Paul, London, 1969, p. 177.

31 J. Foster, *Class Struggle and the Industrial Revolution*, Methuen, London, 1974, p. 41.

32 Thompson, op. cit., p. 663.

33 ibid., p. 733.

34 ibid., p. 753.

35 ibid., p. 780.

36 Foster, op. cit., p. 99.

37 ibid., p. 115.

38 ibid., p. 149.

39 ibid.
40 ibid., p. 207.
41 ibid., p. 208.
42 Perkin, op. cit., p. 177.
43 ibid., p. 196.
44 ibid., p. 37.
45 See E. Laclau, *Politics and Ideology in Marxist Theory*, New Left Books, London, 1977, p. 103n.
46 Moreover it is likely that political consciousness in Portsmouth would be more advanced than elsewhere due to its having been one of the principal foci of the naval mutinies in 1797. For this and the level of political – i.e. jacobinical – consciousness in the navy at this period see R. Wells, *Insurrection: the British Experience 1795–1803*, Alan Sutton, Gloucester, 1983, pp. 79ff.
47 Thompson, op. cit., p. 815.

3 *Frankenstein*: the making of a monster

1 See J. Derrida, '. . . That dangerous supplement . . .', in *Of Grammatology*, trans. G. Spivak, Johns Hopkins University Press, Baltimore, 1976, pp. 141ff.
2 E. P. Thompson *The Making of the English Working Class*, Penguin Books, Harmondsworth, 1968, p. 660.
3 *The Letters of M. W. Shelley*, ed. B. T. Bennet, Johns Hopkins University Press, Baltimore, 1980, vol. I, p. 5.
4 All references to *Frankenstein* are to the Penguin edition, ed. Maurice Hindle, Penguin Books, Harmondsworth, 1985.
5 'A Defence of Poetry' in *Shelley's Prose*, ed. D. Lee Clark, University of New Mexico Press, Albuquerque, 1974, p. 293.
6 ibid., p. 297.
7 ibid., p. 283.
8 ibid., pp. 278–9.
9 ibid., p. 297.
10 ibid., p. 294.
11 M. Foucault, *The Order of Things*, Vintage Books, New York, 1973, p. 237.
12 M. Praz, Introduction to *Three Gothic Novels*, ed. P. Fairclough, Penguin Books, Harmondsworth, 1968, p. 25.
13 Thompson, op. cit., p. 799.

14 See the essay on *Wuthering Heights*, Chapter 4 in this volume.
15 S. Gilbert and S. Gubar, *The Madwoman in the Attic*, Yale University Press, New Haven, 1979.
16 G. Deleuze and F. Guattari, *Anti-Oedipus*, Viking Press, New York, 1977, p. 75.
17 E. Moers, *Literary Women*, Garden City, New York, 1976, pp. 93 ff.
18 *Letters*, p. 12.
19 Thompson, op. cit., p. 768.
20 ibid., p. 819.
21 L. Sterrenberg, 'Mary Shelley's monster: politics and psyche', in *The Endurance of Frankenstein*, ed. G. Levin and U. C. Knoepflmacher, University of California Press, Berkeley, 1982. See also Paul O'Flynn, 'Production and reproduction of *Frankenstein*', in *Literature and History*, Autumn, 1983, pp. 194–213, and E. Jordan, 'Spectres and scorpions: allusion and confusion in *Mary Barton*', in *Literature and History*, Spring, 1981, pp. 48–61.
22 Foucault, op. cit., p. 308.
23 ibid., p. 313.
24 ibid., p. 326.
25 ibid., p. 323.

4 *Wuthering Heights*: the unacceptable texts

1 '*Wuthering Heights*: the unacceptable text', in *Proceedings of the Essex Conference on 'Literature, Society and the Sociology of Literature'*, University of Essex, Colchester, 1977, pp. 154–60.
2 See their 'Presentation' to Renée Balibar's *Les Français fictifs*, Hachette, Paris, 1974.
3 Balibar, op. cit., pp. 231–92.
4 All references to *Wuthering Heights* are to the Penguin edition, ed. D. Daiches, Penguin Books, Harmondsworth, 1972.
5 *The Complete Poems of Emily Jane Brontë*, ed. C. W. Hatfield, Columbia University Press, New York, 1941, p. 69.
6 W. Gérin, *Emily Brontë: A Biography*, Clarendon Press, Oxford, 1971, pp. 17–18.
7 G. Deleuze and F. Guattari, *Anti-Oedipus*, Viking Press, New York, 1977.
8 See Mrs Gaskell, *The Life of Charlotte Brontë*, Penguin Books,

Harmondsworth, 1975, and D. du Maurier, *The Infernal World of Branwell Brontë*, Penguin Books, Harmondsworth, 1972.

9 Gaskell, op. cit., pp. 17–18.

10 Gérin, op. cit., p. 94.

11 The most notorious instance of this is Charlotte's reading of Emily's closely guarded notebook of intensely personal poems. See Gérin, op. cit., pp. 181 ff.

12 F. Ratchford, 'The Gondal story' in Hatfield (ed.), *Poems*, pp. 15–16.

13 Hatfield (ed.), *Poems, passim*.

14 Deleuze and Guattari, op. cit., p. 76.

15 Ratchford, op. cit., p. 19.

16 Deleuze and Guattari, op. cit., p. 77.

17 Hatfield (ed.), *Poems*, pp. 208–9.

18 ibid., 220–1.

19 M. Visick, *The Genesis of 'Wuthering Heights'*, Hong Kong University Press, Hong Kong, 1958.

20 Gérin, op. cit., p. 74. I had not, when I wrote this, read Muriel Spark's brief – and I think excellent – biography of Emily Brontë (*Emily Brontë: her Life and Work*, Peter Owen, London, 1960, reissued Arena, London, 1985). Ms Spark does, in fact, regard the Brussels episode as in some ways 'decisive' (p. 96) but as a factor in what she terms Emily's 'misfortunes'. For Ms Spark the Brussels experience and the encounter with M. Héger resulted in Emily's mind being 'directed away from its proper path' (p. 92). My own view of the significance of the Brussels experience is, therefore, almost the exact reverse of that held by Ms Spark.

21 Gaskell, op. cit., pp. 230–1.

22 See Gérin, 'Appendix A', op. cit., pp. 266–74.

23 H. Dingle, *The Mind of Emily Brontë*, Martin Brian & O'Keeffe, London, 1974, p. 31.

24 Gérin, op. cit., pp. 266–7.

25 ibid., p. 267.

26 ibid., p. 269.

27 ibid., p. 271.

28 ibid., p. 272.

29 Hatfield (ed.), *Poems*, p. 36.

30 Gérin, op. cit., p. 269.

31 ibid., p. 268.

32 This correction does not appear in Gérin and it was brought to my attention by the former librarian at Haworth, Ms Sally Stonehouse who, in turn, was quoting a letter from John Hewish.

33 V. Hugo, 'Sur Mirabeau', in *Littérature et philosophie mélées*, Nelson, Paris, c. 1920, pp. 273–431.

34 ibid., p. 392.

35 ibid., p. 402.

36 ibid., p. 389.

37 D. Cecil, *Early Victorian Novelists*, Pelican, London, 1948, p. 119.

38 Hugo, op. cit., pp. 404, 422, 424.

39 ibid., p. 421.

40 ibid., pp. 384–5.

41 ibid., pp. 426–7.

42 Gaskell, op. cit., p. 239.

43 J. B. Bossuet, 'Oraison funèbre de Henriette-Marie de France, Reine de la Grande Bretagne', in *Oeuvres*, Gallimard, Paris, 1961, pp. 71–2.

44 F. P. G. Guizot, *Historie de la République d'Angleterre*, vol. II, Didier, Paris, 1860, pp. 398–9.

45 T. Carlyle, 'The hero as king' in 'Lectures on Heroes', in *Works*, Ashburton Edition, London, 1889, p. 178.

46 Charlotte Brontë, Preface to *Wuthering Heights*, p. 41.

47 Casimir de la Vigne, *Trois Messeniennes*, Paris, 1819, pp. 46–52.

48 Preface to *Wuthering Heights*, p. 31.

49 See Introduction to Penguin edition of *Wuthering Heights*, p. 8.

50 Hatfield (ed.), *Poems*, pp. 255–6.

5 Notes on a journey to *Vanity Fair*

1 See the Introduction to the Methuen edition of *Vanity Fair* by G. and K. Tillotson, Methuen, London 1963, p. xviii.

2 All references to the text of *Vanity Fair* are to the Penguin edition, ed. J. I. M. Stewart, Penguin Books, Harmondsworth, 1968.

3 See the Introduction to the Methuen edition, p. xxii.

4 Penguin edition of *Vanity Fair*, p. 29.

5 Russell Sturgis in *Scribner's Monthly*, June 1880, quoted by G. and K. Tillotson, op. cit., p. xxxix. See also R. S. Rintoul in the *Spectator*, 22 July 1848, included in *Thackeray: The Critical Heritage*, ed. G. Tillotson and D. Hawes, Routledge & Kegan Paul, London, 1968.

6 G. and K. Tillotson, op. cit., p. xxxix.

7 Methuen edition of *Vanity Fair*, p. 663.

8 See Appendix B to the Methuen edition, pp. 672–4.

9 G. and K. Tillotson, op. cit., p. xxvi.

10 P. Macherey and E. Balibar, in their 'Presentation' to R. Balibar, *Les Français fictifs*, Hachette, Paris, 1974.

11 How little Thackeray is exaggerating popular speech patterns may be judged by comparing the above passages with the examples of Railway Navvy slang offered by Terry Coleman in *The Railway Navvies*, Penguin Books, Harmondsworth, 1965, pp. 125–6.

12 G. Ray, '*Vanity Fair*: one version of a novelist's responsibility', in *Essays by Divers Hands*, XXV, 1949, pp. 87–101.

13 G. and K. Tillotson, op. cit.

14 J. P. Rawlins, *Thackeray's Novels*, University of California Press, Berkeley, 1974.

15 J. A. Sutherland, *Thackeray at Work*, Athlone Press, London, 1974.

16 J. P. Rawlins, op. cit., pp. 6–7.

17 *The Letters and Private Papers of W. M. Thackeray*, ed. G. N. Ray, Oxford University Press, London, 1945, vol. II, p. 423.

18 J. A. Sutherland, op. cit., pp. 24–5.

19 ibid., pp. 26–7.

20 G. Tillotson and D. Hawes (eds), *Thackeray: The Critical Heritage*, p. 85.

21 P. Macherey and E. Balibar, op. cit., *passim*.

22 J. I. M. Stewart, Introduction to Penguin edition of *Vanity Fair*, p. 21.

23 See *The Letters and Private Papers of W. M. Thackeray*, p. 313 f.n.

24 For Thackeray's more general thoughts on the novelist as a 'non-combatant' see his review of Lever's *St Patrick's Eve* in the collections of his *Contributions to the 'Morning Chronicle'*, ed. Gordon Ray, Illinois University Press, Champaign, 1955, pp. 70–7.

25 G. and K. Tillotson, op. cit., p. xxiii.

26 F. R. Leavis, *The Great Tradition*, Penguin Books, Harmondsworth, 1962, p. 32.

27 J. A. Sutherland, op. cit., pp. 35 ff.

28 G. and K. Tillotson, op. cit., p. xxxiii.

29 *The Letters and Private Papers of W. M. Thackeray*, p. 356.

30 J. I. M. Stewart, Introduction to Penguin edition of *Vanity Fair*, p. 19.

31 K. Marx, 'The Eighteenth Brumaire of Louis Bonaparte', in *Surveys from Exile*, Penguin Books, Harmondsworth, 1973, p. 146.

32 I am heavily indebted in much of what follows to Jeffrey Mehlman's brilliant close reading of Marx's essay in his *Revolution and Repetition*, California University Press, Berkeley, 1977.

33 K. Marx, op. cit., p. 182; see also p. 170.

34 ibid., p. 214.

35 ibid., p. 160.

36 ibid., p. 153.

37 ibid., pp. 169–70.

38 ibid., pp. 184–5.

39 J. Coombes, 'The political aesthetics of the "Eighteenth Brumaire of Louis Bonaparte"', in *1848: The Sociology of Literature*, University of Essex, Colchester, 1978, pp. 18–19.

40 W. M. Thackeray, *Notes on a Journey from Cornhill to Grand Cairo*, London, 1846.

41 G. and K. Tillotson, op. cit., p. xvii.

42 Thackeray, *Notes on a Journey from Cornhill to Grand Cairo*, p. 38.

43 ibid., pp. 39–40.

44 ibid., pp. 65 ff.

45 *The Letters and Private Papers of W. M. Thackeray*, p. 182.

46 Thackeray, *Notes on a Journey from Cornhill to Grand Cairo*, p. 62.

47 ibid., p. 98 ff.

48 ibid., p. 192.

49 See G. Deleuze and F. Guattari, *Anti-Oedipus*, Viking Press, New York, 1977.

50 Thackeray, *Notes on a Journey from Cornhill to Grand Cairo*, pp. 79–81.

51 ibid., p. 194.

52 *The Letters and Private Papers of W. M. Thackeray*, p. 183.

53 For the whole of this discussion see Deleuze and Guattari, *Anti-Oedipus*.

54 G. Ray, *The Buried Life*, Oxford University Press, London, 1952, p. 13.

55 ibid., p. 14.

56 *The Letters and Private Papers of W. M. Thackeray*, p. 384.
57 Deleuze and Guattari, op. cit. Anyone familiar with this text will appreciate that it would be otiose to give specific references.
58 *Contributions to the 'Morning Chronicle'*, p. 32.
59 ibid., p. 33.
60 ibid., p. 35.
61 ibid., p. 36.
62 I am indebted to K. Marx for this felicitous image – see 'The Eighteenth Brumaire', p. 171.
63 'The Eighteenth Brumaire', p. 221.
64 ibid., p. 224.
65 ibid., p. 198.
66 ibid., p. 197.
67 'The class struggles in France' in *Surveys from Exile*, p. 72.
68 D. Southgate, *The Passing of the Whigs 1832–86*, Macmillan, London, 1962, p. 193.
69 ibid., p. 142.
70 Deleuze and Guattari, op. cit. – see note 57.
71 M. Foucault, *The History of Sexuality*, Allen Lane, London, 1978.
72 T. Eagleton, 'Tennyson: politics and sexuality in "The Princess" and "In memoriam"', in *1848: The Sociology of Literature*, p. 97.

6 Dickens: the commodification of the novelist

1 R. L. Patten, *Charles Dickens and his Publishers*, Oxford University Press, London, 1978, p. 184.
2 All references to Dickens's letters are to *The Letters of Charles Dickens*, ed. K. Tillotson, Clarendon Press, Oxford, 1977.
3 Quoted by G. Pearson in his 'Towards a reading of *Dombey and Son*, in *Dickens and the Twentieth Century*, ed. J. Gross and G. Pearson, Routledge & Kegan Paul, London, 1962.
4 Patten, op. cit., p. 186.
5 Pearson, op. cit., p. 62.
6 ibid., p. 56.
7 ibid., pp. 57, 66.
8 ibid., p. 57.
9 ibid., p. 57.
10 ibid., p. 56.
11 ibid., p. 58.
12 ibid., p. 57.

13 R. Williams, Introduction to the Penguin edition of *Dombey and Son*, Penguin Books, Harmondsworth, 1970.

14 J. Butt and K. Tillotson, *Dickens at Work*, Methuen, London, 1957, p. 96.

15 All references to *Dombey and Son* are to the Penguin edition, Penguin Books, Harmondsworth, 1970.

16 J. Forster, *The Life of Charles Dickens*, J. M. Dent, London, 1966, vol. I, p. 422.

17 S. Marcus, *Dickens: from Pickwick to Dombey*, Chatto & Windus, London, 1965.

18 ibid., p. 289.

19 ibid., p. 292.

20 ibid.

21 ibid.

22 All references to *The Battle of Life* are to the Penguin volume *Charles Dickens: The Christmas Books*, vol. II, Penguin Books, Harmondsworth, 1971.

23 Forster, op. cit., p. 14.

24 Marcus, op. cit., p. 363.

25 Forster, op. cit., p. 20.

26 ibid., p. 13.

27 ibid., p. 21.

28 ibid., pp. 22–3.

29 ibid., pp. 32–3.

30 Edgar Johnson, *Charles Dickens: his Tragedy and Triumph*, Gollancz, London, 1953, vol. I, p. 145.

31 Forster, op. cit., p. 22.

32 Marcus, op. cit., p. 364.

33 Forster, op. cit., p. 31.

34 ibid.

35 ibid.

36 All references to *Oliver Twist* are to the Penguin edition, Penguin Books, Harmondsworth, 1966.

37 Marcus, op. cit., p. 375.

38 ibid., p. 368.

39 ibid., p. 363.

40 C. Hibbert, *The Making of Charles Dickens*, Longman, London, 1967.

41 Forster, op. cit., p. 9.

42 ibid., pp. 15–16.
43 ibid., p. 17.
44 ibid., p. 31.
45 See G. Deleuze and F. Guattari, *Anti-Oedipus*, Viking Press, New York, 1977, p. 97:

> The father, the mother, the self are at grips with, and directly coupled to, the elements of the political and historical situation – the soldier, the cop, the occupier, the collaborator, the radical, the resister, the boss, the boss's wife – who constantly break all triangulations, and who prevent the entire situation falling back on the familial complex and becoming internalised in it. In a word, the family is never a microcosm in the sense of an autonomous figure, even when inscribed in a larger circle that it is said to mediate and express. The family is by nature eccentric, decentered. . . . There is always an uncle in America; a brother who went bad; an aunt who took off with a military man; a cousin out of work, bankrupt, or a victim of the Crash; an anarchist grandfather; a grandmother in the hospital, crazy or senile.

46 Forster, op. cit., p. 28.
47 ibid., p. 14.
48 See Deleuze and Guattari, op. cit., p. 101:

> Oedipus is always and solely an aggregate of destination fabricated to meet the requirements of an aggregate of departure constituted by a social formation. . . . In the aggregate of departure there is the social formation. . . . In the aggregate of destination there remains only daddy, mommy, and me.

49 Forster, op. cit., p. 9.
50 Hibbert, op. cit., pp. 16–17.
51 Forster, op. cit., p. 11.
52 Forster, op. cit., p. 10. Compare this with Deleuze and Guattari, op. cit., pp. 45–7:

> A child never confines himself to playing house, to playing only at being daddy-and-mommy. He also plays at being a magician, a cowboy, a cop or a robber, a train, a little car. The train is not necessarily daddy, nor is the train station necessarily mommy. The problem has to do not with the sexual nature of desiring machines, but with the family nature of this sexuality. . . . The

unconscious is totally unaware of persons as such. Partial objects are not representations of parental figures or of the basic patterns of familial relations; they are parts of desiring machines, having to do with a process and with relations of production that are both irreducible and prior to anything that may be made to conform to the Oedipal figure. . . . The question, rather, is that of the absolutely *anoedipal* nature of the production of desire. . . . The small child lives with his family around the clock; but within the bosom of this family, and from the very first days of his life, he immediately begins having an amazing nonfamilial experience that psychoanalysis has completely failed to take into account.

53 See G. Deleuze and F. Guattari, *Mille Plateaux*, Éditions de Minuit, Paris, 1980, p. 51:

Or le nom propre ne désigne pas un individu: c'est au contraire quand l'individu s'ouvre aux multiplicités qui le traversent de part en part, à l'issue du plus sévère exercice de dépersonnalisation, qu'il acquiert son véritable nom propre. Le nom propre est l'apprehension instantanée d'une multiplicité.

54 See Deleuze and Guattari, *Anti-Oedipus*, p. 48:

The word 'relate' in this case does not designate a natural productive relationship, but rather a *relation* in the sense of a report or an account, an inscription within the over-all process of inscription.

55 Deleuze and Guattari, *Anti-Oedipus*, p. 119.
56 See J. Lacan, *The Four Fundamental Concepts of Psychoanalysis*, Penguin Books, Harmondsworth, 1977, p. 74.
57 Perhaps Lacan makes a little clearer the kind of shift I am trying to describe: if a bird had to paint it would shed its feathers – the peacock's 'painting' is its display; for the poor unfeathered biped all that he is left with is making patterns in shit. Let me quote:

The authenticity of what emerges in painting is diminished in us human beings by the fact that we have to get our colours where they're to be found, that is to say, in the shit. If I referred to birds who might let fall their feathers, it is because *we* do not have these feathers. The creator will never participate in anything other than the creation of a small dirty deposit, a succession of small dirty deposits juxtaposed.

See *The Four Fundamental Concepts of Psychoanalysis*, p. 117.

58 Forster, op. cit., p. 23.

59 See Deleuze and Guattari, *Anti-Oedipus*, p. 71.

60 Forster, op. cit., p. 27.

61 Deleuze and Guattari, *Anti-Oedipus*, p. 134.

62 Forster, op. cit., p. 19.

63 Forster, op. cit., p. 32.

64 *Charles Dickens: The Public Readings*, ed. P. Collins, Clarendon Press, Oxford, 1975, p. 471.

65 All references to *Sketches by 'Boz'* are to the Oxford Illustrated Dickens edition, Oxford University Press, London, 1957.

66 E. Yeo, 'Mayhew as a Social Investigator', introduction to *The Unknown Mayhew*, Penguin Books, Harmondsworth, 1973, p. 98.

67 Duane DeVries, *Dickens's Apprentice Years*, Harvester Press, Brighton, 1976, pp. 67–76, *passim*.

68 See the essays 'Rhizome' and 'Un seul ou plusieurs loups' in their *Mille Plateaux*.

69 For other important examples of Dickens being within the scene he describes see the description from Todger's roof in *Chuzzlewit* where there is a man sharpening a pen opposite:

> The man who was mending a pen at an upper window over the way, became of paramount importance in the scene, and made a blank in it, ridiculously disproportionate in its extent, when he retired. (p. 188)

and again the trial scene in *Oliver Twist* where we have a young man in the court looking at Fagan looking at him:

> There was one young man sketching his face in a little note-book. He wondered whether it was like, and looked on when the artist broke his pencil point, and made another with his knife, as any idle spectator might have done. (p. 467)

70 In 'Mayhew and the *Morning Chronicle*' in *The Unknown Mayhew*, p. 21.

71 ibid.

72 All references to *The Pickwick Papers* are to the Penguin edition, Penguin Books, Harmondsworth, 1972.

73 All references to *Nicholas Nickleby* are to the Pan edition, Pan Books, London, 1968.

74 All references to *The Old Curiosity Shop* are to the Penguin edition, Penguin Books, Harmondsworth, 1972.

75 Deleuze and Guattari, *Anti-Oedipus*, p. 134.

76 All references to *Martin Chuzzlewit* are to the Penguin edition, Penguin Books, Harmondsworth, 1968.

77 Introduction to the Penguin edition, p. 21.

78 See Lacan's remarks on Diderot's 'Lettre sur les aveugles à l'usage de ceux qui voient' in *The Four Fundamental Concepts of Psychoanalysis*, p. 86.

79 Butt and Tillotson, op. cit., p. 96.

80 All references to *David Copperfield* are to the Pan edition, Pan Books, London, 1967.

81 P. Collins, *Dickens and Crime*, Macmillan, London, 1964, p. 155 ff.

82 ibid., p. 157.

83 Butt and Tillotson, op. cit., p. 175.

84 All references to *Bleak House* are to the Penguin edition, Penguin Books, Harmondsworth, 1971.

85 P. Collins, op. cit., *passim*.

Appendix I   Deleuze and Guattari

1 *On the Line*, Semiotext(e), New York, 1983, p. 4.

2 See also Pierre Clastres, *La Société contre l'État*, Éditions de Minuit, Paris, 1974.

3 *Anti-Oedipus*, Viking Press, New York, 1977, p. 27.

4 D. H. Lawrence, *Fantasia of the Unconscious, Psychoanalysis and the Unconscious*, Penguin Books, Harmondsworth, 1971.

5 *Frankenstein*, ed. M. Hindle, Penguin Books, Harmondsworth, 1985, p. 260.

6 See Alfonso Caso, *The Aztecs*, University of Oklahoma Press, Nosman, Okla., 1953, p. 90.

7 *On the Line*, p. 40.

8 In fact it is Deleuze's theory of language which is to be found most fully worked out in his earlier *Logique du sens*, Éditions de Minuit, Paris, 1969.

9 E. M. Forster, *Passage to India*, Penguin Books, Harmondsworth, 1936, p. 221.

Appendix II Fredric Jameson: *The Political Unconscious*

1 W. C. Dowling, *Jameson, Althusser, Marx*, Methuen, London, 1984, p. 101.
2 ibid., p. 102.
3 *The Political Unconscious*, Methuen, London, 1981, p. 12.
4 ibid., p. 294.
5 ibid.
6 ibid., p. 53.
7 G. Deleuze and F. Guattari, *Anti-Oedipus*, Viking Press, New York, 1977, pp. 42 ff.
8 *The Political Unconscious*, p. 58.
9 ibid., p. 127.
10 ibid., p. 128.
11 ibid., p. 22.
12 ibid., pp. 19–20.
13 ibid., pp. 77 ff.
14 C. Lévi-Strauss, *Tristes tropiques*, Penguin Books, Harmondsworth, 1976, pp. 247–8.
15 ibid., pp. 248–9.
16 ibid., p. 246.
17 ibid., pp. 255–6.
18 *The Political Unconscious*, p. 77.
19 ibid., p. 79.
20 *Tristes tropiques*, p. 244.
21 *The Political Unconscious*, p. 79.
22 *Tristes tropiques*, p. 243.
23 ibid., p. 238.
24 Jacques Derrida, *Of Grammatology*, Johns Hopkins University Press, Baltimore, 1976, pp. 101–40.
25 *Tristes tropiques*, p. 242.
26 ibid., pp. 242–3.
27 ibid., p. 233.
28 *The Political Unconscious*, p. 295.
29 See Eric Hobsbawm's Introduction to his edition of Marx's *Precapitalist Economic Formations*, Lawrence & Wishart, London, 1964, p. 9.
30 *Precapitalist Economic Formations*, p. 80.
31 *The Political Unconscious*, p. 102.

Bibliography

Balibar, Renée, *Les Français fictifs*, Hachette, Paris, 1974.

Bennet, B. T. (ed.), *The Letters of M. W. Shelley*, Johns Hopkins University Press, Baltimore, 1980.

Bossuet, J. B., 'Oraison funèbre de Henriette-Marie de France, Reine de la Grande Bretagne', in *Oeuvres*, Gallimard, Paris, 1961.

Butler, M., *Jane Austen and the War of Ideas*, Clarendon Press, Oxford, 1975.

Butt, J. and Tillotson, K., *Dickens at Work*, Methuen, London, 1957.

Carlyle, T., 'The hero as king' in 'Lectures on Heroes', in *Works*, Ashburton edition, London, 1889.

Caso, A., *The Aztecs*, University of Oklahoma Press, Nosman, 1953.

Cecil, D., *Early Victorian Novelists*, Pelican, London, 1948.

Clastres, P., *La Société contre l'État*, Éditions de Minuit, Paris, 1974.

Coleman, T., *The Railway Navvies*, Penguin Books, Harmondsworth, 1965.

Collins, P., *Dickens and Crime*, Macmillan, London, 1964.

Collins, P. (ed.), *Charles Dickens: the Public Readings*, Clarendon Press, Oxford, 1975.

Corrigan, Philip and Sayer, Derek, *The Great Arch*, Basil Blackwell, Oxford, 1985.

Deleuze, G., *Logique du sens*, Éditions de Minuit, Paris, 1969.

Deleuze, Gilles and Guattari, Felix, *Anti-Oedipus*, Viking Press, New York, 1977.

— *Mille Plateaux*, Éditions de Minuit, Paris, 1980.

— *On the Line*, Semiotext(e), New York, 1983.

Derrida, Jacques, *Of Grammatology*, trans. G. C. Spivak, Johns Hopkins University Press, Baltimore, 1976.

DeVries, D., *Dickens's Apprentice Years*, Harvester Press, Brighton, 1976.

Dickens, C., *The Battle of Life*, in *Charles Dickens: The Christmas Books*, vol. II, Penguin Books, Harmondsworth, 1971.

Dingle, H., *The Mind of Emily Brontë*, Martin Brian & O'Keeffe, London, 1974.

Dowling, W. C., *Jameson, Althusser, Marx*, Methuen, London, 1984.

Duverger, C., *L'Esprit de jeu chez les Azteques*, Mouton, The Hague, 1978.

Faye, Jean-Pierre, *Langages totalitaires*, Hermann, Paris, 1972.

Forster, E. M., *Passage to India*, Penguin Books, Harmondsworth, 1936.

Forster, J., *The Life of Charles Dickens*, J. M. Dent, London, 1966.

Foster, J., *Class Struggle and the Industrial Revolution*, Methuen, London, 1977.

Foucault, M., *The Order of Things*, Vintage Books, New York, 1973.

— *The History of Sexuality*, London, 1978.

Gaskell, E., *The Life of Charlotte Brontë*, Penguin Books, Harmondsworth, 1975.

Gérin, W., *Emily Brontë: A Biography*, Clarendon Press, Oxford, 1971.

Gilbert, S. and Gubar, S., *The Madwoman in the Attic*, Yale University Press, New Haven, 1979.

Gross, J. and Pearson, G., (eds), *Dickens in the Twentieth Century*, Routledge & Kegan Paul, London, 1962.

Guizot, F. P. G., *Histoire de la République d'Angleterre*, Didier, Paris, 1860.

Hatfield, C. W. (ed.), *The Complete Poems of Emily Jane Brontë*, Columbia University Press, New York, 1941.

Hibbert, C., *The Making of Charles Dickens*, Longman, London, 1967.

Hugo, V., 'Sur Mirabeau', in *Littérature et philosophie mélées*, Nelson, Paris, c. 1920.

Jameson, Fredric, *The Political Unconscious*, Methuen, London, 1981.

Johnson, E., *Charles Dickens: his Tragedy and Triumph*, Gollancz, London, 1953.

Lacan, J., *The Four Fundamental Concepts of Psychoanalysis*, Penguin Books, Harmondsworth, 1977.

Laclau, Ernesto, *Politics and Ideology in Marxist Theory*, New Left Books, London, 1977.

Lawrence, D. H., *Fantasia of the Unconscious, Psychoanalysis and the Unconscious*, Penguin Books, Harmondsworth, 1971.

Leavis, F. R., *The Great Tradition*, Penguin Books, Harmondsworth, 1962.

Lecercle, J.-J., *Philosophy through the Looking-Glass*, Hutchinson, London, 1985.

Lee Clark, D. (ed.), *Shelley's Prose*, University of New Mexico Press, Albuquerque, 1974.

Levin G. and Knoepflmacher V. C. (eds), *The Endurance of Franken-stein*, University of California Press, Berkeley, 1982.

Lévi-Strauss, C., *Tristes tropiques*, Penguin Books, Harmondsworth, 1976.

MacGregor, Ian, *The Enemies Within*, Collins, London, 1986.

Marcus, S., *Dickens: from Pickwick to Dombey*, Chatto & Windus, London, 1965.

Marx, K., *Precapitalist Economic Formations*, ed. E. Hobsbawm, Lawrence & Wishart, London, 1964.

— *Surveys from Exile*, Penguin Books, Harmondsworth, 1973.

Maurier, D. du, *The Infernal World of Branwell Brontë*, Penguin Books, Harmondsworth, 1972.

Mehlman, J., *Revolution and Repetition*, California University Press, Berkeley, 1977.

Moers, E., *Literary Women*, Doubleday, Garden City, New York, 1976.

Mudrick, Marvin, *Jane Austen: Irony as Defence and Discovery*, University Press, Princeton, 1952.

Patten, R. L., *Charles Dickens and his Publishers*, Oxford University Press, London, 1978.

Perkin, H., *The Origins of Modern English Society 1780–1880*, Routledge & Kegan Paul, London, 1969.

Rawlins, J. P., *Thackeray's Novels*, University of California Press, Berkeley, 1974.

Ray, G. N., *The Buried Life*, Oxford University Press, London, 1952.

Ray, G. N. (ed.), *The Letters and Private Papers of W. M. Thackeray*, Oxford University Press, London, 1945.

Southgate, D., *The Passing of the Whigs 1832–1886*, Macmillan, London, 1962.

Spark, M., *Emily Brontë: her Life and Work*, Peter Owen, London, 1960, and Arena, London, 1985.

Sutherland, J. A., *Thackeray at Work*, Athlone Press, London, 1974.

Thackeray, W. M., *Contributions to the 'Morning Chronicle'*, ed. Gordon Ray, Illinois University Press, Champaign, 1955.

— *Notes on a Journey from Cornhill to Cairo*, London, 1846.

Thompson, E. P., *The Making of the English Working Class*, Penguin Books, Harmondsworth, 1968.

Tillotson, G. and Hawes, D. (eds) *Thackeray: The Critical Heritage*, Routledge & Kegan Paul, London, 1968.

Tillotson, K. (ed.), *The Letters of Charles Dickens*, Clarendon Press, Oxford, 1977.

Vigne, Casimir de la, *Trois Messeniennes*, Paris, 1819.

Visick, M., *The Genesis of Wuthering Heights*, Hong Kong University Press, Hong Kong, 1958.

Yeo, E. (ed.), *The Unknown Mayhew*, Penguin Books, Harmondsworth, 1973.

Articles

Coombes, J., 'The political aesthetics of the "Eighteenth Brumaire of Louis Bonaparte'", in *1848: The Sociology of Literature*, University of Essex, Colchester, 1978.

Jordan, E., 'Spectres and scorpions: allusion and confusion in *Mary Barton*', in *Literature and History*, Spring, 1981.

Leavis, Q. D., 'A critical theory of Jane Austen's writings', in *Scrutiny*, X, 1–2, June and October, 1941.

— 'The first modern novel in England', in *Casebook on 'Sense and Sensibility' and 'Mansfield Park'*, ed. B. C. Southam, Macmillan, London, 1976.

Lovell, T., 'Jane Austen and gentry society', in *Proceedings of the Essex Conference on 'Literature, Society and the Sociology of Literature'*, University of Essex, Colchester, 1977.

Moler, K., 'The two voices of Fanny Price', in *Jane Austen: Bicentenary Essays*, ed. J. Halpen, Cambridge University Press, Cambridge, 1975.

O'Flynn, P., 'Production and reproduction of *Frankenstein*' in *Literature and History*, Autumn, 1983.

Praz, M., Introduction to *Three Gothic Novels*, Penguin Books, Harmondsworth, 1968.

Ray, G., '*Vanity Fair*: one version of a novelist's responsibility', in *Essays by Divers Hands*, XXV, 1949.

Reitzal, W., '*Mansfield Park* and *Lovers' Vows*' in *Review of English Studies*, IX, Oct. 1933.

Sterrenberg, L., 'Mary Shelley's monster: politics and psyche', in *The Endurance of Frankenstein*, ed. G. Levin and V. C. Knoepflmacher, University of California Press, Berkeley, 1982.

Trilling, L. '*Mansfield Park*', in *Casebook on 'Sense and Sensibility' and 'Mansfield Park'*, ed. B. C. Southam, Macmillan, London, 1976.

Index